D1268030

Gateways to CORRECT SPELLING

REVISED EDITION

by FRED C. AYER

STECK-VAUGHN COMPANY • AUSTIN, TEXAS

Contents

Introduction

It was stated in the Introduction to the 1946 edition of *Gateways to Correct Spelling* that there are two chief things to be done in building a business and general speller for students beyond elementary school age. The first is to select and organize a set of words which students *really* need to study and use. The second is to make use of the best methods by which the needed words can be mastered and retained. How well these ends were achieved is now indicated by the fact that the sales of *Gateways to Correct Spelling* have increased every year since its publication until it has become the leading high school speller in the United States.

An account of the basic research which underlies the first edition of *Gateways to Correct Spelling* may be found in its Introduction, pp. v-xii. The present edition carries on in full measure the content and methods so successfully developed in 1946. In addition, it supplements the fundamental features of the first edition by presenting improvements based on facts gained through new research in the field of spelling instruction and through systematic evaluation of its use as a textbook.

On the basis of the foregoing investigations, the following improvements have been made in the present edition of *Gateways to Correct Spelling:*

1. The Introduction has been completely rewritten.
2. The learning methods have been more sharply delineated.
3. Numerous changes have been made in the Memory Aids; the four illustrations of standard dictionary pages have been brought up to date; and a page of proofreader's marks has been added.
4. Three new lessons have been added to Part 2. They deal with abbreviations, prefixes, and suffixes. One new lesson has been added to Part 3. It deals with words related to psychology.
5. Numerous changes have been made in the vocabulary lessons of Part 3 to bring the key words up to date.

THE VOCABULARY

Gateways to Correct Spelling includes three sets of carefully selected spelling words: (1) The Basic Group; (2) The Practical Group; and (3) The Special Groups.

1. The Basic Group of Spelling Words

The basic group of 720 spelling words is by all odds the most important of the three sets for poor and average spellers and should be studied by all students as an approach to the more advanced aspects of spelling treated in Parts 2 and 3 of this text. These 720 words cause four-fifths of the spelling errors made by persons beyond elementary school age. Students who master this group of words will at the same time develop a method of examining words which will greatly increase their general spelling vocabulary. The method used for the selection of the 720 basic words is described in the paragraph to follow.

The author first prepared a list of the 4,000 words which best reflect the research, thought, and practice of American educators as the group of words that pupils completing the eighth grade should know how to spell. On the basis of tests given by the author, it was discovered that 650 of the 4,000 elementary school words are commonly misspelled by high school pupils. In addition, there are 70 other words which are frequently used by high school pupils and which carry serious spelling difficulties. The total group of 720 words constitutes the basic group of spelling words that are attacked vigorously by direct spelling methods in Part 1 of this textbook.

2. The Practical Group of Spelling Words

The majority of persons who master the basic group of spelling words will have little need for further special instruction in spelling. There will be, however, a substantial body of students who, because of special literary or vocational interests, wish to extend their study of words, and of spelling in particular, beyond the limits of the basic list. These students will be definitely interested in a wider range of good spelling and a wider understanding of word building. Much thought and study have been given to presenting in this text the group of words most useful to supplement the basic list of 720 words.

A painstaking analysis of vocabulary studies and of the words found in recently published high school workbooks and business spellers reveals the need for greater care in the selection of words which appear at the more or less optional levels in high school, business, and adult spellers. The list presented in Part 2 of this book reflects two chief principles of selection: (1) commonly used words in addition to the 720 in the basic list which are known to give spelling difficulty; and (2) words pertinent to business and general correspondence which reflect significant principles and technics of correct spelling and pronunciation. All of these words are arranged in groups to demonstrate practical spelling technics and the best ways of using a dictionary.

3. The Special Groups of Spelling Words

In addition to the basic and general lists of words which are of value to all school students with literary or business interests, there are various sets of key words which are of distinctive value to students who have certain special literary, vocational, or educational interests. Such, for example, are science words, military words, words used in law, or geographical words. Part 3 contains thirty-eight groups of forty key words each, representing the chief fields of educational, social, and business life in the United States.

In making the final choice of words to represent each special interest group out of the considerably larger list at hand, attention was given to three chief criteria of selection: (1) frequency of appearance in related word lists; (2) judgment by experts in the field concerned as to importance; and (3) frequency of appearance in basic textbooks, descriptive accounts, and magazines related directly to the field under consideration. As a result, *Gateways to Correct Spelling* contains by far the most up-to-date selection of key vocabulary words in print.

THE BEST METHODS FOR AN ADVANCED SPELLER

The details of the methods used in this speller may be found only by study of the numerous lessons to follow. The major facts of organization and the general principles of learning to spell at the upper school levels are so different in this text from those used in other spellers that it seems desirable to give them specific discussion at this point.

It is obvious that the large number of commonly used words, already studied in elementary school but *still* commonly misspelled by more advanced students, *should be studied by some other method* than the one which was used in the elementary school. The most important fact in the learning situation is that *the words have to be relearned.* Faulty images and associations have to be destroyed, and new and stronger ones substituted. To do this, the common faults which lie at the basis of the frequent misspellings of these everyday words must be uncovered and the focus of new learning be centered on the points or aspects of the troublesome words which gave the original trouble.

We know, for example, that the word *apology* is misspelled by nearly one-half of the pupils tested at the ninth-grade level in high school, although it appears in most elementary school spellers in or before the eighth grade. We know from Gates' study that 90 per cent or more of the pupils know the meaning of the word *apology* by the end of the seventh grade and that nearly all of the ways of misspelling occur at two hard spots in the word, *p* and *o*. We know from studies by Gilbert and others on photographic eye movements of pupils that good spellers tend to locate and pay special attention to difficult spots in words far more than poor spellers do. With these facts at hand, it is possible to plan specific learning exercises to master the word *apology*. The present text is in full accord with these studies and with other practical contributions of research to the field of spelling. In brief, the scientific methods used in this text encourage students to:

1. Realize that good spelling is important.
2. Assume responsibility for their own progress.
3. Look at words as wholes or in large parts.
4. Focus attention upon spots known to be difficult.
5. Combine vivid sensory impression with aggressive efforts to recall.
6. Combine visualization with pronunciation by syllables.
7. Associate difficult spellings with known forms.
8. Correct all mistakes immediately by fresh study.
9. Review frequently.

The practical application of the foregoing principles is made evident in the directions to pupils which appear on pages 1-4. The following discussion throws additional light upon the general methodology used as a basis for the lessons which appear later in the text.

The present speller, instead of stamping in the old mistakes by use of the same old letter-by-letter drill methods, introduces the *whole-word, hard-spot* study method. This method is justified in general by the practical contributions of organismic psychology and in particular by experimentation in the field of learning to spell. The studies by the Gilberts, for example, show that good spellers do not use the letter-by-letter repetition method. They first see the whole word; then analyze it, or large parts of it, to detect difficult or unusual spots; then with rhythmic sweeps of the eye from left to right, quickly *fuse* the several parts of the word into a *unified whole*. To spell a word correctly, a pupil must look at its parts with sufficient care and detail so that afterward he will be able to see or recall the whole word as a unified group of letters.

Merely printing hard spots, as Tireman has shown, is not enough. The learner's attention must be directed to them and a definite method provided for their speedy fusion into a unified view of the whole word. Studies reported by Gates and elaborate tests by Ayer demonstrate that proper specific attention to hard spots is distinctly helpful in learning to spell. Good visualization is greatly aided by careful word scrutiny and analysis.

Pretesting is sometimes used to locate definite hard spots for individual pupils by noting how they misspell certain words. It is not, however, a good practice to have words misspelled at any time. The present text anticipates most of the hard spots and provides additional exercises to remedy difficulties which may be peculiar to individual pupils. The learning exercises in the text which accompany each word help the student make an aggressive attack upon the special spelling difficulties in the word. They also aid the student to develop a method of attack for the mastery of all spelling words.

Gateways to Correct Spelling places considerably more emphasis on the proper use of a dictionary than do other secondary school spellers. Part 1 is followed by a Basic Dictionary which gives the pronunciation and primary meanings of the 720 words included therein. This enables students to check immediately concerning any uncertainty as to meaning or pronunciation which may arise in connection with a basic word as it is used in the original lessons.

In addition to the dictionary practice afforded by the routine procedure in Part 1, a large share of Part 2 is devoted directly to the more technical aspects of correct dictionary usage. In this connection, *Gateways to Correct Spelling* goes into greater detail than any previous speller. Every spelling and pronunciation presented in this text is based upon one or more leading authorities. Where authorities disagree, the spelling or pronunciation best adapted to correct recall has been selected.

SUGGESTIONS TO TEACHERS

The whole-word, hard-spot study methods used in this text are different from those commonly followed in learning to spell. Inasmuch as the pupil's success depends in large degree upon using these methods, it is important that teachers read carefully:

1. The Introduction (pages iii-viii) which explains the psychology of learning to spell words at upper-grade and mature levels.
2. The introduction for Part 1 (pages 1-4), which explains how pupils are to study.

Gateways to Correct Spelling is designed to serve the needs of variable instructional situations. In schools that so desire, and there are many such, the lessons are arranged so that students, with the occasional supervision of teachers, can make progress according to their own abilities and the time available. On the other hand, the text probably serves at its best when it becomes a significant and highly correlated part of the total language arts program and a special instrument of group or intragroup instruction. In this case, all of the lessons in Part 1 on basic words should be taught or reviewed; most of the lessons in Part 2 on practical spelling and dictionary habits should be taken advantage of; and the lessons in Part 3 should be emphasized to the extent that they strengthen the vocabulary development aims of the language arts course. Part of each day and a whole period each week may best be allotted to this work.

Gateways to Correct Spelling is also highly adapted to the numerous high schools which administer spelling as a separate subject, whether for remedial, review, or graduation credit purposes. The best lessons to use will vary according to the time available and the grade level of pupils. The following schedule is typical of that followed in numerous high schools:

1. Freshman Year—Lessons 1-30. One hour per week.
2. Sophomore Year—Lessons 31-60. One hour per week.
3. Junior Year—Lessons 61-95. Thirty minutes, Tuesday and Thursday.
4. Senior Year—Lessons 96-133. Thirty minutes, Tuesday and Thursday.

Whatever the general methods used, it is advantageous to do some general testing. Words from Part 1 serve well either for diagnostic or classification purposes. Standardized tests[1] with national norms are available for comparative purposes.

[1]*The Ayer Standardized High School Spelling Test,* The Steck Company, Austin, Texas.

PART 1

THE MAIN GATEWAY

SHORT CUTS TO BASIC SPELLING

This gateway opens a series of short cuts to the quick mastery of the basic words which cause four-fifths of all mistakes made in spelling. All users of this book should study with great care the directions which follow.

Experts say that the best way to succeed in learning to spell is to take on responsibility for your own progress. Convince yourself, first of all, that good spelling is a necessity in your education. The knowledge of words is the key to all learning. To study spelling as directed in this book will improve your knowledge of words and ability in writing, in reading, and in speaking. Poor spelling is taken everywhere to be a sign of carelessness and the mark of poor education. It defeats your best efforts in school and later on in the business world. Good spelling, on the other hand, speeds up your education, makes all writing a pleasure, and is a first aid to a successful career in social and business life.

The lessons ahead offer you the best set of words and the easiest ways to learn to spell that American teachers and experts have been able to devise after thousands of hours of study and experimentation. Their work is your gain. All you have to do is to gear yourself up to study with zeal and keep track of your own progress. That is *your* responsibility. How far you go is strictly up to you.

HOW TO STUDY

Learning to spell a word successfully consists of four different phases which go on more or less at the same time: (1) you see the word clearly; (2) you identify the word as to meaning and pronunciation; (3) you drill to memorize the word; and (4) you drill to recall the word. The result is a lasting fusion of sensory and logical memory.

1. How To See a Word Clearly

Most of the words which appear in Parts 1 and 2 of this book are familiar but "tricky" words. They are frequently misspelled by high school and senior students. They need to be looked at very carefully as a first step to achieve correct spelling. The text presents the words in the best manner possible for you to see them clearly, but *you yourself* must look at each word so carefully that you are certain that you see every letter. Note, for example, the word *absence* which appears in the first line of Lesson 1 (page 5) as follows:

1. **absence** His ab′sen*c*e was excused.

Look at the whole word **absence** first. How many letters? Spell it slowly one time. Note the first and last letters. Try to see all of the letters at one glance. If the word is too long, try to see all of the letters in each syllable; for example, *ab* and *sence.*

Pronounce the word correctly (the text will help you) as you look at it in the explanatory sentence, *His ab′sence was excused.* Examine any hard spots (usually printed in italics) in the word, such as the ending *ce.* Then pronounce *ab′sence* to yourself by syllables. At the same time, try to *see* all of the letters in each syllable. Repeat this until you can see *absence* as one word with all of the letters in proper order. Now cover the word and see if you can write it correctly. Probably you can, but you may find that some words still have hard spots. In this case, study the word again as before.

Vigorous practice to see and recall words as just indicated will greatly increase your ability to see words in your "mind's eye," just as you can recall how your name looks on the back of an envelope. These visual images may not stand out very clearly, but their presence in memory is a very important part of successful spelling. You may wish to vary the order a little, but continue *saying* and *seeing* the word by syllables or large parts, and give special attention to the hard spots until you can see the whole word clearly at a single glance.

2. How To Identify a Word

You are, no doubt, fairly well acquainted with most of the 720 words that appear in Part 1 of this text. To spell them correctly, you must be sure that you have exactly the right word in mind. Many mistakes in spelling are made because certain words look or sound a good deal like other words. For example, students frequently confuse *there* with *their, to* with *too,* and *except* with *accept.*

As indicated in the previous section, this textbook is arranged to help you identify the word at the same time that you are seeing it clearly. Each new word is followed by a sentence which illustrates a proper meaning of the word. If you do not recognize the word definitely or are not sure that you can pronounce it correctly after looking at it in the illustrative sentence, look it up in the Basic Dictionary which appears later in this book, beginning on page 65. Learning to recognize a word by syllables is of great value in breaking words correctly at the end of lines when writing or typing.

3. How To Memorize a Word

You have already been told that to combine a clear impression with a sharp recall is the best part of memorizing a spelling word, but this book also presents special memory aids for each word. Your attention is called to certain peculiarities in the word, such as the *ence* ending in *absence.* Similar words are associated in a way that will strengthen your memory of the correct spelling. You are cautioned against faulty associations, such as *wholly* with *solely.* Catchy sayings are given which stick in memory. For example, "A good vocation has a good vacation." When some word is particularly troublesome to you, invent some peculiar association and memorize it. For example, tie up *balance,* the fourth word in Lesson 1, with this memory quip: "*Balance* a *lance* in *Alabama.*" This kind of memory aid is frequently used by memory experts. Thus you will remember not only *balance,* but two other similar words, *lance* and *Alabama.*

4. How To Recall a Word

The three phases of studying a spelling word—seeing clearly, identifying, and memorizing—are essential in learning to recall or revive a word later on. Your ability to recall a word accurately will be quickened and strengthened by doing the Visual Drills which accompany each lesson. After the preliminary study of each word separately as directed up to this point, it will be better for you to take three words at a time for additional practice.

As an illustration of this new practice, take the first three words, *absence, owing,* and *vacation,* in Lesson 1 on page 5. At the bottom of the page you find a special visual drill for these three words in the form of the sentence: *O - ing to the teacher's ab - - - - - , the pupils had a two-day va - - - - on.* As you read this sentence to yourself, try to visualize the correct missing letters. If you have any difficulty, look at the complete word in the lesson above. When you can fill in the missing letters mentally without any delay, cover the page and write from memory the sentence containing the three words. Check the spelling at once. If you have made any mistakes, study the hard parts and test yourself again.

When you have studied all of the twelve words in Lesson 1 in the foregoing manner, have someone give you a test on the twelve words. Better still, see if you can write them all from memory. Take the same test a week later, and give them an occasional review at later dates.

Keep a separate list of your particularly difficult words and, as the coaches say, give them a really "rough tackle." You can down any word in the dictionary for keeps if you tackle it hard enough. The more writing of these words you do in connection with your studies, your letters, or your diary, the better you will be able to recall them later on. Even though you already know how to spell a word, go through the exercises; it will strengthen your permanent recall.

BRIEF STATEMENT OF HOW TO STUDY

(See the preceding pages for details.)

1. Look at the first word in the lesson carefully. Spell it one time letter by letter. Look at the whole word. Note whether it is a three-letter word, a four-letter word, or some other number. Center attention on the first and last letters.
2. Read the explanatory sentence which follows the word. This will help you to recognize the meaning of the word. Note how many syllables there are and where the word is accented.
3. Note how each syllable is spelled as you pronounce the word to yourself. If you are uncertain as to the correct meaning or pronunciation, refer to the Basic Dictionary, pages 65-85.
4. Study any hard or peculiar parts. Most of these are indicated by letters printed in italics. Watch for letters not sounded in the pronunciation.
5. Cover the word and try to see or remember it as a whole. Then write it.
6. Strengthen your memory of the word by doing the related Memory Aid.
7. Study the second and third words in the same manner as the first.
8. Practice the special Visual Drill for the three words at the bottom of the lesson. Then write it from memory.
9. Study the words 4 to 6, 7 to 9, and 10 to 12 in the same way as described above.
10. Take a test on all twelve words; take another test one week later.

In all of these steps correct mistakes immediately and repeat needed study. Keep a list of your difficult words and review them frequently.

Lesson 1 BASIC WORDS

It is important that you study as directed on pages 1-4.

1. **absence** His ab'*sence* was excused.
2. **owing** James left town ow'ing a big debt.
3. **vacation** The summer va ca'*tio*n seemed too short.
4. **balance** The boy on the wire lost his bal'an*ce*.
5. **paid** The debt for the piano was pa*i*d in full.
6. **account** John gave a good a*c*'count of himself.
7. **knew** Charles *k*new everybody there by first name.
8. **just** Washington was a fair and just man.
9. **always** Not just for a day, but al'wa*y*s.
10. **against** The picture hung a g*ai*nst' the wall.
11. **amateur** The am'a t*eu*r played like a professional.
12. **decision** The umpire made a quick de *c*i'*s*ion.

MEMORY AIDS

The heading Copy, as used below and elsewhere, introduces a catchy saying to help fix a spelling in memory.

1. Note that *absence* ends in *ence*. Compare *presence, silence*.
2. Omit the *e* in *owing*. Compare ow*e*, *owing;* mak*e*, *making*.
3. Copy and memorize: A good vocation has a good vacation.
4. Note the *ala* in *balance*. Compare *salary, Alabama*.
5. Compare *pay, paid; lay, laid*. Copy: Paid off and laid off.
6. Focus attention on the *cc* in *account*. Copy: An accurate account according to law.
7. Distinguish *knew* from *new*. Copy: He knew his new knife.
8. Do not pronounce *just*, "*jest*." Copy: Just a junior in June.
9. Copy: Although Alfred was already too big, he almost always ate like a pig.
10. Study the different *ai* sounds in *against (ĕ), certain (ĭ), pain (ā)*.
11. Note the unusual *teur* in *amateur*. Copy: I am an amateur.
12. Note the one *c* and one *s* in *decision*. Compare *precision, vision*.

VISUAL DRILLS

1. O - ing to the teacher's ab - - - - -, the pupils had a two-day va - - - - on.
2. Father p - - d the b - - - - ce on our telephone a - c - - nt.
3. Jones al - - ys said that he - - ew j - st what to do.
4. The faculty made a de - i - ion ag - - nst his am - t - - r standing.

Test yourself by writing each drill from memory.

Lesson 2 BASIC WORDS

One of the best memory drills on these simple but frequently misspelled words is to write them in short sentences.

1. **busy**	The doctor was too b*us*′y to see me.
2. **buy**	Mary planned to b*u*y a new dress.
3. **copy**	Please cop′y this map exactly.
4. **losing**	John has been l*os*′ing weight rapidly.
5. **coming**	I am c*om*′ing to see you soon.
6. **Saturday**	Tomorrow is the last Sat′*ur* da*y* in the month.
7. **handful**	The little boy had a hand′ful of marbles.
8. **bury**	We saw the dog b*ur*′y the bone.
9. **having**	The girls were hav′ing a party.
10. **half**	Please give me ha*l*f of the orange.
11. **duly**	He was du′ly punished for the crime.
12. **truly**	She tru′ly tried to go to the farm.

MEMORY AIDS

1. Spell *busy* with one *s*. Compare *business, busily.*
2. It is *buy*, not *by*. COPY: The busy buyer in business.
3. Note the single *p* in *copy*. Compare *copying;* contrast *poppy.*
4. *Lose* loses an *e* in *losing*. See also *owing, moving, having.*
5. Note the omitted *e* in *coming*. Compare *come, coming; ride, riding; leave, leaving.*
6. *Saturday* is always capitalized. Note the *ur* in *Saturday.*
7. Note that *full* changes to *ful* in *handful*. Compare *useful, grateful.*
8. Note the one *r* in *bury*. See also *busy, copy, duly.*
9. Write three short sentences which include the word *having.*
10. Focus attention on the *l* in *half*. Compare *calf, halfback.*
11. There is only one *l* in *duly*. Compare *truly, unruly.*
12. Compare *true, truly; due, duly; blue, bluing.*

VISUAL DRILLS

First, fill in the missing letters mentally as you read the drill. When you can do this correctly, write the drill from memory.

1. Too b - s - to b - y a co - - of the morning paper.
2. After lo - - ng the game on Sat - - day, the team was co - - ng home.
3. The handf - - of soldiers was not ha - - ng time to b - r - its dead.
4. One ha - f of the letters was du - - signed, "Yours tr - - - ."

Test yourself by writing each drill from memory.

Lesson 3 BASIC WORDS

Some of the most common misspellings are due to carelessness in writing. The simple words in this lesson are very often confused.

1. **to**	It is easy to forget historical dates.
2. **two**	The boy bought t*w*o apples and three oranges.
3. **too**	The hat was much to*o* large for his head.
4. **there**	The firemen went ther*e* quickly.
5. **their**	The Indians spent the*i*r money foolishly.
6. **therefore**	They were ther*e*'for*e* soon out of funds.
7. **its**	The wounded bird spread its wings.
8. **it's**	All men know that it's wrong to steal.
9. **itself**	The car almost ran by it'self.
10. **write**	Please *w*rit*e* a letter home today.
11. **right**	That was the ri*gh*t thing to do.
12. **written**	The letter was *w*rit'*t*en in ink.

MEMORY AIDS

1. Copy: To go to town to give to the poor.
2. *Two* is the correct spelling of the numeral 2.
3. *Too* also means *also.* Mary cried, *too.* Copy: Too much to do.
4. Note the *here* in *there.* Do not confuse *there* with *they're.*
5. The *heir* in *their* suggests possession. It's *their* business.
6. Always put three *e's* in *therefore.* Compare *wherefore.*
7. The word *its* is the possessive case of *it.*
8. The word *it's* is a contraction of *it is.*
9. The word *itself* combines *it* and *self.* Compare *himself, herself.*
10. Center attention on the *wr* beginning of *write.* Compare *wrist, wrinkle.*
11. Consult your Basic Dictionary, beginning on page 65, on this puzzler: "Write *rite* right."
12. Note the two *t's* in *written.* Compare *bite, bitten; smite, smitten.*

VISUAL DRILLS

1. It seems t - - far t - be only t - - miles.
2. They came th - - - first; th - - ef - r - , it was th - i - property.
3. However great it - power, it - - impossible for a machine to repair it - e - - .
4. You should have - rit - - n to the r - g - t place; wr - - - again.

Test yourself by writing each drill from memory.

Lesson 4 BASIC WORDS

You will not learn to spell these words merely by reading the exercises. Study them vigorously.

1. **style**	The old st*y*le is not now in fashion.
2. **stretch**	The story required no stre*t*ch of the imagination.
3. **waist**	The wa*i*st of the old dress was quite small.
4. **flies**	A duck fli*e*s rapidly with the wind.
5. **except**	No one was there ex *c*ept′ two children.
6. **which**	We never knew *wh*ich team won.
7. **whom**	We wondered to *w*hom it belonged.
8. **whose**	Who's the man *w*hose dog is lost?
9. **led**	The poor boy was led astray.
10. **either**	The hunter was e*i*′ther lost or injured.
11. **until**	Keep the letter un til′ I call for it.
12. **maybe**	Maybe he will go and ma*y*′be he will not.

MEMORY AIDS

1. Put a *y* in your *style.* Compare *stylish;* contrast *while.*
2. Note the *tch* in *stretch.* Compare *stretch, scratch, itch.*
3. Do not confuse *waist* with *waste.* Note the *i* in *waist* and the *e* in *waste.*
4. Compare *fly, flies; cry, cries; supply, supplies.*
5. Distinguish *except* from *accept.* STUDY: No one would *accept* a bribe *except* a criminal.
6. Focus on the *wh* in *which.* Compare *where, when, what.*
7. Use the correct forms: *to whom, for whom, by whom.*
8. Do not confuse *whose* with the contraction *who's.*
9. You *lead* a horse now; you *led* the horse yesterday.
10. STUDY: I can see an *i* in *either* with either eye.
11. Note carefully the one *l* in *until.* Contrast *still, till.*
12. Observe that *maybe* is a combination of *may* and *be.*

VISUAL DRILLS

1. This kind and st - l - of w - - st seems to str - - - h the most.
2. It was perfect e - - - pt for the fl - - s w - ich annoyed him.
3. W - ose horse was l - d away and by - - om?
4. M - - be e - - her father or mother will stay unt - - we return.

Test yourself by writing each drill from memory.

Lesson 5 BASIC WORDS

Consult the Basic Dictionary for the correct pronunciation of the words listed below. Study the key to pronunciation on page 65.

1. **severe** The pitcher felt a se vere′ pain in his arm.
2. **cough** The patient suffered from a bad co*ugh.*
3. **ache** His tooth began to a*che* badly.
4. **hoarse** The speaker was too ho*arse* to talk.
5. **stomach** Food is digested in the stom′ac*h.*
6. **grippe** An attack of grip*pe* kept him from work.
7. **hospital** The nurses at the hos′pit al were new.
8. **physician** The *phy* si′*ci*an recognized the symptoms at once.
9. **once** The little boy had been sick only *once.*
10. **benefited** The poor man ben′e fit′ed from your gift.
11. **medicine** The med′i *cine* cured his cold quickly.
12. **immediately** The telegram was delivered *im* me′di at*e* ly.

MEMORY AIDS

1. Note the *ever* in *severe.* Accent the last syllable.
2. Focus on the *ough* in *cough.* COPY: Enough of a rough, tough cough.
3. Note the *che* in *ache.* Contrast *aching.*
4. Distinguish *hoarse* from *horse.* COPY: A hoarse roar from the coarse boar.
5. Note the *tom* in *stomach.* Stress the *a* in *stomach.*
6. Center on the extra *pe* in *grippe.* COPY: The grippe is a gripper.
7. Pronounce *hospital* carefully. Compare *vital;* contrast *pistol.*
8. There is a *y* in *physician.* Compare *physical, musician.*
9. COPY: Once one dunce spelled once, *wunst.* Compare *one.*
10. Stress the three *e* sounds in *benefited.* Note the single *n, f,* and *t.*
11. Stress the two *i*'s in *medicine.* Focus attention on the *cine.*
12. Note the two *m*'s and the final silent *e* in *immediately.* Compare *immediate.*

VISUAL DRILLS

1. The sick boy had a se - er - c - - g - and headac - - .
2. A h - - rs - voice and an upset st - ma - - indicate grip - - .
3. The hosp - t - - ph - - ic - - n treated him at on - - .
4. He ben - fit - - from the med - c - - - almost i - - ediat - - - .

When you have finished this lesson, review Lesson 1.

Lesson 6 BASIC WORDS

Always study the entire lesson. The different parts strengthen each other.

1. **heard** Have you he*a*rd the latest news?
2. **here** The circus arrived her*e* this morning.
3. **friend** Sometimes a dog is a man's best fr*i*end.
4. **says** The speaker *says* the idea is wrong.
5. **weigh** The black bass will w*eigh* five pounds.
6. **coarse** His co*a*rs*e* manners were unpleasant.
7. **wait** We had to wa*i*t ten minutes for the bus.
8. **awful** The thief dreaded the aw′ful disgrace.
9. **because** The player fell be *cause*′ he was tripped.
10. **usually** The sun u′*su al* ly shines in Arizona.
11. **break** The sad news will bre*a*k her heart.
12. **least** It was the le*a*st he could have done.

MEMORY AIDS

1. Note the *ear* in *hear* and *heard.*
2. Do not confuse *here* with *hear. Here* and *there.*
3. Visualize the *ie* in *friend.* Note the two *i*'s in *friendship.*
4. Compare I *say,* he *says.* Note the past tense: he *said.*
5. Compare *weigh, weight.* Remember the *eight* in *weight.*
6. Do not confuse *coarse* with *course.* Think of coarse sand.
7. Center on the *ai* in *wait.* Contrast *wait* and *weight.* COPY: Wait for the bait.
8. *Awful* is shortened from *awe* and *full.* Compare *handful.*
9. Note carefully the *au* in *because.* Compare *cause, pause.*
10. Note the two *u*'s and two *l*'s in *usually.* Compare *awfully.*
11. Distinguish *break* (to separate into pieces) from *brake* (to slow down).
12. Note the *east* in *least.* COPY: At least the beast could eat a feast.

VISUAL DRILLS

1. We he - rd that your fr - - nd was her - .
2. The grocer s - - s the co - rs - sugar does not w - - - h as much.
3. It seemed aw - u - bec - - s - we had to wa - t in the storm.
4. A br - - k us - a - ly comes when l - - st expected.

When you have finished this lesson, review Lesson 2.

Lesson 7 BASIC WORDS

It will help you if you memorize the short quips introduced by the word Copy.

1. **steel**	John's skates were made of ste*e*l.
2. **laid**	The worker la*i*d his shovel down.
3. **straight**	A stra*igh*t line does not curve.
4. **where**	There's wher*e* we long to go.
5. **lose**	Without directions he will l*o*s*e* his way.
6. **nickel**	Mr. Jones paid a nick′el for his newspaper.
7. **though**	I shall go, tho*ugh* it is late.
8. **steal**	A thief may ste*a*l your money.
9. **many**	A great m*a*n′y people live in New York.
10. **believe**	The judge did not be l*ieve*′ his explanation.
11. **theory**	Our teacher explained the the′o ry of evolution.
12. **parallel**	The gymnast performed on the par′*al* lel bars.

MEMORY AIDS

1. Distinguish *steel* from *steal.* Copy: Feel the steel wheel.
2. The word *laid* is the past tense of *lay.* Compare *lay, laid; say, said; pay, paid.*
3. Center on the *aigh* in *straight.* Copy: Paid to be laid straight.
4. Note the *here* in *where.* Compare *there.*
5. Distinguish *lose* from *loose.* Copy: Lose whose loose goose?
6. Note the unusual *el* ending of *nickel.* Contrast *pickle, tickle,* and *fickle.*
7. Note the *thou* in *though.* Compare *through, dough.*
8. Center on the *ea* in *steal.* Copy: Steal a meal of real veal.
9. Pronounced *men i,* but spelled *many.* Compare *any.*
10. Observe the *lie* in *believe.* Compare *relieve, belief.*
11. Sound the *o* in *theory.* Note the three syllables. Copy: Theodore's theory of geography.
12. Sound both *a*'s in *parallel.* Note the final *llel.*

VISUAL DRILLS

1. The ste - l rails were l - - d in a stra - - - t line.
2. Wh - r - did the boy lo - - his ni - k - l?
3. Even tho - - - hungry, not m - n - persons would ste - l food.
4. The professor did not bel - ev - in the th - - ry of par - - l - l lines.

When you have finished this lesson, review Lesson 3.

Lesson 8 BASIC WORDS

Take time to review previous lessons. Frequent review is the key to correct recall.

1.	**clothes**	Everyone should keep his clo*thes* neat and clean.
2.	**beauty**	The b*ea*u'ty of this dress is its color.
3.	**women**	All w*o*m'en like to have beautiful clothes.
4.	**choose**	Which hat do you choo*se* to wear?
5.	**material**	Cotton is a practical ma te'ri al for summer.
6.	**wear**	You must w*ea*r your coat if the weather is cold.
7.	**occasionally**	He came oc ca'*sion* al *ly* to see my father.
8.	**satisfied**	The buyer was not sat'is fi*ed* with the car.
9.	**woman**	The w*o*m'an lost her purse.
10.	**color**	My favorite col'*or* is red.
11.	**blue**	Mary's dress was a light shade of blu*e*.
12.	**prefer**	Which do you pre fer', white meat or dark meat?

MEMORY AIDS

1. Put an *e* in *clothes*. Contrast *cloth, clothe, clothes,* and *clothing.*
2. Note the *beau* in *beauty*. Consult the Basic Dictionary for the pronunciation of *beauty*. Compare *beauty, beautiful.*
3. Center on the *o* in *women*. Compare *man, men; woman, women; gentleman, gentlemen.*
4. Keep the two *o*'s in *choose*. COPY: Choose the loose goose.
5. Note the *mate* in *material*. Compare *serial, financial.*
6. Distinguish *wear* from *ware*. The bearskin will wear, not tear.
7. Note the two *c*'s, one *s*, and two *l*'s in oc*c*a*s*ional*l*y. Compare *occupy*.
8. Center on the *fied* in *satisfied*. Compare *notified, justified.*
9. Note the *man* in *woman*. COPY: Fan the Roman woman.
10. Focus on *olo* in *color*. COPY: A colony of colored colonels.
11. Distinguish *blue* from *blew*. COPY: The best hue is true blue.
12. Accent the *fer* in *prefer*. I *in fer'* you *pre fer'* to *de fer'*.

VISUAL DRILLS

1. Many w-m-n buy clo---- for their b--uty.
2. Others cho-s- a ma----al that will we-r well.
3. There is oc-a-iona--y a w-m-n who is never satisf--d.
4. Most men pref-- the c-l-r of bl--.

When you have finished this lesson, review Lesson 4.

Lesson 9 BASIC WORDS

In taking a Visual Drill, do two things: (1) visualize the missing letters; (2) write the entire sentence from memory.

1. **autumn**	The *au*'tum*n* season seemed short last year.
2. **scenery**	The woodland *sc*en'er y made an attractive view.
3. **sight**	Poor *sig*h*t* is usually aided by wearing glasses.
4. **benefit**	The man received no ben'e fit from the medicine.
5. **junior**	Jones was the j*un*'*io*r partner in the firm.
6. **series**	Our vacation was a se'*ries* of exciting events.
7. **authority**	The principal has *au* thor'i ty over the school.
8. **been**	The children have be*e*n home since noon.
9. **useful**	John's skill with tools makes him us*e*'ful at home.
10. **quiet**	It was particularly qui'et just before dawn.
11. **sincerity**	His sin *c*er'i ty of purpose was very evident.
12. **special**	We went to the game on a spe'*ci*al train.

MEMORY AIDS

1. Compare *autumn, autumnal; column, columnist; hymn, hymnal.*
2. COPY: Scatter the scenery with scented scissors.
3. Distinguish *sight* from *site.* In *sight* (view) of the building *site* (plot).
4. Sound both *e*'s in *benefit.* Compare *benefited, benefiting.*
5. Compare *junior* with *senior.* COPY: Just a junior in June.
6. Focus on the *ie* in *series.* COPY: Many queries about the World's Series.
7. Sound the *i* in *authority.* Compare *authorize, majority.*
8. Note the *bee* in *been,* but pronounce it *bin.* The British say *been.*
9. Use the *e* in *useful,* but not in *using.* Compare *useless.*
10. Distinguish *quiet* from *quite.* Note the two syllables in *qui'et.*
11. Note the *it* in *sincerity.* Compare *authority;* contrast *sincerely.*
12. Focus on the *cia* in *special.* Compare *social, commercial.*

VISUAL DRILLS

1. The s - - nery in a - tu - - was a pretty si - - t.
2. The j - n - - r society gave a ser - - s of ben - fit plays.
3. The judge had b - - n very us - fu - as an a - th - rity on claims.
4. His q - - - t manner and sinc - - - ty of purpose gave him a spe - - - l dignity.

When you have finished this lesson, review Lesson 5.

Lesson 10 BASIC WORDS

Look carefully for the silent letters in the words which follow:

1. **absolutely**	John was ab'so lut*e*'ly certain.
2. **certain**	Be *cer*'t*a*in that you are right.
3. **neither**	The child was ne*i*'ther well nor happy.
4. **catalog**	The cat'*a* log advertised many articles.
5. **manufacture**	Johnson and Sons man'u fac'tur*e* shoes.
6. **item**	No i'tem was too small to be seen.
7. **balloon**	The ba*l* loon' floated out of sight.
8. **nineteen**	It happened nin*e*'te*e*n years ago.
9. **height**	The airplane rose to a great h*e*i*gh*t.
10. **debtor**	The de*b*t'*o*r refused to pay his bill.
11. **merchandise**	Some stores deliver their mer'chan di*s*e.
12. **regard**	The man has no re gard' for the truth.

MEMORY AIDS

1. Note the silent *e* in *absolutely*. Compare *completely, definitely, desperately.*
2. Note the *cer* in *certain.* Compare *certificate, captain.*
3. Study the *e* before *i* combination *ei.* Print the words *neither* and *either* five times.
4. Note the middle *a* in *catalog.* COPY: A cat atop a catalog.
5. Note the two *u*'s in *manufacture.* Compare *manual* labor.
6. Pronounce *i'tem* carefully. Compare *items, itemize, system.*
7. A *balloon* is round and has two *l*'s like a *ball.*
8. Note that *nine, ninety,* and *nineteen* have an *e* after the *n.*
9. Note the *eight* in *height.* COPY: Height – eight feet, eight inches.
10. The word *debtor* is pronounced *det'er.* Compare *debt, doubt.*
11. Put a *hand* in *merchandise.* COPY: A rise in merchandise at the Paradise.
12. Focus on the *gard* in *regard.* Compare *reward, retard.*

VISUAL DRILLS

1. N - - ther speaker was abs - lu - - ly - ert - - n that he knew all of the facts.
2. They man - fact - - - every it - m listed in the cat - l - g.
3. The ba - l - - n went up to a h - i - - t of nin - t - - n hundred feet.
4. The d - - t - r for the merch - n - i - - had no reg - - d for his debt.

When you have finished this lesson, review Lesson 6.

Lesson 11 BASIC WORDS

Try to see all of the letters in these words at one glance. Test yourself three words at a time.

1. **tobacco** The room was full of to bac′*co* smoke.
2. **through** Are you thro*ugh* with my book?
3. **using** We have been u*s*′ing a new brand of coffee.
4. **almost** Jane is al′most sixteen years old.
5. **ready** Are you re*a*d′y to go to the party?
6. **separate** Each class meets in a sep′a rat*e* room.
7. **said** Father s*ai*d that we should meet at six.
8. **entitled** The book is en ti′tl*e*d *Manners for Moderns.*
9. **salary** The sal′a ry is one hundred dollars a month.
10. **anxious** The woman was an*x*′*io*us to see her son.
11. **financial** The firm's chief worry is fi nan′*ci*al.
12. **affairs** The mayor was a man of a*f* fairs′.

MEMORY AIDS

1. Note the one *b* and two *c*'s in *tobacco.* COPY: Recollect tobacco usually disappoints.
2. Distinguish *through* from *threw.* John *threw* the ball *through* the open door.
3. Omit the *e* in *using.* Compare *abuse, abusing; amuse, amusing; fuse, fusing.*
4. Only one *l* in *almost.* COPY: Alfred almost always ate like a pig.
5. Note the *a* in *ready.* COPY: A steady tread and a ready head.
6. Sound both *a*'s in *separate.* Think of preparation for separation.
7. Print *say, said* five times. Compare *pay, paid; lay, laid.*
8. Note that *entitle* begins and ends with an *e.* Compare *encircle.*
9. Sound both *a*'s in *salary.* COPY: A salary balance in Alabama.
10. Center on the *anx* in *anxious.* Compare *anxiety, gracious.*
11. Note the *cia* in *financial.* Compare *special, commercial.*
12. Include two *f*'s in *affairs.* COPY: Affie's affairs of affection.

VISUAL DRILLS

1. The smoker said that he was thr - - - - u - - ng toba - - o.
2. The angry couple were a - - ost re - dy to sep - rate.
3. The clerk s - - d that he was - nti - - ed to a larger sa - - ry.
4. He was an - - - us about his finan - - al af - - irs.

When you have finished this lesson, review Lesson 7.

Lesson 12 BASIC WORDS

Do not use contractions in business or formal letters. In most contractions an apostrophe (') is used in place of one or more missing letters.

1. **couldn't** I am sorry that I co*ul*d'n't come.
2. **wouldn't** Billy wo*ul*d'n't take the medicine.
3. **doesn't** Mary do*es*'n't wish to be in the play.
4. **can't** I can't do what I thought I could.
5. **isn't** The house is'n't in the picture.
6. **didn't** The stranger did'n't know where to go.
7. **don't** Why don't you telephone her?
8. **possessive** He treated her with a pos *s*es'*s*ive manner.
9. **yours** Do you claim that this book is yo*u*rs?
10. **sure** Are you sur*e* that he will come?
11. **etc.** The abbreviation *etc.* means *and other things.*
12. **period** Always put a pe'ri od after an abbreviation.

MEMORY AIDS

1. The contraction *couldn't* is the shortened form of *could not.*
2. The contraction *wouldn't* is the shortened form of *would not.*
3. The contraction *doesn't* is the shortened form of *does not.*
4. The contraction *can't* is the shortened form of *cannot.*
5. The contraction *isn't* is the shortened form of *is not.*
6. The contraction *didn't* is the shortened form of *did not.*
7. The contraction *don't* is the shortened form of *do not.*
8. Note the four *s*'s in *possessive.* Compare *possesses.*
9. Note the *u* in *yours.* Compare *ours, hour, courteous.*
10. Center on the *su* in *sure.* Compare *sugar, surely.*
11. The abbreviation *etc.* is a contraction of *et cetera.*
12. Pronounce the three syllables in *period* carefully.

VISUAL DRILLS

1. Mother do - sn - t know whether John co - - d - 't go or wo - - dn - t go.
2. Anyway, he did - - t go; so you ca - - t say what is - 't so.
3. Don - t use a pos - e - - ive mark (') with yo - rs.
4. Be s - re to place a per - - d after the abbreviation, *e - c.*

When you have finished this lesson, review Lesson 8. Do you know the difference between *cloths* and *clothes?*

Lesson 13 BASIC WORDS

It will help your spelling and writing if you note the separate syllables in each word.

1. **business**	The new b*usi*'ness was profitable.
2. **president**	The pre*s*'i dent was elected for two years.
3. **executive**	The principal is an e*x* ec'u tiv*e* officer.
4. **capacity**	The ca pa*c*'i ty of the tank was fifty gallons.
5. **commercial**	The co*m* mer'*ci*al firm did a large business.
6. **organization**	Our schools have the 6-3-3 plan of or'gan i za'*tio*n.
7. **courteous**	We appreciated the guide's c*ou*r'te *o*us attention.
8. **position**	The ship changed its po *si*'*tio*n during the night.
9. **independent**	The boy was too in'de pend'ent to seek help.
10. **satisfactory**	The secretary's work was sat'is fac'to ry.
11. **service**	The hotel serv'*ice* was unusually poor.
12. **policy**	They adopted the pol'i *c*y of watchful waiting.

MEMORY AIDS

1. The word *business* (biz'ness) has only two syllables.
2. Copy: It is evident that the president is confident.
3. Note the *cuti* in *executive.* Compare *execute, executing.*
4. Note the *city* in *capacity.* Copy: His capacity for veracity.
5. Place two *m*'s in *commercial.* Compare *commence, commerce.*
6. Remember that *organization* is derived from *organize.*
7. Keep the *court* in *courteous.* Compare *courtesy, courtly.*
8. Focus on the *si* in *position.* Compare *ambition, positive.*
9. Copy: The excellent superintendent was independent.
10. Note the three words – *sat, is,* and *factory* – in *satisfactory.*
11. Note the *ice* in *service.* Contrast *serve, service,* and *servant.*
12. Center on the *icy* in *policy.* Copy: The polite police policy.

VISUAL DRILLS

1. As pres - d - nt, Mr. Henry was the chief ex - - utive of a large bu - - ness firm.
2. He showed unusual c - pa - ity in the org - n - - ation of small co - - erc - - l firms.
3. The po - - tion required ind - pend - nt leadership but c - - rt - - - s manners.
4. Mr. Henry said that sat - - fact - - y s - rv - - - was the best pol - - y.

When you have finished this lesson, review Lesson 9.

Lesson 14 — BASIC WORDS

If you are uncertain concerning the pronunciation of any of the following words, refer to the Basic Dictionary, pages 65-85.

1. **bulletin**	The noon bul′*le* tin predicted rain.
2. **official**	The reported election was declared o*f* fi′*ci*al.
3. **bureau**	Please close the bu′r*eau* drawer.
4. **announcement**	The a*n* nounc*e*′ment of the wedding was late.
5. **changeable**	Her mind was chang*e*′a bl*e* from hour to hour.
6. **weather**	Fair we*a*th′er lasted the entire week.
7. **temporary**	Henry served as tem′po ra′ry chairman.
8. **lightning**	The lig*ht*′ning was followed by thunder.
9. **Tuesday**	It happened on Tue*s*′da*y* evening.
10. **possibility**	There was no pos′*s*i bil′i ty of escape.
11. **shining**	The sun was shin′ing brightly.
12. **Wednesday**	It was the first We*d*ne*s*′da*y* in June.

MEMORY AIDS

1. Note the *bullet* in *bulletin.* Compare *bull, bullet, bulletin.*
2. Note the two *f*'s in *official.* COPY: I am off to offer the office to the official officer.
3. Visualize the whole word *bureau.* Remember the two *u*'s.
4. Note the four *n*'s in *announcement.* Compare *ounce, announce.*
5. Keep the *change* in *changeable.* THINK: *able* to *change.*
6. Distinguish *weather* from *whether.* COPY: Heavy leather for wet weather.
7. Pronounce the *o* in *temporary.* Compare *honor, honorary.*
8. Note carefully the *ning* in *lightning.* Distinguish from *lighting.*
9. Center on the *ue* in *Tuesday.* COPY: Dues on Tuesday.
10. Focus on the *ossi* in *possibility.* Compare *possible, possibly.*
11. Omit the *e* in *shining.* Compare: *pine, pining; dine, dining.*
12. Note the *ednes* in *Wednesday.* Compare *Tuesday, Thursday.*

VISUAL DRILLS

1. An of - ic - - l bul - - t - n came from the weather bu - - - - .
2. The an - - un - - ment predicted chan - - - ble w - - ther.
3. There was a tem - - r - ry period of li - - t - ing on T - - sday.
4. There is a good po - s - b - lity that the sun will be shi - - ng on W - - n - - day.

When you have finished this lesson, review Lesson 10.

Lesson 15 BASIC WORDS

Always study the entire lesson as directed in the Brief Statement of How To Study, page 4.

1. **scene**	The lakeside *scene* was beautiful.
2. **appreciate**	We a*p* pre′*c*i at*e* your kindness.
3. **description**	John gave a good de scrip′*tio*n of the man.
4. **error**	You made one er′*ro*r in adding the numbers.
5. **estimate**	Will you es′ti mat*e* the value of the house?
6. **length**	The tailor measured the length of his coat.
7. **traveler**	The trav′el er was going to California.
8. **journey**	We made the j*o*ur′ne*y* on horses.
9. **tired**	His eyes were tir*e*d from reading.
10. **circumstances**	Under the *c*ir′cum stan*c* es, you should stay.
11. **advise**	I would ad vi*s*e′ you not to go.
12. **proceed**	Now we may pro *ce*ed′ with our work.

MEMORY AIDS

1. Copy: The scientific scene of scintillating scissors.
2. Center on the two *p*'s in *appreciate.* Compare *approve, approach.*
3. Pronounce the *des* in *description.* Copy: Destroy the despised description.
4. Count the three *r*'s in *error.* Compare *terror, mirror.*
5. Note the *i* in *estimate.* Compare *intimate, legitimate.*
6. Pronounce *length* carefully. Compare *long, length; strong, strength.*
7. Think of a *lone* traveler. There are no *double* letters.
8. Focus on the *ou* in *journey.* Copy: A journal of our journey.
9. Note the *tire* in *tired.* Copy: Too tired to be inspired.
10. Copy: A circle of circumstances at the circus.
11. Study: We advi*s*e (ad viz′) you to take the doctor's advi*c*e (ad vis′).
12. Copy: To succeed, you must proceed to exceed.

VISUAL DRILLS

1. We ap - re - - - te the vivid d - - crip - - - n of the s - - n - .
2. He made an er - - r in his est - m - te of the l - n - - - of the field.
3. The trav - l - r was t - - - d after the long j - - rn - - .
4. Under the - - rcumstan - - - , how would you advi - e us to proc - - - ?

When you have finished this lesson, review Lesson 11.

Lesson 16 BASIC WORDS

Go through all of the exercises, but do your chief study on the words which are the most difficult to recall.

1. **naturally**	The girl nat′u ral *ly* favors her mother.
2. **rhyme**	Does the word *girl* r*hy*m*e* with *pearl*?
3. **rhythm**	Everyone likes the r*hy*thm of that new song.
4. **icicle**	The dripping water froze into an i′*c*ic l*e*.
5. **minute**	You have one min′*ute* in which to decide.
6. **disappear**	The magician made the egg dis′a*p* pe*a*r′.
7. **early**	It was necessary to begin e*a*r′ly today.
8. **expect**	The officers e*x* pect′ you to be present.
9. **hour**	The plumber will be back in about an *h*our.
10. **automobile**	The stalled *au*′to mo b*i*l*e*′ was out of gas.
11. **especially**	Mother es pe′*c*ial *ly* likes her new hat.
12. **equipped**	The reporter was e *quipped*′ with pad and pencil.

MEMORY AIDS

Memorize the short quips which follow the heading Copy. Each one helps you to remember a spelling.

1. Note the *rally* in *naturally*. Compare *especially, generally*.
2. Center your attention on the *rhy* in *rhyme* and *rhythm*.
3. Copy: Neither rhyme, rhythm, nor rhetoric in rhubarb.
4. Focus on the *cicl* in *icicle*. Contrast *bicycle* and *tickle*.
5. Distinguish *minute* (min′it) from *minute* (mi nut′).
6. Copy: Disappointed because the apple disappeared.
7. Copy: The early eagle earned his earthworm.
8. Focus on the *exp* in *expect*. Distinguish *expect* from *suspect*.
9. Distinguish *hour* from *our*. Copy: An hour in sour flour.
10. Note the *mobile* in *automobile*. Compare *automotive*.
11. Note the *special* in *especially*. Compare *commercially*.
12. Center your attention on the *pp* in *equipped*. Copy: Equipped to be shipped.

VISUAL DRILLS

1. Nat - r - - ly the poem had both rh - m - and r - - th - .
2. The melting ic - - le will dis - p - - - r in a min - t - .
3. The hunters e - - ect to start at an e - rly - o - r.
4. The - - t - mob - - - was - spec - - l - y well equ - p - - d.

When you have finished this lesson, review Lesson 12.

Lesson 17 BASIC WORDS

When you have studied three words, look at the related Visual Drill. Then write it from memory.

1. **belief** His be l*ie*f′ in religion is firm.
2. **religious** Our preacher's re li′*gio*us views are broad.
3. **soul** The miser lost his so*u*l for money.

4. **receipt** Did you receive a re *ceip*t′ for your purchase?
5. **acknowledge** Did the manager a*c* kno*w*l′e*dge* your letter?
6. **shipment** The company expected a ship′ment of new goods.

7. **completely** The runners were com plet*e*′ly exhausted.
8. **forgotten** The visitor had for got′*te*n his hat.
9. **happened** Mary hap′*p*en*e*d to see both trucks coming.

10. **between** The little boy sat be twe*e*n′ his mother's feet.
11. **connection** Our only co*n* nec′*tio*n is in business matters.
12. **source** The reporter located the so*urce* of the rumor.

MEMORY AIDS

1. Distinguish *belief* from *believe.* Compare *relief, relieve.*
2. Note the *ious* in *religious.* Compare *mysterious, superstitious.*
3. Distinguish *soul* (spirit) from *sole* (single). STUDY: His *sole* purpose was saving *souls.*
4. Focus on the *ceip* in *receipt.* Contrast *reception, deceit, conceit.* Do not confuse receipt with *recipe.*
5. Note the *know* and the *ledge* in *acknowledge.*
6. Center on the *ment* in *shipment.* Compare *treatment, enlistment.*
7. Center on the *ete* in *completely.* Compare *complete.*
8. COPY: We got ten forgotten, rotten apples.
9. Center on the *ened* in *happened.* COPY: Happy it happened.
10. COPY: Keen for the screen between fourteen and fifteen.
11. Note the three *n*'s in *connection.* Compare *connect, connected.*
12. COPY: We sought the source of the sour soup.

VISUAL DRILLS

1. The preacher claimed that his rel - g - - - s bel - - - would save his s - - l.
2. The clerk failed to ac - no - l - dg - rec - - p - of the shipm - - t.
3. He had compl - - - ly forg - t - - n what had hap - - - - d.
4. What was the so - r - e of the con - e - - ion betw - - n them?

When you have finished this lesson, review Lesson 13.

Lesson 18 BASIC WORDS

You can strengthen and add to your spelling ability by studying the related words which appear in the Memory Aids.

1. **article** Peggy wrote an ar′ti cl*e* for the newspaper.
2. **science** We studied *sci*′en*c*e in the laboratory.
3. **referred** Miss Adams re *ferre*d′ us to the dictionary.
4. **library** There are fifty new books in the li′brar y.
5. **interesting** *Rifles for Watie* is an in′ter est ing story.
6. **literature** Have you read much lit′er a tur*e* lately?
7. **librarian** Ask the li brar′i an about the new book.
8. **psychology** The study of *psy ch*ol′o gy treats the mind.
9. **volume** The second vol′um*e* is not in the library.
10. **various** The pupils gave var′i *o*us answers.
11. **pamphlet** The pam′*ph*let contained only ten pages.
12. **magazine** He read the new issue of the mag′a zin*e*.

MEMORY AIDS

1. Center on the *cle* in *article.* Copy: An article about the art circle.
2. Focus on the *sci* in *science.* Copy: A scission with scissors in science.
3. Note the *rr* in *referred.* Compare *preferred, conferred.*
4. Pronounce all of the letters in *library* distinctly.
5. Note the *ere* in *interesting.* Compare *interest, interested.*
6. Center on the *era* in *literature.* Compare *literary, illiterate.*
7. Pronounce *librarian* carefully. Compare *barbarian, vegetarian.*
8. Focus on the *psych* in *psychology.* Note the silent letters.
9. Note that *volume* ends in *me.* Contrast the *mn* in *column.*
10. Copy: Curious and furious about the various and spurious.
11. Center on the *ph* in *pamphlet.* Copy: The emphatic pamphlet about camphor.
12. Note the *gaz* in *magazine.* Pronounce both *a*'s.

VISUAL DRILLS

1. Our teacher ref - r - - d us to an art - - l - on sc - - n - e.
2. We found some int - - - sting lit - - - t - r - in the lib - - - y.
3. The lib - - r - an showed us a new vol - - - on - sy - - ol - gy.
4. Besides books, there were var - - - s pam - - l - ts and m - g - z - nes.

When you have finished this lesson, review Lesson 14.

Lesson 19 BASIC WORDS

Note that some words have two accented syllables; one receives a primary accent (ʹ) and another a secondary accent (ˊ).

1. **freight** The men loaded the fr*eigh*t into the boxcars.
2. **passenger** Each pas'*s*en ger on the train had some luggage.
3. **precede** Thought should pre *c*ed*e*' action and speech.
4. **plain** It was pla*i*n to see what was wrong.
5. **engineer** The en'gi ne*e*r' took his place in the cab.
6. **view** The v*ie*w from my window is beautiful.
7. **moving** The men were mov'ing the stove into the house.
8. **territory** The ter'*r*i to'ry of Alaska became a state in 1958.
9. **toward** Suddenly the dog ran to'*w*ard her.
10. **occurred** The thought had not oc cur*r*e*d*' to him before.
11. **tragedy** The death of his puppy was a trag'e dy.
12. **imagine** I can i mag'in*e* how well she looked.

MEMORY AIDS

1. Note the *eight* in *freight.* COPY: The weight of eight freight trains. Contrast *weight* (wāt) with *height* (hīt).
2. Note the *ss* in *passenger.* Compare *passed, messenger.*
3. Center on the *cede* in *precede.* Compare *recede, accede, concede.*
4. Distinguish *plain* from *plane.* A *plane* (flat) surface in *plain* (clear) sight.
5. COPY: Imagine an engine with a queer engineer.
6. Focus on the *iew* in *view.* Print *view the review* three times.
7. Compare *move, moving; shove, shoving; prove, proving.*
8. Note the *rr* in *territory.* Compare *terrible, terror.*
9. STUDY: He ran *toward* her *to ward* off the mad dog.
10. Bear down on *occurred.* Compare *occur, occurred, occurrence.*
11. Pronounce *tragedy* (trăj'ĕ dĭ) carefully. COPY: They staged an aged tragedy.
12. COPY: Imagine an engine with nine engineers.

VISUAL DRILLS

1. The pa - s - nger train had orders to pre - - d - the fr - - - - t train.
2. The eng - n - - r had a pl - - n v - - w of the track ahead.
3. They were mov - - g slowly to - - rd the hilly ter - - t - ry.
4. We could not i - ag - n - why the tr - - e - y oc - - r - ed.

When you have finished this lesson, review Lesson 15.

Lesson 20

BASIC WORDS

There is no rule which covers double letters. You must learn each word separately.

1. **recollect** — Can you rec'*ol* lect the circumstances?
2. **envelope** — Mother needs an en've lop*e* for her letter.
3. **address** — Is Mrs. Jones' a*d* dress' in the directory?
4. **writing** — Helen is *w*rit'ing a theme for English.
5. **invitation** — Mary received an in'vi ta'*tio*n to the dance.
6. **inclose** — Please in clo*s*e' a check for the correct amount.
7. **earnest** — John was e*a*r'nest in his attempt to volunteer.
8. **discussion** — The dis cu*s*'*sio*n soon became a debate.
9. **speech** — The visitor's spe*e*ch to the class was excellent.
10. **mentioned** — My father men'*tio*ne*d* his name two times.
11. **additional** — The doctor made no a*d* di'*tio*n al statements.
12. **information** — These facts give the exact in'for ma'*tio*n.

MEMORY AIDS

1. Note the *ll* in *recollect.* Copy: Recollect a collection of collars in college.
2. Distinguish *en've lope* (a paper container) from *en vel'op* (to surround).
3. Note the *add* in *address.* Copy: Add an accurate address.
4. Omit the *e* in *writing.* Compare *bite, biting; kite, kiting.*
5. Pronounce the middle *i* in *invitation.* Compare *cite, citation.*
6. *Inclose* is also spelled *enclose.* Compare *include, incline.*
7. Note the *ear* in *earnest.* Copy: Learn to be early in earnest.
8. Note the *ss* in *discussion.* Compare *discussed, discussing.*
9. Copy: A speedy speech without a screech.
10. Center on the *tion* in *mentioned.* Compare *invention.*
11. Note the *add* in *additional.* Distinguish from *traditional.*
12. Note the *formation* in *information.* Stress the *tion.*

VISUAL DRILLS

1. Do you re - ol - ec - the ad - re - - on the - nvel - p - ?
2. We should - nclo - - an - nv - ta - - - n in - rit - ng.
3. His sp - - ch was followed by an - - rn - st d - scus - - - n.
4. The speaker men - - - n - d the need for ad - i - - - n - l i - forma - - - n.

When you have finished this lesson, review Lesson 16.

Lesson 21 BASIC WORDS

Always read thoughtfully the illustrative sentence which follows each word. Be certain that you have the right meaning in mind.

1. **loose** The dog broke loos*e*′ from his chain.
2. **aerial** The flyer took an a er′i al photograph.
3. **receiving** Have you been re *cei*v′ing my letters?
4. **response** The girl gave no re spons*e*′ to the question.
5. **could** The pupil co*ul*d give no reason for his absence.
6. **inquiry** An in *qu*ir′y was made concerning the fire.
7. **generally** Boys gen′er al *l*y prefer chocolate to vanilla.
8. **noticeable** The patch in her skirt was not no′ti*ce* a bl*e*.
9. **trouble** The mechanic was having tr*o*u′bl*e* with the engine.
10. **hear** You he*a*r many things on the radio.
11. **satisfactorily** Don did not do his work sat′is fac′to ri ly.
12. **impossible** It is im pos′*s*i bl*e* for her to come today.

MEMORY AIDS

1. Distinguish *loose* from *lose.* You may *lose* a *loose* nickel.
2. Pronounce *aerial* carefully. Compare *serial, material.*
3. Center on the *ei* in *receiving.* Compare *deceiving, receive.*
4. Note that response ends in *se.* Compare *sense, expense.*
5. Focus on the *oul* in *could.* Compare *would, should.*
6. Look at *inquiry* carefully. Compare *inquire, require.*
7. Note the *rally* in *generally.* COPY: A general will generally rally.
8. Keep the middle *e* in *noticeable.* Compare *serviceable.*
9. Center on the *ou* in *trouble.* COPY: Double, double; trouble, trouble.
10. Note the *ear* in *hear.* Distinguish *hear* from *here.*
11. Focus on the *ily* in *satisfactorily.* Pronounce each syllable.
12. Note the *ossi* in *impossible.* Pronounce the *i* in *ible.*

VISUAL DRILLS

1. A l - - s - wire on the a - ri - l prevented us from rec - - v - ng the message.
2. We c - - - d make no r - spon - - to the inq - - r - .
3. The tr - - b - - was gen - r - l - y most noti - - - ble at midday.
4. It was imp - - s - ble to h - - r short words sat - sfactor - - - .

When you have finished this lesson, review Lesson 17.

Lesson 22 BASIC WORDS

The words in this lesson cause many spelling errors. Practice writing them in short sentences.

1. **fertile**	The fer′til*e* valley produces many vegetables.
2. **field**	The farmer was out in the f*i*eld plowing.
3. **yield**	Frank would not y*i*eld his property to the government.
4. **forest**	Have you ever seen a pine for′est?
5. **realize**	The child did not re′al iz*e* that he had done wrong.
6. **necessity**	Salt is a common ne *c*es′*s*i ty of animal life.
7. **often**	The club of′*t*en goes on picnics.
8. **built**	My grandfather b*u*ilt this house years ago.
9. **waste**	To worry is a wast*e* of time.
10. **column**	A col′um*n* of mercury rises with increased heat.
11. **fiery**	The actor's hair was a fi′*e* ry red.
12. **ascend**	The balloon began to as *c*end′ rapidly.

MEMORY AIDS

1. Pronounce *fertile* fur′tĭl. Copy: A hostile fertile reptile.
2. Copy: The field will yield, I know, if you wield, not shield, the hoe.
3. Note the *i* before *e* in *yield, shield, wield,* and *field.*
4. Note the *fore* in *forest.* Copy: Before the forest forever.
5. Note the *a* in *realize.* Pronounce each of the three syllables.
6. Center on the *cess* in *necessity.* Copy: Confess that recess is a necessity.
7. Focus on the *oft* in *often.* Compare *oft, often, soften.*
8. Copy: He built a quilt to hide his guilt.
9. Distinguish *waste* from *waist.* Copy: Don't waste your taste on paste.
10. Center on the *umn* in *column.* Think of a newspaper columnist.
11. Note the three syllables in *fiery.* Contrast *fire, fiery; wire, wiry.*
12. Focus on the *sce* in *ascend.* Compare *descend, scene.*

VISUAL DRILLS

1. A fert - - - f - - ld of corn will y - - ld a large crop.
2. All r - - li - - the ne - e - - ity for protecting the fo - - st.
3. Fires carelessly b - - lt of - - n cause great w - st - .
4. The f - - ry col - - - of smoke began to a - - end still higher.

When you have finished this lesson, review Lesson 18.

Lesson 23

BASIC WORDS

Study the longer words below by syllables. Note the double accents in four of the words.

1. **professor** — The pro fes′*so*r met his classes daily.
2. **knowledge** — We had no *know*l′*edge* of the accident.
3. **thorough** — The doctor gave him a th*o*r′*ough* examination.
4. **university** — Uncle George has a u′ni v*e*r′si ty education.
5. **months** — It has been three m*o*nths since Ted left.
6. **calendar** — The cal′en d*a*r gave the dates of all holidays.
7. **college** — Some of the graduates plan to attend col′*lege*.
8. **dormitory** — The girls liked living in a dor′mi to′ry.
9. **sophomore** — Nancy is a so*ph*′o mor*e* in high school.
10. **laboratory** — We worked an experiment in the lab′o ra to′ry.
11. **examination** — The teacher prepared a final e*x* am′i na′*tio*n.
12. **studying** — The students were stud′y ing their lessons.

MEMORY AIDS

1. Note the *esso* in *professor*. Compare: *profess, professor; confess, confessor.*
2. Note the *know* and the *ledge* in *knowledge.*
3. Focus on the *ough* in *thorough.* COPY: Although he fought, he was thorough in thought.
4. Always spell *university* with two *i*'s. Compare *adversity.*
5. Center on the *ths* in *months.* Write *month, months* three times.
6. Center on the *dar* in *calendar.* COPY: Don't mar the calendar.
7. COPY: A collection of knowledge collected in college.
8. Note the *it* in *dormitory.* Contrast the *at* in *reformatory.*
9. Write three *o*'s in *sophomore.* COPY: The sophomore commodore.
10. Note the *labor* in *laboratory.* Pronounce all five syllables distinctly.
11. Notice the *i* in the middle of *examination.*
12. Center on the *y* in *studying.* Compare *burying, copying, carrying.*

VISUAL DRILLS

1. The pro - es - - r had a tho - - ugh knowle - - e of chemistry.
2. The un - ver - - ty cal - nd - r included dates for nine mon - h - .
3. The so - - - more stayed at the col - - g - dorm - t - ry.
4. He was stud - - ng for an exam - nat - - n on lab - r - t - ry work.

When you have finished this lesson, review Lesson 19.

Lesson 24 BASIC WORDS

Consult the Basic Dictionary whenever you are uncertain about the meaning or pronunciation of a word.

1. **accept**	We hope that you will ac *c*ept′ our invitation.
2. **explanation**	The boy gave an *ex*′pla na′*tio*n for his action.
3. **weird**	The howling of the dog sounded we*i*rd in the night.
4. **does**	His mother do*e*s not know that he is coming.
5. **since**	Mary has not been there sin*c*e her birthday.
6. **very**	The weather has been ver′y hot lately.
7. **popular**	A pop′u l*a*r song seldom lasts over six months.
8. **commission**	The salesman was paid a small co*m* mis′*sio*n.
9. **receive**	Did your mother re *ceive*′ the package?
10. **conceive**	A child cannot con *ceive*′ that much money.
11. **situation**	Our present sit′u a′*tio*n is critical.
12. **deceive**	Do not try to de *ceive*′ him about your age.

MEMORY AIDS

1. Distinguish between *accept* and *except. Accept* gifts *except* from strangers.
2. Note the *plan* in *explanation.* Contrast *explain, explanation.*
3. Focus on the *ei* in *weird.* COPY: Their weird weight.
4. Focus on the *oe* in *does.* Contrast *does, dose,* and *dozen.*
5. Distinguish *since* from *sense.* Compare *convince, prince.*
6. Distinguish *very* from *vary.* Compare *ever, every.*
7. Note the *lar* in *popular.* COPY: The poplar tree is popular with me.
8. Note the *mm* in *commission.* Compare *committee, community.*
9. Focus on the *cei* in *receive.* Compare *deceive, conceive.*
10. COPY: Can you conceive the conceit of the receiver's deceit?
11. Pronounce *situation* distinctly. Compare *valuation, continuation.*
12. Contrast *deceive, deceit* with *receive, receipt.*

VISUAL DRILLS

1. The police did not - - c - pt his expl - nat - on for his w - - rd action.
2. It do - - not seem v - r - long sin - - Christmas.
3. When did the pop - l - r officer rec - - v - his co - mis - - on?
4. We can conc - - v - a sit - - t - on in which he can dec - - v - us.

When you have finished this lesson, review Lesson 20.

Lesson 25 BASIC WORDS

You will not master these words merely by reading the exercises. You must study them vigorously.

1.	**sheriff**	The sher'*iff* wore a broadbrimmed hat.
2.	**road**	This ro*a*d leads to the old rock quarry.
3.	**ninety**	Mother invited nin*e*'ty guests to the party.
4.	**pursuit**	The dog ran in p*ur* su*i*t' of the ducks.
5.	**brief**	Will you make a br*i*ef summary of the book?
6.	**stopped**	The policeman stop*ped* the speeding car.
7.	**meant**	The clerk me*a*nt to call you this morning.
8.	**cancel**	Please can'*c*el my order for the tickets.
9.	**certificate**	Jim was proud of his *c*er tif'i c*ate* of promotion.
10.	**warrant**	The officer had a w*ar*'*r*ant to search the house.
11.	**thought**	The author tho*ugh*t of a name for the play.
12.	**safety**	Carelessness endangers the saf*e*'ty of many workers.

MEMORY AIDS

1. Focus on the *iff* in *sheriff.* COPY: The sheriff had a whiff of sea in a skiff.
2. Distinguish *road* from *rode.* The rider *rode* down the paved *road.*
3. Note the *nine* in *ninety.* COPY: Mine in nineteen-ninety-nine.
4. Center on the *pur* in *pursuit.* COPY: To suit the purpose of his pursuit.
5. Note the *ief* in *brief.* COPY: His belief in the thief was brief.
6. Note the *pp* in *stopped.* Compare *stop, stopped; hop, hopped.*
7. Notice the *ea* in *meant.* COPY: The flea meant to be mean.
8. Focus on the *cel* in *cancel.* Contrast *canceling* with *cancellation.*
9. Note the *cert* in *certificate.* Compare *certain, certify.*
10. Note the *arra* in *warrant.* Compare *narrate;* contrast *parent.*
11. Compare *thought, although, brought, thorough, fought.*
12. Keep the *safe* in *safety.* Contrast *safety* with *crafty.*

VISUAL DRILLS

1. The sh - r - - f drove down the ro - d at n - n - ty miles an hour.
2. After a br - - f p - rs - - t, he st - p - - - a speedster.
3. He m - - nt to can - - l the offender's driving c - rt - fic - t - .
4. The sheriff th - - - - t that public saf - t - would war - - nt this action.

When you have finished this lesson, review Lesson 21.

Lesson 26 BASIC WORDS

It will help you if you memorize the short quips introduced by the word COPY.

1. **cashier**	The cash *ier*′ counted the money carefully.
2. **journal**	The class published a weekly j*our*′nal.
3. **available**	When will the material be a v*ai*l′a bl*e*?
4. **taught**	Miss Smith t*augh*t the class a Spanish song.
5. **tuition**	There is a small tu i′*tio*n for the course.
6. **course**	Two boys failed to pass the music co*urse*.
7. **past**	It was long past the baby's bedtime.
8. **future**	The play will be given in the near fu′tur*e*.
9. **latter**	The lat′*t*er part of the work is the easier.
10. **medium**	The paper is of me′di um quality.
11. **chose**	The boys cho*se* sides for the ball game.
12. **advertising**	Mrs. Smith is ad′ver ti*s*′ing for a maid.

MEMORY AIDS

1. Focus on the *ier* in *cashier.* Compare *frontier, pier, financier.*
2. Note the *our* in *journal.* COPY: Adjourn the journey for our journal.
3. Note the *ail* in *available.* COPY: Ailing Able was not available.
4. Focus on the *augh* in *taught.* Compare *caught;* contrast *ought.*
5. Focus on the *ui* in *tuition.* Pronounce each syllable distinctly.
6. Distinguish *course* from *coarse. Coarse* sand covered the golf *course.*
7. Distinguish *past* from *passed.* Refer to the Basic Dictionary.
8. Stress the *u*'s in pronouncing *future.* Compare *nature, furniture.*
9. COPY: The latter letter was fatter and better.
10. Focus on the *iu* in *medium.* Stress the *u* sound.
11. Stress the *ose* in *chose.* Compare *nose, rose, suppose.*
12. Focus on the *isi* in *advertising.* Compare *advising, rising.*

VISUAL DRILLS

1. The daily j - - rn - l kept by the c - sh - - r was not av - - l - bl - .
2. The instructor ta - - - t the c - - rs - for a small tu - t - on.
3. As to the f - t - r - or the p - st, I know more of the lat - - r.
4. We ch - se the newspaper as the best m - d - - m for adv - rt - s - ng.

When you have finished this lesson, review Lesson 22.

Lesson 27 — BASIC WORDS

Take time to review previous lessons. Frequent review is the key to correct recall.

1. **analyze**	It is difficult to an'a *lyze* a person's motives.
2. **essential**	Exercise is e*s* sen'*ti*al to proper development.
3. **scheme**	The girls thought of a s*ch*em*e* for raising money.
4. **assume**	Mother will a*s* sum*e*' the responsibility for us.
5. **much**	It will take hours to cut that much wood.
6. **doubtful**	It is dou*b*t'ful if they will pay the bill.
7. **certainly**	The baby *ce*r'*ta*in ly likes the little puppy.
8. **proposition**	The farmer's prop'o *si*'*tio*n was to trade horses.
9. **whole**	The *w*hole audience enjoyed the program.
10. **know**	Do you *k*no*w* when he will be back?
11. **portion**	Each boy received an equal por'*tio*n of the pie.
12. **evident**	It is ev'i dent that he dislikes his job.

MEMORY AIDS

1. Focus on the *lyze* in *analyze.* Compare *paralyze;* contrast *sympathize.*
2. Note the *ess* in *essential.* Compare *essay, necessary.*
3. COPY: The schedule of a school is not a scheme for a fool.
4. Note the *ss* in *assume.* Compare *assure, assert, assist.*
5. Center on the *uch* in *much.* Contrast *clutch, crutch.*
6. Observe the *ful* in *doubtful.* Compare *thoughtful, resourceful.*
7. Focus on the *ai* in *certainly.* Compare *certificate, captain.*
8. Note the *sit* in *proposition.* Compare *composition, supposition.*
9. COPY: Whose whole apple is full of holes?
10. COPY: Did he know that the knife would cut his knee?
11. Note the *port* in *portion.* Compare *apportion, distortion.*
12. Focus on the *ide* in *evident.* Compare *confident, accident.*

VISUAL DRILLS

First, visualize the missing letters. Then write the drill from memory.

1. It is e - sen - - al to an - l - ze the s - - em - .
2. We must not a - sum - too m - c - that is do - - tful.
3. C - rt - - nl - , we must look at the - hol - pro - - si - - on.
4. We - no - it is - v - d - nt that a p - rti - - is missing.

When you have finished this lesson, review Lesson 23.

Lesson 28 BASIC WORDS

When you do the Visual Drills, check your memory by trying to recall three words at a time.

1. **accurate**	Measurements for the house must be ac′cu *rate*.
2. **secretary**	A sec′re *tar*′y should be able to type well.
3. **society**	Mother enjoys the so *ci*′e ty of her friends.
4. **statement**	The mayor made a stat*e*′ment to the public.
5. **parliament**	Members of par′li*a* ment are elected.
6. **tomorrow**	Sally's tenth birthday is to mor′*row*.
7. **economy**	A good plan of e con′o my does away with waste.
8. **administration**	The ad min′is tra′*tion* of the project improved.
9. **refer**	When in doubt, re fer′ to a dictionary.
10. **solemn**	The judge always looked sol′em*n* in court.
11. **occasion**	The wedding was a happy oc′ca *sion*.
12. **probably**	The picnic will prob′a bly be postponed.

MEMORY AIDS

1. Note the *rate* in *accurate*. Copy: An accurate account accumulates.
2. Note the *secret* in *secretary*. Contrast *military, dignitary*.
3. Focus on the *iet* in *society*. Contrast *social, sociable*.
4. Copy: The late statement rates early payment.
5. See the Basic Dictionary for the pronunciation of *parliament*.
6. The word *tomorrow* is preferred to the compound *to-morrow*.
7. Stress the two *o*'s in *economy*. Contrast *enemy*.
8. Copy: I admit I admire the administration.
9. Note that *refer* is spelled the same either way.
10. Focus on the *mn* in *solemn*. Copy: The solemn autumn hymn.
11. Emphasize the two *c*'s and one *s* in *occasion*. Compare *occupy*.
12. Stress the *ab* in *probably*. Compare *probable, probably; notable, notably*.

VISUAL DRILLS

1. The secr - t - r - of the so - - - ty kept an ac - - r - t - account.
2. The prime minister will make a st - t - m - nt before the parl - - m - nt tom - r - - w.
3. He will r - f - r to the need for ec - n - - y in a - - in - s - - at - on.
4. It will prob - - - y be a s - l - - n oc - a - - on.

When you have finished this lesson, review Lesson 24.

Lesson 29 BASIC WORDS

Observe the hard spots printed in italics in the syllabified words in the illustrative sentences.

1.	**accommodate**	The manager will be glad to a*c* com′*mo* dat*e* you.
2.	**quite**	The foreigner was *qu*it*e* confused in his words.
3.	**possible**	It is pos′*si* bl*e* that Mary missed the train.
4.	**attorney**	The a*t* tor′ne*y* presented the case clearly.
5.	**persuade**	Perhaps you can per *su*ad*e*′ her to stay.
6.	**seems**	Nothing s*ee*ms to disturb his sleep.
7.	**appeal**	The prisoner made an a*p* pe*a*l′ to the warden.
8.	**modifies**	An adverb is a word that mod′*i* fi*es* a verb.
9.	**governor**	The gov′er n*o*r of the state attended the meeting.
10.	**congratulate**	I am happy to con grat′u lat*e* you on your success.
11.	**innocent**	The jury found the accused man in′*no* *c*ent.
12.	**hoping**	Your friends are hop′ing that you will come.

MEMORY AIDS

1. Focus on the *cc* in *accommodate.* Compare *account, accomplish.*
2. Distinguish *quite* from *quiet.* He was *quiet* for *quite* a while.
3. Stress the *sib* in *possible.* Compare *possibly, possibility.*
4. Note the *torn* in *attorney.* Focus on the *ey* ending.
5. Emphasize the *sua* in *persuade.* Compare *person, persuasion.*
6. Distinguish *seems* from *seams.* This dress *seems* to have no *seams.*
7. Focus on the whole word *appeal.* COPY: Her appearance appeals.
8. Observe the *ifi* in *modifies.* Compare *notifies, dignifies, satisfies.*
9. Stress the *ver* and *nor* in *governor.* Compare *govern, government.*
10. Note the *tu* in *congratulate.* Compare *natural, saturate.*
11. Note the *cent* in *innocent.* COPY: In no century is a murderer innocent.
12. Compare *hope, hoping; rope, roping; type, typing.*

VISUAL DRILLS

1. It is q - - t - p - s - - bl - that the manager will ac - - m - - dat - you.
2. It s - - ms that the at - - rn - - could not p - rs - - d - the jury.
3. The prisoner m - d - f - - s his ap - - - l to the g - v - - n - r.
4. His friends were h - p - - g to c - ngra - - l - t - him as an in - o - - nt man.

When you have finished this lesson, review Lesson 25.

Lesson 30 BASIC WORDS

Refer to the Basic Dictionary for the correct pronunciations of *partner* and *mortgage.*

1. **partner**	The owner of the company took in a part′ner.
2. **extension**	Father plans to build an *ex* ten′*sio*n to the house.
3. **mortgage**	The farmer will mor*t*′g*age* his land to obtain money.
4. **security**	The bank demanded se cu′ri ty for the loan.
5. **customer**	The cus′*to*m er wished to buy a new stove.
6. **remit**	Kindly re mit′ your payment at an early date.
7. **application**	Enter my ap′*pli* ca′*tio*n for the position.
8. **terms**	They agreed on the te*r*ms of the contract.
9. **quote**	May we *quote* your statements in the paper?
10. **approval**	The architect obtained a*p* prov′al for his plans.
11. **concession**	The lawyer made a con *ces*′*sio*n to his opponent.
12. **amount**	The total a mount′ is fifty dollars.

MEMORY AIDS

1. Note the *part* in *partner.* Say *partner,* not *pardner.*
2. Focus on the *sio* in *extension.* Contrast *extension* with *intention.*
3. Note the silent *t* in *mortgage.* COPY: Mort mortgaged the motor.
4. Stress the *it* in *security.* COPY: Pity the necessity for security.
5. Focus on the *usto* in *customer.* Compare *custom, accustomed.*
6. Note the *it* ending in *remit.* Compare *permit, profit.*
7. Focus on the *ppl* in *application.* Compare *apply, applied.*
8. Stress the *erms* ending in *terms.* Compare *germs.* Contrast *firms, worms.*
9. Remember that *q* is always followed by *u.* COPY: He quietly quoted the queer question.
10. COPY: We appreciate the appropriate approval.
11. Focus on the *cess* in *concession.* Contrast *session, possession.*
12. Stress the *ount* in *amount.* Compare *mount, mountain.*

VISUAL DRILLS

1. His business p - r - n - r asked for an ext - n - - on of the m - r - g - g - .
2. The c - st - m - r was unable to r - mi - or to give s - c - r - t - .
3. The ap - - - ca - - on asked the owner to q - - t - new t - rm - .
4. He gave his ap - r - v - l to the am - - nt of the c - n - - s - - on.

When you have finished this lesson, review Lesson 26.

Lesson 31 BASIC WORDS

Focus your attention on the numerous letters in the words of this lesson which are not indicated by the pronunciation.

1. **instructor**	The new in struc′t*o*r has many students.
2. **genius**	The inventor, Edison, was a *g*e′ni us.
3. **brilliant**	The class president has a bril′*li*ant idea.
4. **committee**	The program co*m* mit′*tee* meets today.
5. **recommend**	Please rec′*om* mend′ a good story.
6. **equipment**	The e *qu*ip′ment for the science room is new.
7. **gymnasium**	The *gy*m na′*s*i um was completely filled.
8. **faculty**	The high school fac′ul ty will meet tonight.
9. **preferred**	The girls pre f*erre*d′ not to go.
10. **wholly**	Jack is *w*hol′*l*y responsible for his absence.
11. **procedure**	What pro *c*e′*d*ur*e* should we follow?
12. **concerning**	What are the facts con *c*ern′ing the trouble?

MEMORY AIDS

1. Copy: The professor as instructor was both actor and conductor.
2. Focus on the *ius* in *genius.* Contrast *religious, generous.*
3. Copy: A brilliant illiterate in Illinois.
4. Note the double letters in *committee.* Copy: See the committee of three in Mississippi.
5. Focus on the *mm* in *recommend.* Compare *recollect, necessary.*
6. Note the *equip* in *equipment.* Compare *shipment;* contrast *equipped.*
7. Focus on the *gym* in *gymnasium.* Compare *gymnast, gypsy.*
8. Stress the *ul* in *faculty.* Compare *culture, difficulty.*
9. Focus on the *rr* in *preferred.* Compare *referred, conferred.*
10. Note the unusual *ll* in *wholly.* Contrast *solely, wholesome.*
11. Focus on the *ced* in *procedure.* Contrast *proceed, proceeding.*
12. Note the *cer* in *concerning.* Copy: Concerning a certain concert.

VISUAL DRILLS

1. The new inst - - c - - r was br - l - - - nt, but not a g - n - - s.
2. The com - - - te - decided to rec - m - - nd the new eq - - pm - nt.
3. Most of the f - c - lt - pre - - r - - d the new g - mn - s - - m.
4. They were - hol - - agreed c - n - - rn - ng the best pr - - ed - r - .

When you have finished this lesson, review Lesson 27.

Lesson 32 BASIC WORDS

It will help your spelling and writing if you note the separate syllables in each word.

1. **assure**	Can you as sure′ him that he will get the work?
2. **descend**	Jack began to de scend′ the ladder.
3. **practical**	His ideas came from prac′ti cal experience.
4. **suggest**	Can you sug gest′ a good place to eat?
5. **syllable**	*Chair* is a word of one syl′la ble.
6. **pronounce**	Be careful to pro nounce′ words correctly.
7. **desert**	The giant cactus grows on the des′ert.
8. **attacked**	The Indians at tacked′ the early settlers.
9. **prior**	This sacred duty comes pri′or to all others.
10. **purpose**	Our pur′pose is to be polite at all times.
11. **courtesy**	The visitor was treated with cour′te sy.
12. **oblige**	Please o blige′ me by leaving at once.

MEMORY AIDS

1. Note the *ss* in *assure.* COPY: I assure you, I will assist you.
2. Focus on the *sce* in *descend.* Compare *ascend;* contrast *decent.*
3. Stress the *cal* in *practical.* Compare *medical, vertical.*
4. COPY: I suggest that you suffer from sudden success.
5. Focus on the *syll* in *syllable.* Stress the *able* ending.
6. COPY: Pronounce the *ounce* in *announce* and *denounce.*
7. Note that *des′ert* means a sandy waste; *de sert′*, to abandon.
8. Distinguish *attacked* from *attached.* They *attacked* the gliders *attached* to the plane.
9. Focus on the *or* in *prior.* COPY: Junior is prior to senior.
10. COPY: The purple pup pursued his purpose.
11. Note the *court* in *courtesy.* Compare *courteous, courage.*
12. Focus on the *lige* in *oblige.* Contrast *obligation, privilege.*

VISUAL DRILLS

1. We as - - r - you that it is not pr - ct - c - l to de - - - nd below the surface.
2. We sug - - st that you pr - n - - n - - each s - l - - bl - distinctly.
3. He lived on the d - s - rt pr - - r to the time he was at - - c - - d by Indians.
4. The p - rp - s - of his c - - rt - s - is to obl - g - others.

When you have finished this lesson, review Lesson 28.

Lesson 33 BASIC WORDS

Consult the Basic Dictionary for the correct pronunciation of *g* in *privilege, ought, marriage, league,* and *vinegar.*

1. **Christian** Our country favors the *Chris'tian* religion.
2. **privilege** It was a priv'i lege to hear him speak.
3. **civilization** History classes studied early civ'i li za'*tion*.
4. **ought** You *ought* to return the book at once.
5. **marriage** The mar'*riage* united the happy couple.
6. **jealous** The puppy was jeal'ous of the cat.
7. **association** Students formed an athletic as so'ci a'*tion*.
8. **league** The baseball le*ague* included eight teams.
9. **forty** There were for'ty students in the class.
10. **alcohol** Intoxicating liquors usually contain al'co hol.
11. **vinegar** When fermented, cider changes to vin'e gar.
12. **quantity** A large *quan*'ti ty of soap was wasted.

MEMORY AIDS

1. Note that *Christian* begins with a capital letter.
2. Note the *ivil* in *privilege.* Compare *civil;* contrast *knowledge.*
3. Focus on the *liz* in *civilization.* Note the four *i*'s in *civilization.*
4. COPY: He ought to have thought about what he bought.
5. Note the *age* in *marriage.* Compare *marry, marriage; carry, carriage.*
6. Note the *a* in *jealous.* COPY: Better zealous than jealous.
7. Focus on the *cia* in *association.* Compare *social, sociable.*
8. Note the peculiar *ague* ending in *league.* Contrast *fatigue.*
9. Observe that *forty* omits the *u* correctly found in *four.*
10. Note the *oho* in *alcohol.* Stress the *alco* beginning.
11. Note the *vine* in *vinegar.* Compare *cigar;* contrast *beggar.*
12. Center on the *ity* in *quantity.* COPY: Vanity about charity has more quantity than quality.

VISUAL DRILLS

1. It is a pr - v - le - - to live in a C - r - st - - n civ - l - z - t - - n.
2. A new couple o - - - t not to be j - - l - - s after mar - - a - - .
3. The l - - g - - was an as - - c - - t - - n of f - rt - teams.
4. A large q - - nt - t - of wine containing alc - h - l changed to v - n - g - r.

When you have finished this lesson, review Lesson 29.

Lesson 34 BASIC WORDS

Review the directions on How To Study beginning on page 1 to see if you are following them properly.

1. **athletics**	Skill in ath let′ics requires much practice.
2. **pleasure**	It was a ple*as*′ur*e* to see our team win.
3. **exercise**	Playing basketball is good ex′er *cise*.
4. **athlete**	The ath′let*e* increased in strength.
5. **perspiration**	The per′spi ra′*tio*n dripped from his brow.
6. **tournament**	Ten teams played in the t*o*ur′na ment.
7. **develop**	Try to de vel′op correct posture.
8. **strength**	The wrestler's muscular strength is enormous.
9. **physical**	Recruits must pass a *phy*′*si* cal examination.
10. **practically**	The game was prac′ti cal *ly* over.
11. **exhausted**	The boys were ex *haus*t′ed from running.
12. **bicycle**	Mary rode her new bi′*cy* cle to school.

MEMORY AIDS

1. Limit *athletics* to three syllables. Compare *athlete.*
2. Focus on the *lea* in *pleasure.* COPY: Treasure a measure of pleasure.
3. Focus on the *cise* in *exercise.* COPY: It's wise to rise and exercise.
4. Limit *athlete* to two syllables. Compare *complete.*
5. Focus on the *per* and the *spi* in *perspiration.*
6. Note the *tour* in *tournament.* Compare *tourist, touring.*
7. *Develop* is also spelled *develope.* Compare *envelop, development.*
8. Focus on the *gth* in *strength.* Compare *length, width.*
9. Note the *physic* in *physical.* Compare *physician, physics.*
10. Note the *ally* in *practically.* Compare *medically, vertically.*
11. Focus on the *haus* in *exhausted.* Remember the silent *h.*
12. Remember that the *bi* in *bicycle* means two. Compare *biplane.*

VISUAL DRILLS

1. Ath - - t - cs give both pl - - s - re and ex - r - i - e.
2. Each ath - - t - in the t - - rn - m - nt was covered with p - - - p - ration.
3. We take - h - sic - l exercise to dev - lo - stren - - - .
4. The b - c - cle rider was pra - t - c - l - y ex - - - sted.

When you have finished this lesson, review Lesson 30.

Lesson 35 BASIC WORDS

There is no rule to govern the spelling of words ending in *ance*. Learn to associate them with each other. Contrast these endings with those which appear in Lesson 39.

1. **resistance** The team's re *s*ist'an*ce* is weakening.
2. **remittance** The book company received his re mit'*t*an*ce*.
3. **insurance** Father purchased a life in sur'an*ce* policy.
4. **acceptance** His a*c* *c*ept'an*ce* of the gift pleased us.
5. **nuisance** John's behavior at the party was a nu*i*'san*ce*.
6. **accordance** His acts are in a*c* cord'an*ce* with law.
7. **remembrance** This poem revives a re mem'bran*ce* of childhood.
8. **acquaintance** Mr. Brown is an a*c* *qu*a*i*nt'an*ce* of my mother.
9. **appearance** It was his first a*p* pe*a*r'an*ce* on the stage.
10. **assurance** He gave me every a*s* sur'an*ce* of success.
11. **maintenance** The ma*i*n'te nan*ce* of food is essential to life.
12. **assistance** She worked the problem without a*s* sist'an*ce*.

MEMORY AIDS

1. Copy and memorize the following story: The appearance of the sick man was better. He had just received a remembrance from an old acquaintance, as well as assurance of financial assistance in the maintenance of his health. His quick acceptance was in accordance with his improved condition. Although a nuisance, he made no resistance to paying a remittance on his insurance.
2. Arrange the twelve *ance* words of this lesson in a column in alphabetical order. If any pronunciation or meaning is not clear, consult the Basic Dictionary.

VISUAL DRILLS

1. He made no re - ist - n - e to paying the re - it - - nce for his - nsu - - n - e.
2. His - c - ept - n - e of the nu - s - - c - was in ac - ord - n - e with his good feeling.
3. The ap - e - r - n - e of his old a - q - - - nt - nc - brought back many a rem - - br - n - e.
4. He received as - ur - nc - for continued as - ist - nc - in health m - - nt - n - n - e.

When you have finished this lesson, review Lesson 31.

Lesson 36 BASIC WORDS

The following list contains six pairs of similar words which are frequently confused. Consult the Basic Dictionary for the exact meaning of each word.

1. **forth**	Columbus set forth to discover a new route.
2. **fourth**	Helen sat in the f*o*urth seat of the first row.
3. **piece**	The p*ie*ce of cloth was torn in two places.
4. **peace**	A policeman is a guardian of the pe*ace*.
5. **principal**	The prin′*ci* pal color of the room is tan.
6. **principle**	Honesty is a good prin′*ci* pl*e* to follow.
7. **prophesy**	No one could pro*ph*′e *sy* the outcome of the game.
8. **prophecy**	The class pro*ph*′e *cy* predicted many changes.
9. **counsel**	The girls went to the dean for coun′sel.
10. **council**	The Indians held a coun′*c*il around the campfire.
11. **compliment**	The teacher gave Mary's theme a com′pli ment.
12. **complement**	The plain dress needed a com′ple ment.

MEMORY AIDS

1. Distinguish *forth* from *fourth*. Compare *forthwith, forthright.*
2. Note the *four* in *fourth*. Compare *fourteen;* contrast *forty-one.*
3. Distinguish *piece* from *peace*. COPY: A piece of pie.
4. Focus on the *eace* in *peace*. Compare *peaceful;* contrast *pacific.*
5. Distinguish *principle* from *principal*. COPY: A sensible principle.
6. COPY: My school principal is my principal pal.
7. Distinguish *prophesy* (to foretell) from *prophecy* (a prediction).
8. Stress the *cy* (sĭ) ending of prophecy. Focus on the *phe.*
9. Distinguish *counsel* from *council*. Focus on the *sel.*
10. Focus on the *cil* in *council*. Think of a *city* council.
11. Focus on the *pli* in *compliment*. COPY: A sublime compliment.
12. Focus on the *ple* in *complement*. COPY: The first complement was completely competent.

VISUAL DRILLS

1. The clerk brought f - - th the f - - rth p - - ce of goods.
2. The princ - p - - argument was over the princ - p - - of pe - c - .
3. Knowing John's ability to pro - he - y, we took coun - - - over his pro - he - y of rain.
4. Compl - m - nt the coun - - - for its compl - m - nt of members.

When you have finished this lesson, review Lesson 32.

Lesson 37 — BASIC WORDS

Do your main study on the words most difficult to recall.

1. **opportunity**	There was no op′*por* tu′ni ty to advance.
2. **altogether**	The judges were not al′to geth′er fair.
3. **fulfil**	The salesman tried to ful fil′ his promise.
4. **passed**	The circus parade pass*ed* our house at noon.
5. **tariff**	Congress put a tar′i*ff* on imported furs.
6. **unanimous**	John was elected by a u nan′i m*ous* vote.
7. **sugar**	How much sug′*ar* do you like in your tea?
8. **enough**	There was not e n*ough*′ cloth for the curtains.
9. **restaurant**	We ate at the new res′t*au* rant last night.
10. **invoice**	The in′voi*ce* stated the correct amount.
11. **potatoes**	We had sweet po ta′to*es* for dinner.
12. **supplies**	The medical su*p* pli*es*′ were sent by express.

MEMORY AIDS

1. Note the *port* in *opportunity.* Compare *oppose, opposite.*
2. Distinguish *altogether* from *all together.*
3. *Fulfil* is also spelled *fulfill,* but never *fullfill.*
4. Distinguish *passed* from *past.* Compare *passing, passenger.*
5. Note the *riff* in *tariff.* COPY: The sheriff had a tiff with the tariff.
6. Stress each syllable in *unanimous.* Compare *famous.*
7. Focus on the *ar* in *sugar.* COPY: Surely there is no sugar in vinegar.
8. Focus on the *ough* in *enough.* COPY: Rough enough for any tough.
9. Focus on the *tau* in *restaurant.* COPY: The pleasant restaurant.
10. Note the *oice* in *invoice.* Compare *choice, voice.*
11. Note the *toes* in *tomatoes.* Compare *potato, potatoes.*
12. Focus on the *lies* in *supplies.* Compare *supply, supplies; apply, applies.*

VISUAL DRILLS

1. He did not f - lf - l the op - - rt - n - ty a - t - g - th - r.
2. The t - r - - f law was pas - - - by a un - n - m - - s vote.
3. The r - st - - r - nt did not have en - u - - s - g - r.
4. The inv - - c - listed new p - t - t - - s and other s - - pl - - s.

When you have finished this lesson, review Lesson 33.

Lesson 38 BASIC WORDS

Always do the Visual Drills. They check your accuracy and strengthen your memory.

1.	**terrible**	The little boy had a ter′*ri* bl*e* dream.
2.	**forehead**	He had a bump on his for*e*′*he*ad.
3.	**awkward**	The colt was very *aw*k′ward when he walked.
4.	**folks**	The old fo*l*ks seemed very happy.
5.	**cemetery**	In the *c*em′e ter y were many new graves.
6.	**grieve**	The unhappy husband continued to gr*ie*ve.
7.	**grateful**	We are very grat*e*′ful to you for your help.
8.	**extremely**	The weather has been e*x* trem*e*′ly warm.
9.	**sympathy**	A friend expressed his s*y*m′pa thy with flowers.
10.	**further**	There is no need for fur′ther questioning.
11.	**acknowledgment**	They sent an ac *k*now*l*′*edg* ment of your letter.
12.	**later**	The judge will decide at a lat′er date.

MEMORY AIDS

1. Note the *rri* in *terrible.* Compare *horrible, irritation.*
2. Think of *forehead* as before-head. Compare *forenoon, foretell.*
3. Focus on the *awk* in *awkward.* Copy: An awkward hawk.
4. Focus on the *ol* in *folks.* Copy: John talks to the old folks.
5. Focus on the unusual *tery* ending in *cemetery.* Stress the three *e*'s.
6. Note the *rie* in *grieve.* Compare *retrieve, brief, friend.*
7. Note the *ate* in *grateful.* Compare *hateful, wakeful.*
8. Focus on the *eme* in *extremely.* Contrast *seem, stream.*
9. Stress the *path* in *sympathy.* Compare *sympathize, pathetic.*
10. Note the *fur* in *further.* Distinguish *fur* from *far.*
11. The preferred spelling is *acknowledgment.* Compare *judgment.*
12. John and Tom are here, but the *latter* (Tom) came *later.*

VISUAL DRILLS

1. The a - kw - rd fighter received a t - - r - bl - blow on the f - r - h - - d.
2. The dead boy's f - - ks continued to gr - - v - at the c - m - t - r - .
3. They were extr - m - l - gr - t - f - l for the many expressions of s - mp - th - .
4. They made f - rth - r ackn - - le - gm - nt at a l - t - r date.

When you have finished this lesson, review Lesson 34.

Lesson 39 BASIC WORDS

This lesson will help you associate the words ending in *ant, ense,* and *ience* with other words having the same endings. Contrast these endings with those in Lesson 35.

1. **ignorant**	She was quite ig′no rant of the fact.
2. **pleasant**	It was a ple*as*′ant task to accomplish.
3. **attendant**	John is a regular church a*t* tend′ant.
4. **assistant**	The nurse served as a*s* sist′ant to the doctor.
5. **expense**	The rent was an additional e*x* pens*e*′.
6. **defense**	The team maintained an excellent de fens*e*′.
7. **sense**	Good common sens*e* prevents many mistakes.
8. **nonsense**	The one-act play was full of non′sens*e*.
9. **conscience**	The prisoner had a guilty con′*science*.
10. **experience**	The e*x* pe′ri en*ce* taught her a lesson.
11. **patience**	He waited for the train with great pa′*tience*.
12. **inconvenience**	The loss of our car was an in′con ven′*ience*.

MEMORY AIDS

Frequent writing of the words in this lesson is the best way to learn to spell them correctly.

1. COPY: The ignorant ant was a pleasant attendant, but a poor assistant.
2. COPY: Enough expense for American defense is always sense, and never nonsense.
3. COPY: Science is the result of long experience, strict conscience, great patience, and much inconvenience.
4. Arrange the twelve words of Lesson 39 in a column in alphabetical order. If any meaning or pronunciation is not clear, consult the Basic Dictionary .

VISUAL DRILLS

1. Although he seemed to be ign - r - nt, the man was a pl - - s - nt a - tend - nt.
2. The firm went to great exp - n - - for the def - n - - of their as - ist - nt.
3. There was more s - n - - than nons - n - - to his strict cons - - - n - - .
4. The doctor learned from long exp - r - - n - - to meet each inconv - n - - n - - with pat - - n - - .

When you have finished this lesson, review Lesson 35.

Lesson 40 — BASIC WORDS

Examine the following words with great care. They are the cause of many misspellings.

1. **language**	The only lan′*guage* he could speak was Spanish.
2. **communication**	The telephone increased co*m* mu′ni ca′*tion*.
3. **chief**	His ch*ie*f ambition was to make money.
4. **misspell**	What words do you mis *s*pell′ most frequently?
5. **endeavor**	We will en de*av*′*o*r to fill your order.
6. **grammar**	The speaker used excellent gram′*ma*r.
7. **describe**	Try to de scrib*e*′ his appearance.
8. **discuss**	They agreed to dis cus*s*′ the problem.
9. **would**	I wo*ul*d go if I could.
10. **evidence**	The wet grounds were ev′i den*c*e of rain.
11. **opinion**	We value your o pin′*io*n on this subject.
12. **judgment**	The doctor withheld ju*dg*′ment in the case.

MEMORY AIDS

1. Focus on the *uage* in *language.* Note the *age* in *language.*
2. Focus on the *mm* in *communication.* Compare *common, community.*
3. Note the *ie* in *chief.* Copy: The chief thief came to grief.
4. Focus on the *ss* in *misspell.* Contrast *mistake* and *mischief.*
5. Note the *eav* in *endeavor.* Stress the *end* and the *or.*
6. Center on the final *ar* in *grammar.* Contrast *stammer.*
7. Focus on the *des* in *describe.* Stress the pronunciation.
8. Note the *cuss* in *discuss.* Compare *discussed, discussion.*
9. Focus on the *oul* in *would.* Copy: He should, and he would if he could.
10. Focus on the *vid* in *evidence.* Note the *ence* words in Lesson 39.
11. Focus on the *nion* in *opinion.* Compare *onion, union.*
12. Cut the *judge* to *judg* in *judgment.* Compare *acknowledgment.*

VISUAL DRILLS

1. Lang - - - - is the ch - - f means of co - m - n - cat - - n.
2. End - - v - r not to mis - p - - l words or to make mistakes in gr - m - - r.
3. He w - - - d neither d - scr - b - nor d - sc - - s the accident.
4. The ju - - m - nt was based on ev - d - n - - and not on op - n - - n.

When you have finished this lesson, review Lesson 36.

Lesson 41 BASIC WORDS

There is no rule which covers the use of double letters in spelling. You must learn each word separately.

1. **route** — They advised her to take another r*oute.*
2. **original** — The class composed an o rig′i nal song.
3. **advice** — The principal's ad v*ice*′ was helpful.

4. **already** — They have al re*a*d′y taken the books.
5. **regretting** — Joyce was re gret′*t*ing her hasty decision.
6. **numerous** — The track team received nu′mer *o*us rewards.

7. **similar** — The twins are sim′i l*a*r in appearance.
8. **mutual** — The two girls developed a mu′tu al admiration.
9. **surprise** — The party was a complete *sur* pri*se*′.

10. **village** — We drove through a small vil′*lage.*
11. **together** — The family came to geth′er at dinner.
12. **community** — Helen lived in a rural co*m* mu′ni ty.

MEMORY AIDS

1. Distinguish *route* (way or road) from *rout* (defeat and flight).
2. Focus on the *igi* in *original.* Stress the vowel sounds.
3. Distinguish the noun *advice* (suggestion) from the verb *advise* (to counsel).
4. Distinguish *already* (by this time) from *all ready.*
5. Focus on the *tt* in *regretting.* Compare *letting, betting.*
6. Stress the *mer* in *numerous.* Compare *number;* contrast *humorous.*
7. Stress the vowel sounds in *similar.* Compare *regular, popular.*
8. Focus on the *ual* in *mutual.* Compare *actual, visual, manual.*
9. Focus on the *sur* in *surprise.* Compare *surface, survey.*
10. Note the *age* in *village.* COPY: The village will age.
11. Note the *get* in *together.* Compare *whether;* contrast *weather.*
12. COPY: A city is a community with common commercial communication.

VISUAL DRILLS

1. The guide's advi - - was to follow the or - g - n - l r - - t - .
2. The num - r - - s voters were alr - - d - regr - - t - ng their choice.
3. Their s - m - l - r views were a matter of m - t - - l s - rpr - s - .
4. The whole vil - - - - worked t - g - th - r to better the c - - m - n - t - .

When you have finished this lesson, review Lesson 37.

Lesson 42 BASIC WORDS

Always read thoughtfully the illustrative sentence which follows each word. Be sure that you have the right meaning in mind.

1. **barrel** The bar′*r*el was almost filled with water.
2. **shoes** The bootblack shines black and tan sho*e*s.
3. **shipped** Six boxes were ship*ped* by express.

4. **holiday** The entire city observed the Easter hol′i da*y*.
5. **eighth** The *eigh*th locker in the row was open.
6. **twelfth** December is the twelfth month of the year.

7. **forward** The group moved for′w*a*rd rapidly.
8. **banquet** The ban′*qu*et was in honor of the visitor.
9. **annual** The spring picnic is an an′*n*u al affair.

10. **preliminary** Our team played a pre lim′i nar y game.
11. **comparatively** His estimate was com par′a tiv*e* ly correct.
12. **preparation** There was little time for prep′a ra′*tio*n.

MEMORY AIDS

1. Focus on the *rel* in *barrel*. Compare *quarrel, tunnel.*
2. Focus on the *oes* in *shoes*. COPY: Our foes had woes, but no shoes.
3. Note the two *p*'s in *shipped*. Compare *shipping, slipped.*
4. Stress the *i* in *holiday*. COPY: A solid holiday policeman.
5. Focus on the *eigh* in *eighth*. COPY: The eighty-eighth freight.
6. Note the *elf* in *twelfth*. Stress each of the seven letters.
7. Note the *for* in *forward*. COPY: Force forward for forty steps.
8. Pronounce the two syllables in *banquet* distinctly.
9. COPY: Anne announced our annual anniversary.
10. Focus on the *imi* in *preliminary*. COPY: Limit the preliminary.
11. Focus on the *ara* in *comparatively*. Contrast *comparison.*
12. Stress the *par* in *preparation*. Compare *prepare, separation.*

VISUAL DRILLS

1. The Boy Scouts ship - - - a b - r - - l of old sh - - s to the needy.
2. The h - l - da - lasted from the ei - - th day to the tw - l - th day in April.
3. The members looked f - rw - rd to the an - - - l b - n - - et.
4. The committee has made c - mp - r - t - vely little pr - l - m - n - ry pr - p - r - t - on.

When you have finished this lesson, review Lesson 38.

Lesson 43 BASIC WORDS

Note that some words have two accented syllables, one receiving a primary accent (ʹ) and another a secondary accent (ʹ).

1. **co-operation**	The club's co-op′er a′*ti*on was appreciated.
2. **attitude**	Jane assumed an at′*ti* tud*e* of indifference.
3. **all right**	Your corrected theme is al*l* rig*h*t now.
4. **suppose**	Do you su*p* pose′ that he is lost?
5. **conscientious**	The con′sci en′*tio*us worker did his best.
6. **succeed**	John tried to suc *cee*d′ at everything he tried.
7. **earliest**	The e*a*r′li est morning train arrived at five.
8. **humorous**	The artist drew some hu′m*o*r *o*us cartoons.
9. **exception**	It was an ex *c*ep′*tio*n to the rule.
10. **prompt**	It is important to be prompt at all times.
11. **practice**	The team had to prac′ti*c*e for the game.
12. **cordial**	The visitor was given a cor′*d*ial welcome.

MEMORY AIDS

1. Pronounce each hyphenated *o* distinctly in *co-operation.*
2. Focus on the *atti* in *attitude.* Contrast *gratitude, latitude.*
3. Note the two *l's* in *all right.* Compare *all wrong.*
4. Focus on the *pp* in *suppose.* Compare *supper, supply, support.*
5. Focus on the *tious* in *conscientious.* Compare *conscious.*
6. *Succeed* is one of the only three words ending in *ceed.* COPY: To succeed, you must proceed to exceed.
7. Note the *lie* in *earliest.* Compare *early, earlier, earliest.*
8. Focus on the *mor* in *humorous.* Compare *odorous;* contrast *numerous.*
9. Distinguish *exception* (omission) from *acceptance* (approval).
10. Note the two *p's* in *prompt.* Pronounce all of the letters.
11. The spelling *practice* is preferred to *practise.* Compare *practical.*
12. Note the *dial* in *cordial.* Print *with cordial regards* three times.

VISUAL DRILLS

1. The beginner's at - - t - d - of c - - - per - t - on was al - r - - - t.
2. Do you s - - pos - that he is c - ns - - - nt - - us in his efforts to suc - - ed?
3. His e - rl - - st efforts, without e - - ept - on, had been h - m - r - - s.
4. He made a pr - ct - c - of always being pr - - - t and c - r - - al.

When you have finished this lesson, review Lesson 39.

Lesson 44 BASIC WORDS

This lesson contains some particularly deceptive words. Consult the Basic Dictionary for correct pronunciations.

1. **necessary**	Exercise and rest are nec′es sar′y for health.
2. **maintain**	Try to main tain′ a good record of attendance.
3. **discipline**	Strict dis′ci pline is necessary in that class.
4. **soldier**	The sol′dier won a medal for his brave act.
5. **arctic**	Little vegetation grows in the arc′tic regions.
6. **transferred**	The student trans′ferred to another college.
7. **campaign**	The politician made a good cam paign′ speech.
8. **lieutenant**	The lieu ten′ant gave the command to fire.
9. **colonel**	Her father is a colo′nel in the Army.
10. **conquer**	It was Hitler's desire to con′quer the world.
11. **country**	China is a coun′try of ancient origin.
12. **enemies**	Our en′e mies were numerous and well equipped.

MEMORY AIDS

1. Focus on the *nec* in *necessary.* Compare *necessity, necessarily.*
2. COPY: Strain to maintain the main mountain train.
3. Note the *scip* in *discipline.* Contrast *disappear, disappoint.*
4. Note the *die* in *soldier.* Pronounce it *sol′jer.*
5. *Arctic* is capitalized in proper names, such as *Arctic Circle, Arctic Ocean.*
6. Note the *err* in *transferred.* Compare *conferred, deferred.*
7. Focus on the *aign* in *campaign.* Note carefully the silent *ig.*
8. Note that *lieutenant* ends in *ant.* Center on the *lieu.*
9. Distinguish *colonel* from *kernel.* The *colo* in *colonel* is pronounced *kur.*
10. Focus on the *que* in *conquer.* Compare *conquest, conqueror.*
11. Note the *ou* in *country.* COPY: You can count on our country.
12. Note the three *e*'s in *enemies.* Center on *emie.*

VISUAL DRILLS

1. It was ne - es - - ry to m - - nt - - n strict di - - ipl - n - .
2. The sol - - - r tran - f - r - - - to an ar - t - c regiment.
3. He began the camp - - - n as a l - - - ten - nt and ended as a c - - - n - l.
4. Attempt to con - - - r the en - m - - s of our c - - ntr - .

When you have finished this lesson, review Lesson 40.

Lesson 45 BASIC WORDS

Study and review these words until you *know* that they belong to the group of words ending in *ence.*

1. **existence** The disease threatened our *ex* ist'en*ce.*
2. **reference** We reply with ref'er en*ce* to your request.
3. **preference** Walter has a distinct pref'er en*ce* for blue.
4. **conference** The three met in con'fer en*ce* at dinner.
5. **correspondence** His secretary answered all cor'*re* spond'en*ce.*
6. **influence** Mr. Jones has little in'flu en*ce* over his son.
7. **confidence** Everyone has great con'fi den*ce* in Dr. Harper.
8. **presence** No one expected his pre*s*'en*ce* at the party.
9. **consequence** It happened in con'se *quence* of carelessness.
10. **occurrence** The *oc* cur'*rence* of a fire was unexpected.
11. **sentence** The sen'ten*ce* contained only five words.
12. **residence** Their re*s*'i den*ce* is located on Palm Street.

MEMORY AIDS

1. COPY and memorize the following story: This is a tearful story in reference to the existence of a thirsty man who showed a preference for strong drink. Under the influence of said drink he became so filled with confidence that he arranged a conference with a policeman. The policeman found evidence of the presence of too much whiskey. In consequence of the said occurrence, the poor man was given a sentence to take up residence in the local jail. His absence from home led to much serious correspondence.
2. Give special study to the word *occurrence.* It is one of the most difficult of all commonly used words. Compare *occur, occurring; recur, recurring.*

VISUAL DRILLS

1. The psychologist made ref - r - n - e to man's pref - r - n - - for long e - ist - n - - .
2. There was much written co - r - spond - n - - because the confer - n - - had so little infl - - n - - .
3. We were filled with conf - d - n - - as a cons - qu - n - - of his pres - n - - .
4. A single sent - n - - described the strange o - - ur - - n - - at the victim's res - d - n - - .

When you have finished this lesson, review Lesson 41.

Lesson 46 BASIC WORDS

You can strengthen your memory of many of the following words by giving special attention to the separate syllables.

1. **formerly**	Is this where you for′mer ly lived?
2. **doctor**	The boy required the aid of a doc′t*o*r.
3. **rheumatism**	Her r*he*u′ma tism was difficult to cure.
4. **every**	The basketball team won ev′er y game.
5. **repetition**	There will be no rep′e ti *tio*n of the play.
6. **sacrifice**	She made a sac′ri fi*ce* by giving so much.
7. **aggravate**	It is easy to ag′gra vat*e* him to anger.
8. **relieve**	A good rest will re l*ieve*′ your fatigue.
9. **considerably**	The new problems are con sid′er a bly harder.
10. **leisure**	Helen reads during her le*i*′s*u*r*e* time.
11. **agreeable**	The new arrangement was a gre*e*′a bl*e* to all.
12. **minimum**	They reduced the fine to a min′i mum.

MEMORY AIDS

1. Note the *former* in *formerly*. Distinguish from *formally*.
2. Note the *tor* in *doctor*. Compare *actor, victor, debtor*.
3. Focus on the *rheu* in *rheumatism*. Print *rheuma* three times.
4. Note the *eve* in *every*. COPY: Is every evening everywhere?
5. Note the *titi* in *repetition*. Compare *competition, petition*.
6. Note the *ri* in *sacrifice*. COPY: I sacrifice the price of ice.
7. Focus on the *gg* in *aggravate*. Compare *aggregate;* contrast *agree, agriculture*.
8. Note the *lie* in *relieve*. Compare *believe, relief*.
9. Note the *consider* and *ably* in *considerably*. Compare *probably, honorably*.
10. Focus on the *lei* in *leisure*. Note the final *sure*.
11. Note the *agree* and *able* in *agreeable*. Compare *passable*.
12. Pronounce each syllable in *minimum* distinctly.

VISUAL DRILLS

1. He told the d - ct - r that he f - rm - rl - had r - - um - t - sm.
2. He made - v - ry s - cr - f - ce to prevent a r - p - t - t - on.
3. It would ag - r - v - t - him c - ns - d - r - bly, and never r - l - - v - him.
4. Even a min - m - m of l - - s - r - would be agre - - bl - .

When you have finished this lesson, review Lesson 42.

Lesson 47 BASIC WORDS

Remember the slogan: "Much writing makes a good speller."

1. **ascertain** They studied at length to as'*cer* ta*i*n' the facts.
2. **precious** The emerald is a pre'*cio*us stone.
3. **valuable** The woman's jewels were very val'u a bl*e*.
4. **convenient** The meeting came at a con ven'*i*ent hour.
5. **dining** The meals were served in the din'ing room.
6. **breakfast** It is important to eat a good bre*a*k'fast.
7. **guess** Can you g*u*ess how many persons were there?
8. **stationery** The box of sta'*tio*n er y was a welcome gift.
9. **positive** The doctor was po*s*'i tiv*e* in his opinion.
10. **pierce** The savage used his spear to p*i*er*ce* the body.
11. **plane** The carpenter used a plan*e* to smooth the board.
12. **easily** Her directions could be followed *eas*'i ly.

MEMORY AIDS

1. Focus on the *sce* in *ascertain.* COPY: Certain to ascend to ascertain.
2. Stress the *cio* in *precious.* Compare *delicious, conscious.*
3. Note the *lua* in *valuable.* Contrast *value* with *valuable.*
4. Focus on the *ent* in *convenient.* Compare *patient, ancient.*
5. Note the *ini* in *dining.* Compare *dine, dining; line, lining.*
6. Note the *break* in *breakfast.* COPY: Break the fast at breakfast.
7. Focus on the *ue* in *guess.* Contrast *guessed* with *guest.*
8. Distinguish *stationery* (writing materials) from *stationary* (not moving).
9. Note the *s* in *positive.* Compare *position;* contrast *possible.*
10. COPY: Pierce his shield in the fierce, fiery field.
11. Distinguish *plane* from *plain.* Note the *lane* in *plane.*
12. COPY: The early sun came up easily in the east.

VISUAL DRILLS

1. Can you as - - rt - - n how v - l - - bl - the pre - - - us stones are?
2. The kitchen was c - nv - n - - nt to the d - n - ng and the br - - kf - st rooms.
3. Was he p - s - t - v -, or did he g - - ss where he put the st - t - on - ry?
4. The bullet seemed to p - er - - the armor of the pl - n - e - s - ly.

When you have finished this lesson, review Lesson 43.

Lesson 48 BASIC WORDS

It will help you if you learn the memory quips introduced by the word COPY.

1. **advisable**	It will be ad vis'a bl*e* to leave early.
2. **immigration**	Our population increased by im'*mi* gra'*tio*n.
3. **foreign**	We traveled in three for'*e*ign countries.
4. **government**	The students took a course in gov'ern ment.
5. **control**	The cowboy gained con trol' of the wild horse.
6. **people**	There were many peo'ple at the theater.
7. **schedule**	The new sc*h*ed'ul*e* is on the bulletin board.
8. **planned**	The committee plan*ne*d the spring dance.
9. **carrying**	Are you car'*ry* ing your books to school?
10. **delivery**	The letter went by special de liv'er y.
11. **guarantee**	The manager will g*u*ar'an te*e* good service.
12. **machinery**	The ma *ch*i*n*'er y suddenly stopped running.

MEMORY AIDS

1. Focus on the *able* in *advisable.* Compare *admirable, movable, comparable.*
2. Stress the *immi* in *immigration.* Distinguish from *emigration.*
3. Focus on the *reign* in *foreign.* COPY: Feign to reign in foreign Spain.
4. Note the *govern* in *government.* Compare *governor, governing.*
5. COPY: Sole control of the whole government dole.
6. Focus on the unusual *eo* of *people.* Print *peop* three times.
7. COPY: The schedule is a scheme to rule the school.
8. Focus on the *nn* in *planned.* COPY: Anne planned to get tanned.
9. Keep the *y* in *carrying.* Compare *marrying, studying.*
10. Note the *live* in *delivery.* Compare *deliver, delivering.*
11. Focus on the *ua* in *guarantee.* COPY: Guard the dual guarantee.
12. COPY: The machinery of the refinery was used by the winery.

VISUAL DRILLS

1. It seemed adv - - abl - to restrict f - r - - - n im - - gr - t - on.
2. Democratic g - v - r - m - nt is under c - ntr - l of the p - - pl - .
3. They insisted on car - - - ng out the sc - - d - l - as plan - - d.
4. The company would not g - - r - nte - prompt d - l - v - ry of the m - ch - n - ry.

When you have finished this lesson, review Lesson 44.

Lesson 49 BASIC WORDS

Take time to review previous lessons. Frequent review is the key to correct recall.

1.	**magnificent**	The palace is a mag nif′i *c*ent building.
2.	**prominent**	Our most prom′i nent citizen is the mayor.
3.	**recent**	The new book is a re′*c*ent publication.
4.	**equivalent**	Was the payment e *qu*iv′a lent to the damage?
5.	**intelligent**	The professor was unusually in tel′*l*i gent.
6.	**excellent**	Jack made e*x*′*c*el *l*ent grades in geometry.
7.	**accident**	The automobile ac′*c*i dent was tragic.
8.	**confident**	The student assumed a con′fi dent manner.
9.	**superintendent**	The board elected a new su′per in tend′ent.
10.	**management**	The cafeteria is under excellent man′*age* ment.
11.	**permanent**	They expect to install per′ma nent fixtures.
12.	**competent**	The secretary is com′pe tent in her work.

MEMORY AIDS

1. Copy and memorize the following story: The magnificent display of tennis in the recent tournament makes it evident that excellent play is no accident. There is no equivalent for steady practice. We are confident that the intelligent management by the competent superintendent will be made permanent.
2. Arrange the twelve words of Lesson 49 in a column in alphabetical order. Compare them with the words in Lessons 35, 39, and 45. The accompanying stories will aid you in keeping these words in the proper spelling groups.

VISUAL DRILLS

Writing words in sentences is one of the best ways to learn them. Write the following sentences:

1. The re - ent portrait by the prom - n - nt artist is a magn - fi - - nt painting.
2. He tried to make ex - e - l - nt manners the equ - v - l - nt of inte - l - g - nt action.
3. The sup - - intend - nt was c - nf - d - nt that he could prevent another ac - - d - nt.
4. It is good man - g - m - nt to employ comp - t - nt workers on a perm - n - nt basis.

When you have finished this lesson, review Lesson 45.

Lesson 50 — BASIC WORDS

Do two things in the Visual Drills below: (1) visualize the missing letters; (2) write the entire sentence from memory.

1. **beginning**	At the be gin'*n*ing of the game, we were ahead.
2. **paragraph**	You should indent each new par'a gra*ph*.
3. **capital**	Names of months begin with cap'i t*a*l letters.
4. **difficult**	The story was dif'*fi* cult for me to understand.
5. **continually**	She sang the same song con tin'u al *ly*.
6. **license**	The sportsman obtained a li'*cense* to hunt.
7. **exceed**	The number of players should not ex *cee*d' ten.
8. **tries**	Nancy always tri*es* to do her best.
9. **achievement**	To learn to skate is a difficult a ch*ieve*'ment.
10. **success**	The actors made a great suc *cess*' of the play.
11. **sufficient**	The money must be su*f* fi'*ci*ent to pay the debt.
12. **partial**	Naturally he is par'*ti*al to his own son.

MEMORY AIDS

1. Focus on the *nn* in *beginning.* Compare *winning, grinning.*
2. Note the middle *a* in *paragraph.* Compare *parallel, parachute;* contrast *telegraph, phonograph.*
3. Distinguish *capital* (head) from *capitol* (building).
4. Focus on the *iffi* in *difficult.* Contrast *deficit, different.*
5. Stress the *ua* in *continually.* Compare *annually, visually.*
6. Focus on the *cens* in *license.* Compare *expense;* contrast *absence.*
7. *Exceed* is one of the only three words ending in *ceed.* COPY: To succeed, you must proceed to exceed.
8. Note that *tries* ends in *ies.* Compare *flies, supplies, dries.*
9. Note the *achieve* in *achievement.* Compare *retrieve, believe.*
10. Focus on the *cc* and *ss* in *success.* Compare *access, succeed.*
11. Focus on the *cie* in *sufficient.* Compare *efficient, deficient.*
12. Note the *tia* in *partial.* Compare *initial, confidential.*

VISUAL DRILLS

1. Put a c - p - t - l letter at the beg - n - - ng of a par - gra - - .
2. The hunters were cont - n - - - ly having dif - - c - lty in getting a li - en - - .
3. A good student tr - - s to ex - - ed his first ach - - v - m - nt.
4. To achieve par - - - l suc - es - is not su - fi - - - nt.

When you have finished this lesson, review Lesson 46.

Lesson 51

BASIC WORDS

There is no rule which covers the use of double letters in spelling. Learn each word as a distinct word.

1. **disappoint**	The weather seemed to dis *ap* point' everyone.
2. **site**	This is the sit*e* for the new building.
3. **beautiful**	The lovely flowers made a b*eau*'ti ful picture.
4. **across**	John sat a cros*s*' the table from Jane.
5. **particular**	Our librarian is par tic'u l*ar* about the books.
6. **accidentally**	He ac *ci* dent'al *ly* dropped the papers.
7. **brought**	The students bro*ugh*t their books to school.
8. **February**	Feb'ru *ar* y is the second month of the year.
9. **variety**	There is a large va ri'e ty to select from.
10. **effect**	The medicine had no *ef* fect' upon the patient.
11. **raise**	She asked the pupils to ra*ise* their hands.
12. **spirits**	The picnic put them in good spir'its.

MEMORY AIDS

1. Note the one *s* and two *p*'s in *disappoint.* Compare *disappear, disapprove.*
2. Distinguish *site* (position) from *sight* (vision).
3. Focus on the *eau* in *beautiful.* Compare *beauty, bountiful.*
4. Note the *cross* in *across.* COPY: Alive, alone, across the sea.
5. Distinguish *particular* from *peculiar.* Note the *part* beginning.
6. Note the *cc* in *accidentally.* COPY: An accidentally accurate account.
7. Compare *think, thought* with *bring, brought.* COPY: He thought he brought the bread he bought.
8. Pronounce both the *r*'s in *February.* Focus on the *bru.*
9. Pronounce each syllable in *variety* distinctly.
10. Focus on the *ff* in *effect.* Compare *affect;* contrast *defect.*
11. Note the *ai* in *raise.* COPY: Praise the rain and raise the grain.
12. Note the *it* in *spirits.* Pronounce each syllable distinctly.

VISUAL DRILLS

1. The b - - ut - ful scenes at the s - t - did not d - sa - p - - nt us.
2. We came acr - - s this p - rt - c - l - r spot ac - - d - nt - - ly.
3. F - br - - ry br - - - - t forth a great v - r - - ty of weather.
4. The ef - - ct served to r - - s - our sp - r - ts.

When you have finished this lesson, review Lesson 47.

Lesson 52 BASIC WORDS

Look carefully at the words in this lesson. Be sure that you see all of the letters.

1. **ancient**	The history of an′*ci*ent civilization is interesting.
2. **interest**	You must pay in′ter est on borrowed money.
3. **great**	The building cost a gr*e*at amount of money.
4. **whether**	I wonder *wh*eth′er or not we can go?
5. **duplicate**	The one twin was a du′pli cat*e* of the other.
6. **genuine**	The purse was made of gen′u in*e* leather.
7. **ghost**	John claimed that a g*h*ost haunted the attic.
8. **familiar**	They sang the old, fa mil′*i*ar songs.
9. **picture**	This pic′tur*e* was taken last year.
10. **although**	Mary came, al thou*gh*′ she was not invited.
11. **seize**	The thief attempted to se*ize* the money.
12. **determine**	You must de ter′min*e* what to do next.

MEMORY AIDS

1. Note the unusual *cie* in *ancient.* Contrast *receive, deceive.*
2. Stress the *ter* in *interest.* COPY: Enter winter interest.
3. Distinguish *great* (large) from *grate* (iron bars).
4. Distinguish *whether* (which of two) from *weather* (cold, wet, etc.).
5. Focus on the *pli* in *duplicate.* Compare *triplicate, implicate.*
6. Focus on the *uine* in *genuine.* Place the accent on *gen.*
7. Note the *host* in *ghost.* COPY: The ghastly ghost was a hostile host.
8. Note the *liar* in *familiar.* Compare *peculiar;* contrast *similar.*
9. Distinguish *picture* (photograph) from *pitcher* (a ballplayer).
10. Note the one *l* in *although.* Also correctly spelled *altho.*
11. Focus on the *ei* in *seize.* Distinguish *seize* from *cease.*
12. Note the *mine* in *determine.* Compare *genuine, feminine.*

VISUAL DRILLS

1. The buyer showed gr - - t int - r - st in an - - - nt art.
2. He wondered wh - th - r the painting was g - n - - ne or a d - pl - c - te.
3. He was not f - m - l - - r with a weird p - ct - re of a g - - st.
4. Altho - - - present, he could not d - t - rm - ne to s - - z - the ghost.

When you have finished this lesson, review Lesson 48.

Lesson 53 BASIC WORDS

Make sure that you know the correct pronunciation and meaning of each word. Refer to the Basic Dictionary.

1. **performance** The actors gave a good per form′an*ce*.
2. **affect** The change in rates did not a*f* fect′ us.
3. **appreciation** The audience showed its a*p* pre′*ci* a′*tion*.
4. **neighbor** The cat belongs to our n*eigh*′bor.
5. **criticism** The crit′i *c*ism of the book was bitter.
6. **dying** The beautiful rose is slowly d*y*′ing.
7. **grievous** The injured man had a griev′*o*us wound.
8. **disposition** Miss Jones has a cheerful dis′po *si*′*tion*.
9. **profession** He belongs to the medical pro fes′*sion*.
10. **guardian** Mr. Andrews is Mary's legal g*u*ard′i an.
11. **handling** The officers are han′dling the crowd well.
12. **responsible** The driver was re spon′si bl*e* for the accident.

MEMORY AIDS

1. Note the *ance* ending in *performance*. Compare words in Lesson 35.
2. Distinguish *affect* (to influence) from *effect* (to cause to happen). Compare *affection;* contrast *defect*.
3. Focus on the *cia* in *appreciation*. Compare *appreciate, approve*.
4. Focus on the *eigh* in *neighbor*. COPY: Weigh eight neighbors.
5. Note the *critic* in *criticism*. Compare *critical, criticize*.
6. Distinguish *dying* (expiring) from *dyeing* (coloring).
7. Focus on the *ie* in *grievous*. Compare *retrieve;* contrast *receive*.
8. Note the *position* in *disposition*. Compare *positive, dispose*.
9. Note the single *f* in *profession*. Compare *profess, professor*.
10. Note the *ua* in *guardian*. Distinguish *guardian* from *garden*.
11. Focus on the *dli* in *handling*. Compare *trembling, assembling*.
12. Focus on the *sible* ending in *responsible*. Compare *indefensible*.

VISUAL DRILLS

1. Lack of ap - re - - - ti - n did not af - - ct the p - rf - rm - n - - .
2. The bitter cr - ti - - sm of the new n - - - - bor was d - - ng out.
3. His pr - f - - si - n had a gr - - v - - s effect on his d - sp - s - ti - n.
4. The girl's g - - rd - - n was r - sp - ns - bl - for h - ndl - ng her affairs.

When you have finished this lesson, review Lesson 49.

Lesson 54 BASIC WORDS

Study carefully the differences in the spelling and pronunciation of *kerosene* and *gasoline.*

1. **chauffeur** The *chauf feur'* drove the car away.
2. **mileage** The speedometer records the mil*e'age.*
3. **getting** The team is get'*t*ing ready to play.
4. **kerosene** Much ker'o sen*e'* is burned in oil lamps.
5. **gasoline** There was no gas'o l*ine* in the tank.
6. **carburetor** The mechanic repaired the car'bu ret'*o*r.
7. **scarcely** The room is scar*ce'*ly ever open.
8. **mountain** The moun'*ta*in was covered with pine trees.
9. **climb** The little boy liked to clim*b* trees.
10. **finally** They fi'nal *l*y finished the long game.
11. **compelled** The rain com pel*l*ed' them to go indoors.
12. **carriage** The typewriter car'*riage* is broken.

MEMORY AIDS

1. Consult the Basic Dictionary for the pronunciation of *chauffeur.*
2. Note the *mile* and the *age* in *mileage.* Contrast *village.*
3. Note the *tt* in *getting.* Compare *get, getting; bet, betting.*
4. Focus on the *ene* in *kerosene.* Contrast *gasoline, vaseline.*
5. Note the *so* in *gasoline.* COPY: Old line gasoline gas.
6. Note the *bur* in *carburetor.* Stress the *or* ending.
7. Focus on the *rce* in *scarcely.* Compare *fiercely, pierce.*
8. Focus on the *ai* in *mountain.* COPY: Captain of a certain mountain fountain.
9. Note the *limb* in *climb.* COPY: Climb the limber limb.
10. Note the *ally* in *finally.* Compare *usually, naturally.*
11. Note the *ll* in *compelled.* COPY: He rebelled, but spelled when compelled.
12. Focus on the *arri* in *carriage.* Compare *marriage;* contrast *mileage.*

VISUAL DRILLS

1. The ch - - f - - - r was g - - t - ng low m - l - - g - out of the car.
2. The k - r - s - n - mixed with g - s - l - n - choked the c - rb - r - t - r.
3. They could sc - r - - ly cl - m - the m - - nt - - n road.
4. They f - n - - ly were c - mp - - led to go by c - - r - - ge.

When you have finished this lesson, review Lesson 50.

Lesson 55 BASIC WORDS

Focus your attention on the hard spots which appear in italics.

1. **villain** The vil'*la*in escaped through the jail window.
2. **character** The judge was a man of fine c*h*ar'ac ter.
3. **establish** The firm tried to es tab'lish a good reputation.
4. **possession** The new owner of the house claimed po*s* *s*e*s*'*s*ion.
5. **principally** We were prin'*c*i pal *ly* concerned about the game.
6. **treasurer** The class tre*as*'ur er collected the dues.
7. **decide** The picnickers could not de *c*ide' where to go.
8. **majority** Jack was elected by a ma jor'i ty of votes.
9. **arrangement** Who made the a*r* range'ment for the trip?
10. **American** The A mer'i can flag is an emblem of democracy.
11. **niece** Aunt Jane bought the gift for her n*ie*ce.
12. **allowance** Father increased John's monthly a*l* lo*w*'an*ce*.

MEMORY AIDS

1. COPY: The villain of the mountain fountain.
2. Note the *act* in *character*. Contrast *chorus, chemistry*.
3. Focus on the *est* in *establish*. COPY: Establish an estimate.
4. Note the four *s*'s in *possession*. COPY: The Mississippi possession.
5. Note the *ally* in *principally*. Compare *practically, accidentally*.
6. Note the *sure* in *treasurer*. Compare *measure, pleasure*.
7. Focus on the *c* in *decide*. Compare *decision;* contrast *beside*.
8. Note the *major* in *majority*. COPY: The majority of city mayors.
9. Focus on the *ge* in *arrangement*. Compare *management, changeable*.
10. Always begin *American* with a capital *A*. Stress the *i*.
11. Focus on the *ie* in *niece*. COPY: Our niece would lie for a piece of pie.
12. Stress the *ance* in *allowance*. COPY: An advance allowance.

VISUAL DRILLS

1. The guilty v - - l - - n could not est - bl - sh a good c - ar - ct - r.
2. The tr - - s - r - r obtained p - - ses - - - n pr - nc - p - - ly by his promptness.
3. It took a m - j - r - ty to d - c - d - the new ar - - ng - m - nt.
4. Her Am - r - c - n n - - c - received the largest al - - w - nc - .

When you have finished this lesson, review Lesson 51.

Lesson 56 BASIC WORDS

The words in this lesson cause many spelling errors. Practice writing them in short sentences.

1. **volunteer**	He will vol'un *tee*r' to do his duty.
2. **allowed**	Smoking is not *al* lo*we*d' in this building.
3. **captain**	The cap'*ta*in said farewell to his crew.
4. **different**	The sisters are dif'*f*er ent in appearance.
5. **apartment**	The a part'ment is small, but convenient.
6. **convenience**	Telephones are a con ven'*ience* to our homes.
7. **basis**	Visual learning is the ba'sis of this book.
8. **definite**	He made def'i nit*e* plans for his trip.
9. **criticize**	We usually crit'i *cize* what we disapprove.
10. **personal**	Evidence means more than per'*so*n al opinion.
11. **argument**	The ar'gu ment was in the field of politics.
12. **prejudice**	The farmer held a prej'*u* di*ce* against the city.

MEMORY AIDS

1. Focus on the *un* in *volunteer.* Compare *voluntary, profiteer.*
2. Note the *owe* in *allowed.* Distinguish *allowed* (permitted) from *aloud* (with full sound).
3. Focus on the *tai* in *captain.* Compare *mountain, fountain.*
4. Note the *ent* in *different.* Copy: Silent, violent, and different.
5. Note the *apart* in *apartment.* Copy: A part of an apartment.
6. Focus on the *ience* in *convenience.* Compare *science, experience.*
7. Note the *is* in *basis.* Copy: His basis is the oasis.
8. Stress the *ite* ending in *definite.* Compare *infinite;* contrast *deposit.*
9. Keep the *critic* in *criticize.* Compare *critical, criticism.*
10. Note the *al* in *personal.* Copy: A personal pal is not critical.
11. Note the omitted *e* when *argue* changes to *argument.*
12. Focus on the *ej* in *prejudice.* Compare *judicial, injustice.*

VISUAL DRILLS

1. The clerk a - lo - - d the v - l - nt - er to see the c - pt - - n.
2. A d - f - - r - nt ap - rtm - nt might have greater c - nv - n - - n - - .
3. The lawyer found a d - f - n - t - b - s - s to cr - t - c - ze the decision.
4. The lengthy arg - m - nt was due to p - rs - n - l pr - j - di - - .

When you have finished this lesson, review Lesson 52.

Lesson 57 BASIC WORDS

Give special attention to the different syllables which make up the words in this lesson.

1. **disease** The strange dis *ease'* is very contagious.
2. **stating** The professor was stat'ing a fact.
3. **extraordinary** The giraffe is an ex tr*a*or'di nar y animal.
4. **recognize** He did not rec'og nize his old friend.
5. **difference** There is much dif'*f*er en*ce* of opinion.
6. **sensible** Mary is a bright and sen'si bl*e* girl.
7. **divided** John di vid'ed the apple into three parts.
8. **fundamental** The fun'da men'tal cause is his ignorance.
9. **opposite** They spoke on op'*po* sit*e* sides of the debate.
10. **merely** He viewed the fight mer*e*'ly as a spectator.
11. **pressure** Great pres'*s*ur*e* of steam exploded the boiler.
12. **vicinity** The two towns are in the same vi *c*in'i ty.

MEMORY AIDS

1. Stress the *dis* in *disease.* COPY: Dispose the distant disease.
2. Omit the *e* in *stating.* Compare *state, stating; skate, skating.*
3. Note that *traor* is one syllable in *extraordinary.*
4. Pronounce the *g* in the middle syllable of *recognize.*
5. Note the *ence* in *difference.* COPY: A difference in evidence.
6. Focus on the *sib* in *sensible.* Compare *defensible, responsible.*
7. Stress the *i*'s in *divide.* Compare *inside, division.*
8. Pronounce each syllable in *fundamental* distinctly.
9. Stress the *po* in *opposite.* Compare *opportunity, opposition.*
10. Note the *mere* in *merely.* Compare *sincerely;* contrast *nearly.*
11. COPY: Be sure to stress the *press* in *pressure.*
12. Focus on the *cin* in *vicinity.* Stress the three *i*'s in *vicinity.*

VISUAL DRILLS

1. She kept st - t - ng that it was an extr - - rd - n - ry d - s - - se.
2. I did not r - c - gn - ze any s - ns - bl - d - f - - r - nc - in temperature.
3. They were d - v - d - d into op - - s - te groups as to its f - nd - m - nt - l cause.
4. It was m - r - l - a harmless pr - s - - re in the vi - - n - ty of the heart.

When you have finished this lesson, review Lesson 53.

Lesson 58 BASIC WORDS

Note that some words have two accented syllables, one receiving a primary accent (ʹ) and another a secondary accent (ˈ).

1. **attention** The audience paid *a*t ten'*tio*n to the speaker.
2. **sincerely** We are sin *cere*'ly sorry about the misfortune.
3. **respectfully** The minister was treated very re spect'ful *ly*.
4. **affectionately** Arthur spoke a*f* fec'*tio*n at*e* ly of his parents.
5. **really** Did your dream re'al *ly* come true?
6. **characteristic** Kindness is his most c*h*ar'ac ter is'tic trait.
7. **comparison** There is no com par'i *so*n between the books.
8. **relative** The fact is not rel'a tiv*e* to the question.
9. **competition** The com'pe ti'*tio*n between the two was keen.
10. **representative** Mr. Johnson went as our rep're *se*nt'a tiv*e*.
11. **conscious** He was con'*scio*us although badly hurt.
12. **individual** She greeted each in'di vid'u al differently.

MEMORY AIDS

1. Note the three *t*'s in *attention*. Compare *invention, attended.*
2. Keep the *sincere* in *sincerely*. Compare *merely, entirely*.
3. Note the *respect* and the *fully* in *respectfully*.
4. Focus on the *ely* in *affectionately*. Compare *approximately*.
5. Focus on the *all* in *really*. Compare *totally, locally, naturally.*
6. Compare *characteristic* with *character* in Lesson 55.
7. Focus on the *ison* ending of *comparison*. Contrast with *compare*.
8. Focus on the *la* in *relative*. Pronounce the *a* distinctly.
9. Note the *petition* in *competition*. Focus on the *eti*.
10. Focus on the *at* in *representative*. Stress the *a* sound.
11. Focus on the *scio* in *conscious*. Compare *glorious, conscience.*
12. Pronounce each syllable distinctly in *individual*.

VISUAL DRILLS

1. Your at - - nt - - n is s - n - - r - ly and r - sp - ctf - - ly requested.
2. John's af - - ct - - n - t - ly written letter was r - - - ly c - - r - ct - rist - c of him.
3. He made no c - mp - r - s - n r - l - t - ve to the close c - mp - t - t - - n.
4. R - pr - s - nt - t - ve government is c - n - - - ous of the ind - v - d - - l voter.

When you have finished this lesson, review Lesson 54.

Lesson 59 BASIC WORDS

Refer to the Basic Dictionary for the correct pronunciation of the difficult words in this lesson.

1. **vacuum** — An empty space is called a vac′u um.
2. **apparently** — They were *ap* par′ent ly waiting for someone.
3. **instead** — Please use your own pencil in ste*a*d′ of mine.
4. **forfeit** — The winner must for′f*e*it the prize.
5. **guest** — We are having a g*u*est for dinner.
6. **embarrass** — It would em bar′*r*as*s* him if he lost.
7. **purchase** — She went to the shop to pur′chas*e* a suit.
8. **orchestra** — They employed an or′*ch*es tra for the dance.
9. **piano** — Myrtle plays the pi an′o in the orchestra.
10. **mysterious** — The m*y*s te′ri *o*us murder remained unsolved.
11. **superstitious** — Some persons are su per sti′*ti*ous about Friday.
12. **shepherd** — The shep′*h*erd cared for hundreds of sheep.

MEMORY AIDS

1. Focus on the *uu* in *vacuum.* Stress all three syllables.
2. Note the *rent* in *apparently.* Compare *transparent, parent.*
3. Focus on the *ea* in *instead.* Copy: Lead instead of bread.
4. Note the *ei* in *forfeit.* Compare *surfeit, counterfeit.*
5. Focus on the *ue* in *guest.* Distinguish *guest* (visitor) from *guessed* (supposed).
6. Focus on the *rr* and the *ss* in *embarrass.* Print *embarrass* three times.
7. Note the *pur* in *purchase.* Copy: Purchase the purple purse.
8. Focus on the *ch* in *orchestra.* Stress the *tra* syllable.
9. Pronounce the three syllables in *piano* distinctly.
10. Focus on the *mys* in *mysterious.* Note the *ious* ending.
11. Focus on the *tious* in *superstitious.* Compare *superstition.*
12. Note the *shep* and the *herd* in *shepherd.* Focus on the silent *h.*

VISUAL DRILLS

1. Ap - - r - ntly it was full of air, inst - - d of being a va - - - m.
2. The game included a f - rf - - t to embar - - - s each g - - st.
3. The orc - - str - arranged to p - rch - s - a concert p - - n - .
4. The m - st - r - - - s noise at night scared the s - p - rst - t - - - s sh - p - - rd.

When you have finished this lesson, review Lesson 55.

Lesson 60 BASIC WORDS

Frequent review is the key to correct recall.

1.	**irresistible**	He had an *ir*'re *s*ist'i bl*e* desire to sneeze.
2.	**apparatus**	The new laboratory ap *p*a ra'tus is complicated.
3.	**current**	It is one of the cur'*r*ent books of the month.
4.	**destroy**	They plan to de stroy' the old building.
5.	**siege**	Grant led the *sie*g*e* of Vicksburg in 1863.
6.	**concrete**	The house had a con'cret*e* foundation.
7.	**substitute**	Oleomargarine is a sub'sti tut*e* for butter.
8.	**auxiliary**	The sailboat had to use its *aux* il'*i*a ry engine.
9.	**propeller**	The small airplane used a wooden pro pel'*l*er.
10.	**anything**	Is there *a*n'y thing wrong with the plan?
11.	**stationary**	The weather conditions remained sta'*tio*n ar'y.
12.	**desirable**	Honesty and diligence are de *s*ir'a bl*e* traits.

MEMORY AIDS

1. Focus on the *rr* in *irresistible.* Note the *ible* ending carefully.
2. Focus on the *pp* in *apparatus.* COPY: Apply the apparatus.
3. Note the *rr* in *current.* COPY: The excellent current officers should be made permanent.
4. Focus on the *des* in *destroy.* Compare *destruction, despise.*
5. Focus on the *ie* in *siege.* COPY: Relieve the field by siege.
6. Note the *ete* ending of *concrete.* Compare *complete, athlete.*
7. Focus on the *sti* in *substitute.* Compare *constitute, institute.*
8. Note the *liar* in *auxiliary.* Focus on the unusual *aux* beginning.
9. Focus on the *elle* in *propeller.* Compare *speller;* contrast *propel.*
10. Note that *any* and *thing* combine to make *anything.*
11. Distinguish *stationary* (fixed) and *stationery* (paper, etc.).
12. Note the *rable* ending of *desirable.* Compare *admirable.*

VISUAL DRILLS

1. The electric cur - - nt from the new ap - - r - t - s was almost ir - - s - st - ble.
2. The aim of the s - - g - was to d - str - y the c - ncr - t - pill-boxes.
3. The crippled ship was forced to s - bst - t - te an a - x - l - - ry prop - - l - r.
4. To remain st - t - - n - ry was an - th - ng but d - s - r - ble.

When you have finished this lesson, review Lesson 56.

Basic Dictionary

The following Basic Dictionary gives the pronunciation and primary meanings of the 720 basic words which appear in Part 1 of this speller. Together with the illustrative sentences given earlier in the text, the Basic Dictionary helps the student identify clearly each basic spelling word. The Lesson in which a word occurs is indicated by the number at the end of the definition.

The Basic Dictionary presents only those facts which are essential to basic spelling. The more extensive uses of the dictionary are treated in detail in Part 2. Each word in the Basic Dictionary is followed by its prevailing pronunciation in parentheses; for example, *absence* (ăb′sĕns). To show the pronunciation, each word is divided into syllables, the proper syllables are accented, and special marks indicate the vowel sounds. The regular and secondary accents are indicated respectively by the strong and weak accent marks; for example, application (ăp′lĭ kā′shŭn). The Key to Pronunciation below illustrates what the marks mean.

When two meanings are given for a word, the numbers 1 and 2 are used. The first meaning given is the one used previously in the text. When the same word is commonly used either as a noun or a verb or an adjective, the different definitions are preceded by *n.*, *v.*, or *adj.*, as the case may be.

KEY TO PRONUNCIATION

ā as in āte	ī as in īce	ō as in gō	ū as in cūbe
ă as in ăt	ĭ as in hĭt	ŏ as in tŏp	ŭ as in ŭp
ä as in ärm	ē as in bē	ô as in ôrb	û as in bûrn
ȧ as in ȧsk	ĕ as in gĕt	ŏ̂ as in sŏ̂ft	*th* (thick sound) as in fea*th*er
â as in câre	ẽ as in watẽr	o͞o as in mo͞on	
		o͝o as in fo͝ot	th (thin) as in thin

absence (ăb′sĕns), the state of being away; lack. **1.**

absolutely (ăb′sō lūt′lĭ), 1. positively. 2. in an unrestricted manner. **10.**

accept (ăk sĕpt′), 1. to receive with approval. 2. to take. **24.**

acceptance (ăk sĕp′tăns), 1. receiving with approval. 2. the act of taking. **35.**

accident (ăk'sĭ dĕnt), a mishap; an unexpected event. **49.**

accidentally (ăk'sĭ dĕn'tăl ĭ), unexpectedly; by chance. **51.**

accommodate (ă kŏm'ō dāt), 1. to make room for. 2. to adapt. **29.**

accordance (ă kôr'dăns), agreement; conformity. **35.**

account (ă kount'), *n.* 1. an explanation. 2. a financial statement.—*v.* to compute. **1.**

accurate (ăk'ū răt), correct; exact; free from error. **28.**

ache (āk), *v.* to have continuous pain.—*n.* pain. **5.**

achievement (ă chēv'mĕnt), accomplishment; something completed. **50.**

acknowledge (ăk nŏl'ĕj), 1. to express thanks for. 2. to admit to be true. 3. to confess. **17.**

acknowledgment (ăk nŏl'ĕj mĕnt), 1. a notice of recognition or receipt. 2. expression of thanks. 3. admission of truth. **38.**

acquaintance (ă kwān'tăns), 1. a person whom one knows slightly. 2. personal knowledge of persons or things. **35.**

across (ă krŏs'), 1. on the other side of. 2. from one side to the opposite side. **51.**

additional (ă dĭsh'ŭn ăl), added; extra. **20.**

address (ă drĕs'), *n.* 1. place of residence. 2. a formal speech.—*v.* to speak or write to. **20.**

administration (ăd mĭn'ĭs trā'shŭn), 1. the management of business or public affairs. 2. the persons collectively who manage. **28.**

advertising (ăd'vĕr tīz'ĭng), asking by public notice; calling attention to. **26.**

advice (ăd vīs'), 1. opinion about what should be done. 2. notification. **41.**

advisable (ăd vīz'ȧ bl), in agreement with good judgment; prudent. **48.**

advise (ăd vīz'), 1. to offer an opinion to. 2. to take counsel. **15.**

aerial (ā ē'rĭ ăl), *adj.* 1. relating to the air. 2. like air.—*n.* radio antenna. **21.**

affairs (ă fârz'), 1. matters of public concern. 2. one's personal interests. **11.**

affect (ă fĕkt'), 1. to influence. 2. to be fond of. 3. to pretend. **53.**

affectionately (ă fĕk'shŭn ĭt lĭ), devotedly; lovingly; warmly. **58.**

against (ȧ gĕnst'), 1. in contact with. 2. directly into. 3. in preparation for. **1.**

aggravate (ăg'rȧ vāt), 1. to add to; to intensify. 2. to irritate. **46.**

agreeable (ȧ grē'ȧ bl), 1. acceptable. 2. willing. 3. suitable. **46.**

alcohol (ăl'kō hŏl), a liquid used in intoxicating beverages; a colorless, inflammable liquid. **33.**

allowance (ă lou'ăns), 1. a definite sum or quantity granted. 2. an amount added to or subtracted from something; concession. **55.**

allowed (ă loud'), 1. permitted. 2. admitted. 3. added or subtracted in consideration of something. **56.**

all right (ôl rīt), correct; certainly. **43.**

almost (ôl'mōst), nearly; in large part. **11.**

already (ôl rĕd'ĭ), by this time; previously. **41.**

although (ôl *th*ō'), in spite of the fact; even if. **52.**

altogether (ôl'to͞o gĕ*th*'ĕr), 1. completely. 2. on the whole. **37.**

always (ôl'wāz), 1. at all times. 2. continually. **1.**

amateur (ăm'ȧ tûr'), *n.* 1. a nonprofessional performer. 2. person who does something poorly. —*adj.* of an amateur. **1.**

American (ȧ mĕr'ĭ kăn), *adj.* of or pertaining to America.—*n.* a citizen of America. **55.**

amount (ă mount'), the sum total; aggregate. **30.**

analyze (ăn'ȧ līz), to examine; to find out the essential features of. **27.**

ancient (ān'shĕnt), *adj.* 1. very old. 2. pertaining to the past.—*n.* one who lived long ago. **52.**

announcement (ă nouns'mĕnt), 1. formal notice. 2. act of announcing. **14.**

annual (ăn'ū ăl), 1. happening once a year. 2. yearly. **42.**

anxious (ăngk'shŭs), 1. earnestly desirous. 2. deeply concerned. **11.**

anything (ĕn'ĭ thĭng), something; any happening, act, or object. **60.**

apartment (ȧ pärt'mĕnt), a room or set of rooms used as a residence. **56.**

apparatus (ăp ȧ rā'tŭs), an outfit of tools, or instruments for any work. **60.**

apparently (ă pâr'ĕnt lĭ), obviously; evidently; seemingly. **59.**

appeal (ă pēl'), *n.* 1. a call for sympathy or aid. 2. a resort to a higher court.—*v.* to call for aid or sympathy. **29.**

appearance (ă pēr'ăns), 1. act of coming before the public. 2. an act of becoming visible. 3. aspect. **35.**

application (ăp'lĭ kā'shŭn), 1. a request. 2. act of applying. 3. a remedy. **30.**

appreciate (ă prē'shĭ āt), 1. to esteem highly. 2. to recognize the worth of. 3. to raise the value of. **15.**

appreciation (ă prē'shĭ ā'shŭn), 1. a just recognition of worth. 2. a sympathetic understanding. **53.**

approval (ă prōōv'ăl), an act of approving; consent. **30.**

arctic (ärk'tĭk), relating to the North Pole region; frigid. **44.**

argument (är'gū mĕnt), 1. a discussion or debate. 2. proofs presented for or against something. **56.**

arrangement (ă rānj'mĕnt), 1 plan or system. 2. preparation. 3. settlement. 55.

article (är'tĭ kl), 1. a literary composition. 2. a section of any written material. 3. a particular thing. **18.**

ascend (ă sĕnd'), 1. to go up; to rise. 2. to slope upward. 3. to exalt. **22.**

ascertain (ăs'ẽr tān'), to make sure; to find out. **47.**

assistance (ă sĭs'tăns), help; support. **35.**

assistant (ă sĭs'tănt), *n.* a helper; an aid.—*adj.* helping. **39.**

association (ă sō'sĭ ā'shŭn), 1. corporation; union. 2. act of uniting. **33.**

assume (ă sūm'), 1. to take upon oneself. 2. to take for granted. 3. to pretend to possess. **27.**

assurance (ă shŏŏr'ăns), 1. act of inspiring confidence; confidence. 2. certainty. 3. guarantee. 4. insurance. **35.**

assure (ă shŏŏr'), 1. to make certain. 2. to inspire confidence in. 3. to insure. **32.**

athlete (ăth'lēt), one trained in physical agility. **34.**

athletics (ăth lĕt'ĭks), 1. athletic sports. 2. any system of athletic training. **34.**

attacked (ă tăkt'), 1. assaulted. 2. offended. **32.**

attendant (ă tĕn'dănt), *n.* one who attends, serves, or accompanies. —*adj.* 1. present. 2. accompanying. **39.**

attention (ă tĕn'shŭn), 1. heed. 2. act of courtesy. 3. readiness to receive orders. **58.**

attitude (ăt'ĭ tūd), 1. apparent state of mind. 2. pose. **43.**

attorney (ă tûr'nĭ), one legally qualified to act for another; a lawyer. **29.**

authority (ô thŏr'ĭ tĭ), 1. a right to command or act; jurisdiction. 2. expert or specialist. **9.**

automobile (ô'tō mō bēl'), *n.* 1. a motor driven vehicle.—*adj.* having to do with automobiles. **16.**

autumn (ô'tŭm), 1. the season between summer and winter. 2. period of decline or decay. **9.**

auxiliary (ôg zĭl'yȧ rĭ), *adj.* assisting; helping; giving aid.—*n.* a helper; an ally. **60.**

available (ȧ vāl'ȧ bl), 1. at disposal; obtainable. 2. usable. **26.**

awful (ô'fo͝ol), 1. causing awe; terrible. 2. dreadful. **6.**

awkward (ôk'wẽrd), 1. ungraceful; clumsy. 2. embarrassing. **38.**

balance (băl'ăns), *n.* 1. equilibrium. 2. weighing device. 3. surplus. 4. mental poise.—*v.* 1. to weigh. 2. to bring to equilibrium. 3. to compare. **1.**

balloon (bă lo͞on'), a large bag filled with gas or heated air, which will float in the air. **10.**

banquet (băng'kwĕt), *n.* an entertainment feast.—*v.* to feast. **42.**

barrel (băr'ĕl), a cylindrical vessel. **42.**

basis (bā'sĭs), 1. first principle. 2. base; foundation. 3. chief ingredient. **56.**

beautiful (bū'tĭ fo͝ol), qualities delightful to the mind and senses; lovely. **51.**

beauty (bū'tĭ), qualities which are pleasing to the eye. 2. particular grace or charm. **8.**

because (bē kôz'), for the reason that; since. **6.**

been (bĭn), past participle of *be.* **9.**

beginning (bē gĭn'ĭng), first part; origin; starting point. **50.**

belief (bē lēf'), 1. conviction. 2. opinion. **17.**

believe (bē lēv'), 1. to accept as true. 2. to hold an opinion. 3. to place confidence in. **7.**

benefit (bĕn'ē fĭt), *n.* advantage.—*v.* 1. to receive good. 2. to profit. **9.**

benefited (bĕn'ē fĭt'ĕd), 1. received good from. 2. profited from. **5.**

between (bē twēn'), 1. in the middle of two objects. 2. concerning; involving. **17.**

bicycle (bī'sĭk l), *n.* a two-wheeled vehicle for riding.—*v.* to ride a bicycle. **34.**

blue (blo͞o), 1. of the color of the sky. 2. down-spirited. **8.**

break (brāk), *v.* 1. to injure; to damage. 2. to burst; to shatter. —*n.* breach; gap. **6.**

breakfast (brĕk'fȧst), *n.* the first meal of the day.—*v.* to eat breakfast. **47.**

brief (brēf), *adj.* 1. concise; condensed. 2. short.—*n.* outline of an argument. **25.**

brilliant (brĭl'yănt), 1. distinguished; clever. 2. sparkling; glittering. **31.**

brought (brôt), past tense of *bring.* **51.**

built (bĭlt), 1. constructed. 2. formed by art. 3. established. **22.**

bulletin (bo͝ol'ĕ tĭn), 1. latest news statement. 2. periodical pamphlet or journal. 3. official report. **14.**

bureau (bū'rō), 1. chest of drawers. 2. an office. **14.**

bury (bĕr'ĭ), 1. to place in the ground. 2. to forget. 3. to absorb deeply. **2.**

business (bĭz'nĕs), 1. occupation; profession. 2. commercial enterprise; employment. **13.**

busy (bĭz'ĭ), 1. at work; active. 2. meddlesome. **2.**

buy (bī), to purchase. **2.**

calendar (kăl'ĕn dẽr), 1. table showing days, weeks, and months of the year. 2. register; list. **23.**

campaign (kăm pān'), *n.* 1. planned course of action for a purpose. 2. related military operations.—*v.* to take part in a campaign. **44.**

cancel (kăn'sĕl), *v.* 1. to abolish; do away with. 2. to cross out.—*n.* the part canceled. **25.**

can't (känt), contraction of *cannot;* to be unable. **12.**

capacity (kȧ păs'ĭ tĭ), 1. amount of room or space inside; content. 2. ability. 3. position. **13.**

capital (kăp'ĭ tăl), *n.* 1. upper case letter. 2. money used to run a business. 3. city where state government is located. — *adj.* punishable with death. **50.**

captain (kăp'tĭn), commanding officer of a company, troop, or ship. **56.**

carburetor (kär'bū rĕt'ẽr), device for mixing air with gasoline to feed to cylinders of a gasoline engine. **54.**

carriage (kăr'ĭj), 1. any part of a machine which carries another part. 2. the act, cost of, or charge for transportation. 3. vehicle on wheels. 4. bearing. **54.**

carrying (kăr'ĭ ĭng), 1. taking from one place to another. 2. influencing. 3. winning. 4. possessing. **48.**

cashier (kăsh ēr') *n.* an official who pays bills, debts, and receives remittances. — *v.* to dismiss in disgrace. 2. to reject. **26.**

catalog (kăt'ȧ lôg), *n.* a systematic list.—*v.* to enter in or make a catalog. **10.**

cemetery (sĕm'ē tĕr'ĭ), burial ground; graveyard. **38.**

certain (sûr'tĭn), 1. sure. 2. fixed. 3. dependable. 4. definite person, place, or thing, but not named. **10.**

certainly (sûr'tĭn lĭ), surely, without doubt. **27.**

certificate (sẽr tĭf'ĭ kĭt), *n.* a formal, written statement. — *v.* to write a formal statement vouching the worth of something. **25.**

changeable (chān'jȧ bl), 1. fickle; unstable. 2. having form or color that changes. **14.**

character (kăr'ăk tẽr), 1. individuality; mental and moral qualities. 2. a letter, figure, or mark. 3. person in play or story. **55.**

characteristic (kăr'ăk tẽr ĭs'tĭk), *adj.* distinguishing mark or quality.—*n.* a distinctive mark; trait. **58.**

chauffeur (shō fûr'), driver of an automobile; paid driver. **54.**

chief (chēf), *adj.* principal; main. —*n.* a leader; highest in rank. **40.**

choose (chōōz), 1. to select. 2. to see fit. **8.**

chose (chōz), past tense of *choose.* **26.**

Christian (krĭs'chăn), *n.* a believer in Christ.—*adj.* believing in, or practicing the religion of Christ. **33.**

circumstances (sûr'kŭm stăns'ĕz), 1. the condition of affairs. 2. surroundings. 3. details. **15.**

civilization (sĭv'ĭ lĭ zā'shŭn), 1. advanced stage in social development. 2. progressive state. 3. culture and ways of living. **33.**

climb (klīm), 1. to go up. 2. to slope upward. **54.**

clothes (klōthz), 1. wearing apparel. 2. bed coverings. **8.**

coarse (kōrs), 1. unrefined; rude. 2. inferior. 3. made of large particles. **6.**

college (kŏl'ĕj), 1. an educational institution above high school. 2. the buildings of an educational institution. **23.**

colonel (kûr'nĕl), chief officer of a regiment. **44.**

color (kŭl'ẽr), *n.* 1. hue or tint. 2. paint. 3. pigment. 4. pretext. —*v.* 1. to tint or dye. 2. to misrepresent. **8.**

column (kŏl'ŭm), 1. an upright pillar, or anything suggesting one. 2. series of figures or words placed vertically. **22.**

coming (kŭm'ĭng), *adj.* drawing near; approaching.—*n.* 1. an approaching. 2. occurring as a result. **2.**

commercial (kŏ mûr'shăl), 1. pertaining to business of buying and selling. 2. made to be sold. **13.**

commission (kŏ mĭsh'ŭn), *n.* 1. compensation allowed an agent. 2. act of doing. 3. a charge. 4. publicly authorized body.—*v.* 1. to authorize. 2. to empower. **24.**

committee (kŏ mĭt′ĭ), one or more persons appointed to consider any matter. **31.**

communication (kŏ mū′nĭ kā′shŭn), 1. means of passing or sending information from one place to another. 2. news. **40.**

community (kŏ mū′nĭ tĭ), body of people living under the same general conditions. **41.**

comparatively (kŏm păr′ȧ tĭv lĭ), relatively; not absolutely. **42.**

comparison (kŏm păr′ĭ sŭn), act of comparing; relative resemblance. 58.

compelled (kŏm pĕld′), forced; urged; obliged. **54.**

competent (kŏm′pē tĕnt), capable; fit; able. **49.**

competition (kŏm′pē tĭsh′ŭn), 1. a contest; a match. 2. rivalry. **58.**

complement (kŏm′plē mĕnt), *n.* that which completes. — *v.* to complete. **36.**

completely (kŏm plēt′lĭ), fully; totally. **17.**

compliment (kŏm′plĭ mĕnt), *n.* polite expression of approval or admiration. — *v.* to praise or flatter. **36.**

conceive (kŏn sēv′), 1. to understand. 2. to imagine; to think. **24.**

concerning (kŏn sûrn′ĭng), relating to; about. **31.**

concession (kŏn sĕsh′ŭn), 1. act of granting or admitting. 2. the thing conceded. **30.**

concrete (kŏn′krēt), *adj.* formed into a mixture of sand, gravel, and cement.—*n.* a solid object. **60.**

conference (kŏn′fẽr ĕns), 1. discussions. 2. assembly for discussion. **45.**

confidence (kŏn′fĭ dĕns), 1. trust; belief. 2. boldness. **45.**

confident (kŏn′fĭ dĕnt), having confidence. **49.**

congratulate (kŏn grăt′ū lāt), to wish joy to. **29.**

connection (kŏ nĕk′shŭn), 1. relationship; union. 2. a thing that connects. **17.**

conquer (kŏng′kẽr), 1. to win by fighting. 2. to overcome; to subdue. **44.**

conscience (kŏn′shĕns), one's moral sense or knowledge of right and wrong. **39.**

conscientious (kŏn′shĭ ĕn′shŭs), guided by conscience. **43.**

conscious (kŏn′shŭs), 1. mentally awake. 2. aware of one's thoughts and actions. 58.

consequence (kŏn′sē kwĕns), 1. a result. 2. importance; significance. **45.**

considerably (kŏn sĭd′ẽr ȧ blĭ), notably, as in size or value. **46.**

continually (kŏn tĭn′ū ăl ĭ), going on without interruption; continuous. **50.**

control (kŏn trōl′), *n.* 1. restraint. 2. act or power of directing.—*v.* 1. to govern; to direct. 2. to regulate. **48.**

convenience (kŏn vēn′yĕns), 1. anything that gives advantage or comfort. 2. fitness. 3. suitable time; opportunity. **56.**

convenient (kŏn vēn′yĕnt), 1. suited to one's comfort or ease. 2. easy to reach. **47.**

co-operation (kō ŏp′ẽr ā′shŭn), 1. act of working together in harmony. 2. collective action. **43.**

copy (kŏp′ĭ), *v.* to make a thing like something else; to imitate. —*n.* one thing made like another; an example or the thing from which another like it is made. 2.

cordial (kôr′jăl), warm and friendly; hearty. 43.

correspondence (kŏr′ē spŏn′dĕns), 1. communication between persons by letters. 2. the letters. 3. agreement between certain things. **45.**

cough (kôf), *n.* the act of coughing.—*v.* to force air from the lungs with effort and noise. 5.

could (ko͝od), past tense of *can.* **21.**

couldn't (ko͝od″nt), contraction of *could not.* **12.**

council (koun′sĭl), a group of people gathered to act on some matters. **36.**

counsel (koun′sĕl), *n.* advice; instruction.—*v.* to advise. **36.**

country (kŭn′trĭ), 1. all the land of a nation. 2. land outside of cities or towns. **44.**

course (kōrs), 1. planned program of study. 2. progress; passage. 3. portion of a meal. **26.**

courteous (kûr′tē ŭs), polite; considerate of others. **13.**

courtesy (kûr′tĕ sĭ), politeness. **32.**

criticism (krĭt′ĭ sĭzm), the art of careful judgment. **53.**

current (kûr′ĕnt), *adj.* of the present day.—*n.* flowing or passing, as of water. **60.**

customer (kŭs′tŭm ĕr), patron; purchaser. **30.**

debtor (dĕt′ĕr), one who owes a debt. **10.**

deceive (dē sēv′), to mislead; to trick. **24.**

decide (dē sīd′), to settle; to make up one's mind. **55.**

decision (dē sĭzh′ŭn), 1. settlement; conclusion. 2. firmness. **1.**

defense (dē fĕns′), 1. act of defending or protecting. 2. players defending a goal in a game. 3. action, speech, or writing in favor of something. **39.**

definite (dĕf′ĭ nĭt), 1. clear; exact. 2. limited. **56.**

delivery (dē lĭv′ĕr ĭ), 1. act of delivering or transferring. 2. rescue. 3. manner of speaking. **48.**

descend (dē sĕnd′), 1. to come down from a higher place to a lower one. 2. to come from; to pass by inheritance. 3. to stoop. **32.**

describe (dē skrīb′), to tell or write about. **40.**

description (dē skrĭp′shŭn), 1. act of giving a picture or account in words. 2. kind; sort. **15.**

desert (dĕz′ĕrt), 1. dry, barren region, usually sandy and without trees. 2. not inhabited. **32.**

desirable (dē zīr′ȧ bl), worth wishing for; pleasing; agreeable. **60.**

destroy (dē stroi′), 1. to ruin; to do away with. 2. to kill. **60.**

determine (dē tûr′mĭn), 1. to decide; to resolve. 2. to find out exactly. **52.**

develop (dē vĕl′ŭp), 1. to unfold and grow. 2. to expand. 3. to improve. **34.**

didn't (dĭd″nt), contraction of *did not.* **12.**

difference (dĭf′ĕr ĕns), 1. unlikeness between persons or things. 2. amount by which one number differs from another. 3. a dispute. **57.**

different (dĭf′ĕr ĕnt), 1. unlike another person or thing. 2. separate. 3. unusual. **56.**

difficult (dĭf′ĭ kŭlt), hard to do or understand; not easy. **50.**

dining (dīn′ĭng), eating. **47.**

disappear (dĭs′ă pēr′), 1. to cease to be seen. 2. to be lost. **16.**

disappoint (dĭs′ă point′), to fail to fulfill a hope or expectation. **51.**

discipline (dĭs′ĭ plĭn), *n.* 1. strict training that corrects or strengthens. 2. control gained through obedience or strict training.—*v.* to train in self-control or obedience. **44.**

discuss (dĭs kŭs′), to debate fully and openly. **40.**

discussion (dĭs kŭsh′ŭn), act of debating fully and openly. **20.**

disease (dĭ zēz′), illness; sickness. **57.**

disposition (dĭs′pō zĭsh′ŭn), 1. natural mental attitude toward things or people. 2. tendency. 3. the act of managing; disposal. **53.**

divided (dĭ vīd′ĕd), 1. parted; separated. 2. kept apart. 3. given out in shares. **57.**

doctor (dŏk′tĕr), 1. physician; surgeon. 2. person with the highest degree given by a college. **46.**

does (dŭz), third person singular, present tense of *do*. **24.**

doesn't (dŭz''nt), contraction of *does not*. **12.**

don't (dōnt), contraction of *do not*. **12.**

dormitory (dôr'mĭ tō'rĭ), 1. building with many beds. 2. sleeping room. **23.**

doubtful (dout'fo͝ol), 1. not clear or certain. 2. questionable. **27.**

duly (dū'lĭ), in due manner, time, or degree; properly. **2.**

duplicate (dū'plĭ kāt), *n.* a thing that looks exactly like some other thing; a copy.—*v.* to make an exact copy. **52.**

dying (dī'ĭng), 1. about to die. 2. death. **53.**

earliest (ûr'lĭ ĕst), first in point of time. **43.**

early (ûr'lĭ), 1. before usual time. 2. at or near the beginning. **16.**

earnest (ûr'nĕst), sincere; with serious purpose. **20.**

easily (ēz'ĭ lĭ), 1. in an easy manner. 2. naturally; informally. 3. comfortably. **47.**

economy (ē kŏn'ō mĭ), 1. thrift. 2. management so as to avoid waste. 3. organization; system. **28.**

effect (ĕ fĕkt'), *n.* 1. result. 2. meaning; intent. 3. fact. 4. influence.—*v.* 1. to bring about. 2. to make. **51.**

eighth (ātth), 1. next after seventh. 2. one of eight equal parts of anything. **42.**

either (ē'*th*ẽr), 1. one or the other of two. 2. each of two. **4.**

embarrass (ĕm băr'ăs), 1 to make confused or upset in mind. 2. to disturb and hinder. **59.**

endeavor (ĕn dĕv'ẽr), *v.* to try; to strive.—*n.* an effort; an attempt. **40.**

enemies (ĕn'ē mĭz), 1. foes. 2. things that harm persons or things. **44.**

engineer (ĕn'jĭ nēr'), *n.* 1. a man who operates an engine. 2. a man who is skilled in engineering.—*v.* to lay out, manage, or construct. **19.**

enough (ē nŭf'), *adj.* plenty; sufficient.—*n.* a sufficient quantity. **37.**

entitled (ĕn tī'tld), 1. named. 2. qualified. **11.**

envelope (ĕn'vĕ lōp), a cover or container for a letter. **20.**

equipment (ē kwĭp'mĕnt), 1. articles which make up an outfit. 2. things needed for some activity. **31.**

equipped (ē kwĭpt'), 1. fitted out. 2. furnished. **16.**

equivalent (ē kwĭv'ȧ lĕnt), *adj.* equal or alike in meaning.—*n.* something alike in meaning, value. **49.**

error (ĕr'ẽr), 1. a mistake; a blunder. 2. a sin. **15.**

especially (ĕs pĕsh'ăl ĭ), particularly; chiefly. **16.**

essential (ĕ sĕn'shăl), *adj.* 1. necessary; very important. 2. fundamental; basic. — *n.* something which is essential. **27.**

establish (ĕs tăb'lĭsh), 1. to fix firmly; to settle. 2. to appoint. **55.**

estimate (ĕs'tĭ māt), *v.* 1. to form an opinion of; to judge. 2. to calculate.—*n.* 1. an opinion; a judgment. 2. a calculation. **15.**

etc., abbreviation of *et cetera,* and other things. **12.**

every (ĕv'ẽr ĭ), each and all. **46.**

evidence (ĕv'ĭ dĕns), 1. proof; facts. 2. sign; indication. **40.**

evident (ĕv'ĭ dĕnt), clear to the sight or mind; plain. **27.**

examination (ĕg zăm'ĭ nā'shŭn), 1. an examining. 2. a test. **23.**

exceed (ĕk sēd'), 1. to go beyond; to be more or greater than. 2. to surpass. **50.**

excellent (ĕk'sĕ lĕnt), first-class; unusually good. **49.**

except (ĕk sĕpt'), *prep.* 1. other than. 2. leaving out. — *v.* to omit. **4.**

executive (ĕg zĕk'ū tĭv), *adj.* concerned with the management of things.—*n.* a managing official 13.

exercise (ĕk'sẽr sīz), *n.* 1. something that gives practice; physical activity. 2. program.—*v.* 1. to use. 2. to drill. **34.**

exhausted (ĕg zôs'ted), 1. tired out; fatigued. 2. drawn out, or let out completely. **34.**

existence (ĕg zĭs'tĕns), 1. life; living. 2. actual occurrence. **45.**

expect (ĕks pĕkt'), 1. to look for; to think something will happen. to suppose. **16.**

expense (ĕks pĕns'), 1. cost; charge. 2. loss. **39.**

experience (ĕks pēr'ĭ ĕns), *n.* 1. the actual living through an event or events. 2. skill or knowledge gained by practice.—*v.* to feel; to live through. **39.**

explanation (ĕks'plȧ nā'shŭn), 1. the act of making clear. 2. thing that explains. **24.**

extension (ĕks tĕn'shŭn), 1. an addition. 2. an extending; an increasing. **30.**

extraordinary (ĕks trôr'dĭ nĕr'ĭ), unusual; uncommon. **57.**

extremely (ĕks trēm'lĭ), much more than usual; very. **38.**

faculty (făk'ŭl tĭ), 1. teachers of a school or college; members of a profession. 2. ability. 3. power. **31.**

familiar (fȧ mĭl'yẽr), 1. well-known. 2. intimate. 3. informal. **52.**

February (fĕb'ro͝o ĕr'ĭ), the second month of the year. **51.**

fertile (fûr'tĭl), 1. fruitful, rich. 2. capable of developing or growing. **22.**

field (fēld), 1. cleared land used for some special purpose. 2. sphere of activity. **22.**

fiery (fī'ẽr ĭ), 1. hot or glowing, as if on fire. 2. blazing; on fire. **22.**

finally (fī'năl ĭ), at last; at the end. **54.**

financial (fĭ năn'shăl), having to do with money matters. **11.**

flies (flīz), *v.* 1. moves through the air with wings. 2. goes quickly. —*n.* two-winged insects. **4.**

folks (fōks), 1. people. 2. one's relatives. **38.**

forehead (fŏr'ĕd), 1. the part of the face above the eyes. 2. the front part of anything. **38.**

foreign (fŏr'ĭn), 1. outside of one's own country. 2. having to do with other countries. 3. not related. **48.**

forest (fŏr'ĕst), a large area of land covered with trees. **22.**

forfeit (fôr'fĭt), *v.* to lose because of some crime, penalty, neglect, fault, etc.—*n.* something which is lost because of some crime, penalty, neglect, etc. **59.**

forgotten (fŏr gŏt'n), past participle of *forget.* **17.**

formerly (fôr'mẽr lĭ), in time past. **46.**

forth (fōrth), 1. forward; onward. 2. out into view. **36.**

forty (fôr'tĭ), number; four times ten. **33.**

forward (fôr'wẽrd), *adv.* or *adj.* 1. near or at the front part. 2. toward what is front.—*v.* 1. to send on. 2. to advance. **42.**

fourth (fōrth), 1. next after the third. 2. one of four equal parts. **36.**

freight (frāt), 1. load of goods carried on train or ship. 2. amount paid for carrying goods. **19.**

friend (frĕnd), person who knows and likes another person. **6.**

fulfill (fo͝ol fĭl'), to bring to pass. **37.**

fundamental (fŭn'dȧ mĕn'tăl), *adj.* basic; essential. — *n.* principle, rule, or law that forms a foundation. **57.**

further (fûr'*th*ẽr), *adj.* farther; additional.—*adv.* moreover. **38.**

future (fū'tūr), *n.* future time.—*adj.* coming after the present. **26.**

gasoline (găs′ō lēn), an inflammable liquid, used as a motor fuel and as a cleansing material. **54.**

generally (jĕn′ẽr ăl ĭ), for the most part; usually. **21.**

genius (jēn′yŭs), 1. a very gifted person. 2. great natural ability. **31.**

genuine (jĕn′ū ĭn), real; true. **52.**

getting (gĕt′tĭng), 1. obtaining; receiving. 2. learning. **54.**

ghost (gōst), 1. spirit of a dead person. 2. a faint image. **52.**

government (gŭv′ẽrn mĕnt), 1. the system of governing. 2. the governing body. **48.**

governor (gŭv′ẽr nẽr), 1. an official elected to rule a state. 2. one who manages or directs. **29.**

grammar (grăm′ẽr), the study of the relations of words within sentences. **40.**

grateful (grāt′fo͝ol), 1. thankful. 2. pleasing. **38.**

great (grāt), 1. big. 2. numerous. 3. noble. 4. famous. **52.**

grieve (grēv), 1. to sorrow. 2. to cause grief or sorrow. **38.**

grievous (grēv′ŭs), 1. full of grief. 2. severe; intense. 3. serious; grave. **53.**

grippe (grĭp), influenza. **5.**

guarantee (găr′ăn tē′), *v.* to assure the quality or permanence of a thing.—*n.* something that is given or held as a security. **48.**

guardian (gär′dĭ ăn), a person who takes care of another person or his property. **53.**

guess (gĕs), *v.* 1. to say without being sure. 2. to suppose.—*n.* a try at the answer. **47.**

guest (gĕst), 1. a visitor. 2. a patron. **59.**

gymnasium (jĭm nā′zĭ ŭm), a place or building for athletic exercises. **31.**

half (hȧf), *n.* one of two equal parts.—*adj.* being a half. **2.**

handful (hănd′fo͝ol), a small amount or number. **2.**

handling (hăn′dlĭng), 1. managing; directing. 2. touching with the hand. **53.**

happened (hăp′ĕnd), 1. chanced. 2. occurred by chance. 3. met by chance. **17.**

having (hăv′ĭng), possessing; owning; bearing. **2.**

hear (hēr), 1. to take in through the ear. 2. to listen to. 3. to receive information as if through the ear. **21.**

heard (hûrd), past tense of *hear.* **6.**

height (hīt), 1. altitude. 2. measurement from top to bottom. 3. highest point; greatest degree. **10.**

here (hēr), 1. in this place. 2. to this place. 3. in this life. **6.**

hoarse (hōrs), 1. harsh or grating in sound. 2. sounding rough and deep. **5.**

holiday (hŏl′ĭ dā), a day of freedom from work. **42.**

hoping (hōp′ĭng), desiring; expecting with faith. **29.**

hospital (hŏs′pĭt ăl), a place where sick or injured people are cared for. **5.**

hour (our), 1. 60 minutes; 1/24 of a day. 2. time of day. 3. particular time. **16.**

humorous (hū′mẽr ŭs), full of humor; funny. **43.**

icicle (ī′sĭk l), a hanging, pointed mass of ice formed by dripping water. **16.**

ignorant (ĭg′nō rănt), 1. not knowing about something. 2. having little knowledge or education. **39.**

imagine (ĭ măj′ĭn), 1. to picture in one's mind; to fancy. 2. to suppose; to believe. **19.**

immediately (ĭ mē′dĭ ĭt lĭ), 1. at once. 2. with nothing between. 3. next. 4. directly. **5.**

immigration (ĭm′ĭ grā′ shŭn), a coming into a foreign country or region to live. **48.**

impossible (ĭm pŏs′ĭ bl), not possible. **21.**

inclose (ĭn klōz′), 1. to put in an envelope along with a letter. 2. to contain. 3. to surround. **20.**

inconvenience (ĭn′kŏn vēn′yĕns), *n.* 1. discomfort. 2. trouble.—*v.* to cause inconvenience. **39.**

independent (ĭn′dē pĕn′dĕnt), 1. not dependent. 2. self-reliant. 3. separate. **13.**

individual (ĭn′dĭ vĭd′ū ăl), *n.* 1. a person. 2. a single member.—*adj.* of or belonging to an individual. **58.**

influence (ĭn′flo͞o ĕns), *n.* 1. power to produce an effect. 2. power caused by wealth, position, character.—*v.* to change. **45.**

information (ĭn′fŏr mā′shŭn), 1. knowledge. 2. valuable facts. **20.**

innocent (ĭn′ō sĕnt), 1. not guilty. 2. not knowing evil; pure. **29.**

inquiry (ĭn′kwĭ rĭ), 1. act of asking. 2. a question. 3. an examination by questioning. **21.**

instead (ĭn stĕd′), in place of; rather. **59.**

instructor (ĭn strŭk′tĕr), a teacher. **31.**

insurance (ĭn sho͝or′ăns), 1. an insuring of property, person, or life. 2. the sum for which anything is insured. **35.**

intelligent (ĭn tĕl′ĭ jĕnt), 1. being able to learn and understand. 2. showing understanding. **49.**

interest (ĭn′tĕr ĕst), 1. the price paid for the use of borrowed money. 2. a share; a part. 3. a feeling of wanting to know, see, do, own, share in. **52.**

interesting (ĭn′tĕr ĕs tĭng), arousing interest; engaging the attention. **18.**

invitation (ĭn′vĭ tā′shŭn), 1. a request to come some place or do something. 2. the act of inviting. **20.**

invoice (ĭn′vois), 1. a priced list of goods sent to a purchaser. 2. a shipment of such goods. **37.**

irresistible (ĭr′rē zĭs′tĭ bl), not to be resisted. **60.**

isn't (ĭz′′nt), contraction of *is not.* **12.**

item (ī′tĕm), 1. separate thing, part, or article. 2. a piece of news or information. **10.**

its (ĭts), of or belonging to it. **3.**

it's (ĭts), contraction of *it is.* **3.**

itself (ĭt sĕlf′), 1. reflexive form of *it.* 2. emphatic form of *it.* **3.**

jealous (jĕl′ŭs), 1. wanting attention paid to no one else; envious. 2. watchful; careful. **33.**

journal (jûr′năl), 1. newspaper; magazine. 2. a diary. 3. a book to record business transactions. **26.**

journey (jûr′nĭ), *n.* trip. — *v.* to travel from one place to another. **15.**

judgment (jŭj′mĕnt), 1. act of judging. 2. decision; decree. 3. opinion. 4. good sense. **40.**

junior (jo͞on′yĕr), *adj.* 1. lower in standing. 2. younger.—*n.* 1. a person lower in rank. 2. a younger person. **9.**

just (jŭst), *adj.* 1. righteous; fair. 2. lawful. 3. reasonable.—*adv.* 1. exactly. 2. almost; nearly. 3. only a moment ago. **1.**

kerosene (kĕr′ō sēn′), a thin oil; coal oil. **54.**

knew (nū), past tense of *know.* **1.**

know (nō), 1. to be sure of; to have information about. 2. to recognize. 3. to be acquainted. 4. to have practical skill in doing a thing. **27.**

knowledge (nŏl′ĕj), 1. what one knows. 2. range of information. 3. learning. **23.**

laboratory (lăb′ō rȧ tō′rĭ), a room or building where scientific work is done. **23.**

laid (lād), 1. placed; caused to lie. 2. constructed according to plan. **7.**

language (lăng′gwĭj), 1. the speech of one nation or race. 2. human speech spoken or written. 3. form, style, or kind of expression. **40.**

later (lāt′ĕr), by and by. **38.**

latter (lăt'ẽr), 1. near the end; later. 2. second of two things. **26.**

league (lēg), association of persons, parties, or countries formed to help one another. **33.**

least (lēst), *n.* smallest or slightest amount; lowest degree. — *adj.* smallest; shortest; lowest. **6.**

led (lĕd), 1. guided; conducted. 2. was ahead of the others. **4.**

leisure (lē'zhẽr), *adj.* unemployed; at ease.—*n.* freedom from work. **46.**

length (lĕngth), 1. the distance from end to end. 2. long stretch or extent. **15.**

librarian (lī brâr'ĭ ăn), a person who has charge of a library. **18.**

library (lī'brĕr'ĭ), 1. a place where books are kept for use and not sale. 2. a collection of books. **18.**

license (lī'sĕns), 1. permission given by law to do something. 2. paper, card, etc., showing this permission. **50.**

lieutenant (lū tĕn'ănt), 1. army officer next below a captain. 2. naval officer next below a lieutenant commander. **44.**

literature (lĭt'ẽr ȧ tūr), 1. writings of a period or of a country. 2. all the books and articles on a subject. **18.**

loose (lo͞os), *adj.* 1. free. 2. not fastened. 3. not exact.—*v.* to make loose. **21.**

lose (lo͞oz), 1. to go astray. 2. to mislay. 3. to suffer the loss of. **7.**

losing (lo͞oz'ĭng), suffering the loss of; going astray. **2.**

machinery (mȧ shēn'ẽr ĭ), 1. the working parts of a machine or engine; machines as a group. 2. the means by which something is done. **48.**

magazine (măg'ȧ zēn'), 1. a publication appearing regularly and containing stories, articles, etc. by various writers. 2. a storehouse. **18.**

magnificent (măg nĭf'ĭ sĕnt), 1. splendid; richly ornamented. 2. lofty; noble. **49.**

maintain (mān tān'), 1. to carry on. 2. to support. **44.**

maintenance (mān'tē năns), 1. support; livelihood. 2. upkeep of a thing. **35.**

majority (mȧ jŏr'ĭ tĭ), a number greater than half of a total. **55.**

management (măn'ăj mĕnt), the act of conducting administration. **49.**

manufacture (măn'ū făk'tūr), 1. to make by hand or by machine. 2. to make something into useful form. **10.**

many (mĕn'ĭ), *adj.* numerous; not few.—*n.* a large number. **7.**

marriage (măr'ĭj), 1. wedlock. 2. a wedding. **33.**

material (mȧ tēr'ĭ ăl), *n.* 1. cloth. 2. substance; goods; parts. — *adj.* 1. belonging to or having a body. 2. important. **8.**

maybe (mā'bĭ), perhaps. **4.**

meant (mĕnt), 1. intended; designed. **25.**

medicine (mĕd'ĭ sĭn), a substance taken to make one well. **5.**

medium (mē'dĭ ŭm), *adj.* having a middle position, degree.—*n.* 1. that which is in the middle. 2. environment. **26.**

mentioned (mĕn'shŭnd), specified; referred to by name. **20.**

merchandise (mûr'chăn dīz), goods bought and sold. **10.**

merely (mēr'lĭ), simply; only. **57.**

mileage (mīl'ĭj), a measuring in miles; distance in miles. **54.**

minimum (mĭn'ĭ mŭm), least possible amount; lowest. **46.**

minute *n.* (mĭn'ĭt), sixty seconds. —*adj.* (mĭ nūt'), very small. **16.**

misspell (mĭs spĕl'), to spell incorrectly. **40.**

modifies (mŏd'ĭ fīz), 1. describes. 2. limits. 3. qualifies. **29.**

months (mŭnths), one of the twelve portions of the year. **23.**

mortgage (môr'gĭj), *v.* 1. to place a house or land under a mortgage. 2. to pledge.—*n.* pledge of property; security for the payment of a debt. **30.**

mountain (moun'tĭn), land rising higher than hills above surrounding country. **54.**

moving (mo͞ov'ĭng), 1. causing motion or action. 2. affecting the passions. 3. in motion. **19.**

much (mŭch), *adj.* great in quantity, extent, or duration. — *adv.* greatly; nearly. — *n.* a great quantity. **27.**

mutual (mū'tū ăl), 1. something given and received back and forth. 2. something had by two persons. **41.**

mysterious (mĭs tēr'ĭ ŭs), full of mystery; secret. **59.**

naturally (năt'ū răl ĭ), 1. in a natural way. 2. of course. **16.**

necessary (nĕs'ĕ sĕr'ĭ), impossible to do without; essential. **44.**

necessity (nē sĕs'ĭ tĭ), 1. a very necessary thing. 2. very great need of help. **22.**

neighbor (nā'bẽr), 1. a person who lives near another. 2. a fellow being. **53.**

neither (nē'*th*ẽr), not the one or the other. **10.**

nickel (nĭk'ĕl), 1. a five-cent piece. 2. a hard, silver-white metal. **7.**

niece (nēs), a daughter of one's brother or sister. **55.**

nineteen (nīn'tēn'), nine more than ten. **10.**

ninety (nīn'tĭ), nine times ten. **25.**

nonsense (nŏn'sĕns), foolish talk or doings. **39.**

noticeable (nō'tĭs ȧ bl), 1. easily seen. 2. worth noticing. **21.**

nuisance (nū'săns), a person or thing that is annoying or troublesome. **35.**

numerous (nū'mẽr ŭs), 1. many. 2. in great numbers. **41.**

oblige (ō blīj'), 1. to do a favor. 2. to compel; to force. **32.**

occasion (ŏ kā'zhŭn), 1. a special event. 2. a good chance. **28.**

occasionally (ŏ kā'zhŭn ăl ĭ), at times; now and then. **8.**

occurred (ŏ kûrd'), 1. came to the mind. 2. happened. **19.**

occurrence (ŏ kûr'ĕns), 1. event. 2. happening. **45.**

official (ŏ fĭsh'ăl), *adj.* having to do with an office or officers. — *n.* a person holding a position of authority. **14.**

often (ôf'ĕn), many times; frequently. **22.**

once (wŭns), 1. one time only. 2. on any occasion. 3. formerly. **5.**

opinion (ō pĭn'yŭn), 1. a belief; a judgment. 2. a statement by an expert after careful study. **40.**

opportunity (ŏp'ŏr tū'nĭ tĭ), a favorable chance; a favorable time. **37.**

opposite (ŏp'ō zĭt), 1. as different as possible. 2. in front of. 3. hostile. **57.**

orchestra (ôr'kĕs trȧ), 1. a band or company of musicians. 2. the first floor in a theater. **59.**

organization (ôr'găn ĭ zā'shŭn), 1. the action, condition, or process of organizing. 2. group of persons united for some purpose. **13.**

original (ō rĭj'ĭ năl), *n.* a thing of which all similar things are copies.—*adj.* 1. not copied. 2. newly thought out. **41.**

ought (ôt), 1. to have a duty. 2. to be suitable. 3. to be expected. 4. to be very likely. **33.**

owing (ō'ĭng), 1. due to be paid. 2. because of. **1.**

paid (pād), 1. settled. 2. remunerated. 3. was profitable. **1.**

pamphlet (păm'flĕt), a few printed sheets bound together. **18.**

paragraph (păr'ȧ grȧf), 1. a group of sentences that belong together. 2. separate note or item of news. **50.**

parallel (păr'ă lĕl), *adj.* 1. at or being the same distance apart everywhere. 2. like; similar.—*n.* 1. a parallel line, curve, or surface. 2. likeness. **7.**

parliament (pär′lĭ mĕnt), an assembly which is the lawmaking body of a country. **28.**

partial (pär′shăl), 1. favoring unfairly. 2. not complete; not total. **50.**

particular (pär tĭk′ū lẽr), 1. very careful. 2. separate; individual. 3. special; noteworthy. **51.**

partner (pärt′nẽr), 1. one who shares something with another or others. 2. a player on the same side in a game. **30.**

passed (påst) 1. went by. 2. was approved. **37.**

passenger (păs′ĕn jẽr), a traveler in a train, bus, boat, etc. **19.**

past (påst), *adj.* or *adv.* gone by or passed; beyond.—*n.* time gone by. **26.**

patience (pā′shĕns), 1. calm endurance or waiting. 2. steady effort. **39.**

peace (pēs), 1 an agreement to end war. 2. public quiet and order. 3. harmony between persons. **36.**

people (pē′pl), persons. **48.**

performance (pẽr fôr′măns), 1. a doing of a task. 2. a public entertainment. **53.**

period (pēr′ĭ ŭd), 1. dot marking the end of a sentence or showing an abbreviation. 2. portion of time. **12.**

permanent (pûr′må nĕnt), lasting; enduring. **49.**

personal (pûr′sŭn ăl), 1. individual; private. 2. of the person or body. **56.**

perspiration (pûr′ spĭ rā′ shŭn), sweat. **34.**

persuade (pẽr swād′), 1. to convince. 2. to win over by urging, arguing. **29.**

physical (fĭz′ĭ kăl), 1. of the human body. 2. relating to nature. **34.**

physician (fĭ zĭsh′ăn), doctor of medicine. **5.**

piano (pĭ ăn′ō), a large musical instrument with many tones which come from wires when struck by padded hammers. **59.**

picture (pĭk′tūr), 1. a likeness; an image. 2. a drawing; a painting; a photograph. **52.**

piece (pēs), *n.* a portion; a part; a fragment.—*v.* to mend. **36.**

pierce (pērs), 1. to go into; to go through. 2. to make a hole in something. **47.**

plain (plān), 1. clear; easily understood. 2. flat; level. 3. simple. 4. homely; without beauty. **19.**

plane (plān), *n.* a tool for smoothing wood.—*v.* to level with a plane. **47.**

planned (plănd), arranged; projected; schemed; designed. **48.**

pleasant (plĕz′ănt), 1. pleasing; agreeable. 2. fair; not stormy. **39.**

pleasure (plĕzh′ẽr), enjoyment; delight. **34.**

policy (pŏl′ĭ sĭ), 1. plan of action. 2. practical wisdom. 3. written agreement about insurance. **13.**

popular (pŏp′ū lẽr), 1. pleasing to many people. 2. having to do with the common people. **24.**

portion (pōr′shŭn), a share; a part. **27.**

position (pō zĭsh′ŭn), 1. the place where a person or thing is. 2. ways of being placed. 3. job. **13.**

positive (pŏs′ĭ tĭv), certain; sure. **47.**

possession (pŏ zĕsh′ŭn), 1. something possessed. 2. the act of possessing. 3. control. **55.**

possessive (pŏ zĕs′ĭv), 1. showing the desire to possess, own, or control. **12.**

possibility (pŏs′ ĭ bĭl′ ĭ tĭ), that which is possible. **14.**

possible (pŏs′ĭ bl), capable of being done or permitted. **29.**

potatoes (pō tā′tōz), starchy, edible tubers. **37.**

practical (prăk′tĭ kăl), 1. having to do with action or practice. 2. useful. **32.**

practically (prăk′tĭ kăl ĭ), 1. almost. 2. in a useful way. **34.**

practice (prăk'tĭs), *n.* 1. a thing done as a regular matter. 2. exercise to improve skill; drill. —*v.* 1. to drill. 2. to work at a profession. **43.**

precede (prē sēd'), 1. to go before; to come before. 2. to be higher than in rank or importance. **19.**

precious (prĕsh'ŭs), 1. of great value or worth. 2. dear; cherished. **47.**

prefer (prē fûr'), 1. to like better than something else. 2. to raise; to promote. **8.**

preference (prĕf'ẽr ĕns), 1. a special liking for one thing over another thing. 2. choice. **45.**

preferred (prē fûrd'), liked better. **31.**

prejudice (prĕj'o͝o dĭs), 1. opinion without reason. 2. injury; damage. **56.**

preliminary (prē lĭm'ĭ nĕr'ĭ), coming before the main business; introductory. **42.**

preparation (prĕp'ȧ rā'shŭn), 1. a making ready in advance. 2. readiness. **42.**

presence (prĕz'ĕns), 1. the fact of being in a certain place. 2. the place where a person is. 3. appearance. **45.**

president (prĕz'ĭ dĕnt), 1. the chief executive officer. 2. a person who presides over a meeting. **13.**

pressure (prĕsh'ẽr), 1. the continued action of a weight or force. 2. state of trouble. 3. urgency. **57.**

principal (prĭn'sĭ păl), *adj.* main; chief.—*n.* 1. a chief official in a school. 2. sum of money drawing interest. **36.**

principally (prĭn'sĭ păl ĭ), chiefly; mainly; primarily. **55.**

principle (prĭn'sĭ pl), 1. a truth which is the basis of other truths. 2. a rule of conduct. **36.**

prior (prī'ẽr), being or happening before something else. **32.**

privilege (prĭv'ĭ lĭj), special right, advantage, or favor. **33.**

probably (prŏb'ȧ blĭ), more likely than not. **28.**

procedure (prō sē'dūr), 1. way of proceeding. 2. manner or way of conducting business. **31.**

proceed (prō sēd'), 1. to go forward or onward. 2. to go or act by an orderly method. **15.**

profession (prō fĕsh'ŭn), 1. an occupation requiring an education. 2. an open claim or declaration. **53.**

professor (prō fĕs'ẽr), 1. college teacher of highest rank. 2. a person who professes. **23.**

prominent (prŏm'ĭ nĕnt), 1. well-known; important. 2. easy to see; standing out. **49.**

prompt (prŏmpt), *n.* 1. quick; on time. 2. done at once.—*v.* 1. to cause someone to do something. 2. to suggest. **43.**

pronounce (prō nouns'), to speak aloud. **32.**

propeller (prō pĕl'ẽr), a device fitted with revolving blades which gives motion to airplanes, ships, etc. **60.**

prophecy (prŏf'ē sĭ), 1. a foretelling of future events. 2. the sayings of a prophet. **36.**

prophesy (prŏf'ē sī), to foretell; to predict. **36.**

proposition (prŏp'ō zĭsh'ŭn), a proposal; that which is offered to be considered. **27.**

psychology (sī kŏl'ō jĭ), the study of the mind; mental nature and behavior. **18.**

purchase (pûr'chĭs), *v.* to buy for a price.—*n.* a thing bought. **59.**

purpose (pûr'pŭs), 1. a plan; an aim; an intention. 2. the result aimed at. **32.**

pursuit (pûr sūt'), 1. act of pursuing. 2. an occupation. **25.**

quantity (kwŏn'tĭ tĭ), an amount or portion. **33.**

quiet (kwī'ĕt), *adj.* 1. still. 2. peaceful; gentle.—*n.* 1. stillness. 2. state of rest or peace.—*v.* 1. to calm. 2. to become still. **9.**

quite (kwīt), 1. completely; wholly. 2. actually; really. **29.**

quote (kwōt), to repeat exactly the words of another or a passage from a book. **30.**

raise (rāz), 1. to cause to rise up. 2. to increase. **51.**

ready (rĕd'ĭ), 1. prepared for use or action. 2. willing. 3. quick; prompt. 4. handy. **11.**

realize (rē'ăl īz), 1. to understand clearly. 2. to gain. 3. to cause to seem real. **22.**

really (rē'ăl ĭ), actually; in truth. **58.**

receipt (rē sēt'), 1. written statement that money or something has been received. 2. receiving. 3. recipe. **17.**

receive (rē sēv'), 1. to take what is offered or sent. 2. to accept. 3. to take in. **24.**

receiving (rē sēv'ĭng), 1. taking what is offered or sent. 2. accepting. 3. taking in. **21.**

recent (rē'sĕnt), 1. done or made not long ago. 2. not long past; modern. **49.**

recognize (rĕk'ŏg nīz), 1. to know again. 2. to admit; to accept. 3. to take notice of. **57.**

recollect (rĕk'ŏ lĕkt'), to call to mind; to remember. **20.**

recommend (rĕk'ŏ mĕnd'), 1. to suggest favorably. 2. to advise. **31.**

refer (rē fûr'), 1. to direct attention to. 2. to hand over. 3. to assign. **28.**

reference (rĕf'ĕr ĕns), 1. the act of referring. 2. relation; regard. 3. person who can give information. **45.**

referred (rē fûrd'), directed attention to. **18.**

regard (rē gärd'), *n.* 1. heed; care. 2. respect; esteem.—*v.* 1. to pay attention to. 2. to respect. **10.**

regretting (rē grĕt'ĭng), feeling sorry for; mourning the loss of. **41.**

relative (rĕl'ȧ tĭv), *adj.* 1. being related or connected. 2. belonging. 3. comparative.—*n.* person who belongs to the same family as another. **58.**

relieve (rē lēv'), 1. to give ease, aid, or sympathy to someone. 2. to take the place of a person on duty. **46.**

religious (rē lĭj'ŭs), 1. having to do with religion. 2. strict; done with care. **17.**

remembrance (rē mĕm'brăns), 1. memory. 2. state of being remembered. 3. souvenir. **35.**

remit (rē mĭt'), 1. to send money to a person or place. 2. to forgive. 3. to cancel. **30.**

remittance (rē mĭt'ăns), 1. sending money to someone at a distance. 2. the money that is sent. **35.**

repetition (rĕp'ē tĭsh'ŭn), 1. the act of repeating; doing over. 2. the thing repeated. **46.**

representative (rĕp'rē zĕn'tȧ tĭv), *n.* person appointed to act or speak for others. 2. a member of the House of Representatives.—*adj.* 1. acting as the agent. 2. typical. **58.**

residence (rĕz'ĭ dĕns), 1. house; home. 2. staying; dwelling in a place. **45.**

resistance (rē zĭs'tăns), 1. the act of resisting. 2. opposition. **35.**

respectfully (rē spĕkt'fo͝ol ĭ), with respect; politely. **58.**

response (rē spŏns'), act of replying; an answer. **21.**

responsible (rē spŏn'sĭ bl), 1. obliged or expected to account for. 2. trustworthy; reliable. **53.**

restaurant (rĕs'tō rănt), a place where meals or food may be bought. **37.**

rheumatism (ro͞o'mȧ tĭzm), a disease with soreness, swelling, and stiffness in one's muscles and joints. **46.**

rhyme (rīm), *v.* 1. to cause words or lines to end with the same sound. 2. to end with the same sound.—*n.* agreement in final sounds. **16.**

rhythm (rĭ*th*m), a flow of sound marked by regular accented beats. **16.**

right (rīt), *adj.* or *adv.* 1. suitable; correct. 2. straight. 3. just; upright.—*n.* anything that is true or correct. **3.**

rite (rīt), a solemn ceremony; a religious practice. **3.**

road (rōd), 1. a highway. 2. a course or wide path. **25.**

route (ro͞ot), the road; the way to go. **41.**

sacrifice (săk′rĭ fīs), *n.* the giving-up of something precious. —*v.* 1. to give up something. 2. to offer to a god. **46.**

safety (sāf′tĭ), freedom from harm or danger. **25.**

said (sĕd), expressed in words. **11.**

salary (săl′ȧ rĭ), a fixed pay for regular work. **11.**

satisfactorily (săt′ĭs făk′tō rĭ lĭ), satisfying; good enough to satisfy. **21.**

satisfactory (săt′ĭs făk′tō rĭ), satisfying; good enough to satisfy. **13.**

satisfied (săt′ĭs fīd), 1. made content. 2. freed from doubt. **8.**

Saturday (săt′ẽr dā), the seventh day of the week. **2.**

says (sĕz), states in words; asserts. **6.**

scarcely (skârs′lĭ), 1. very probably not. 2. barely; not quite. 3. decidedly not. **54.**

scene (sēn), 1. a place; a setting. 2. one part of a stage play or drama. 3. a showing of feelings. **15.**

scenery (sēn′ẽr ĭ), 1. the general appearance of a place. 2. the painted scenes or hangings of a stage. **9.**

schedule (skĕd′ūl), *n.* a written or printed statement of details; a list.—*v.* to make a schedule of. **48.**

scheme (skēm), *n.* 1. plan. 2. plot. —*v.* 1. to plan; to plot. **27.**

science (sī′ĕns), 1. knowledge of facts and laws arranged in an orderly system. 2. a branch of such knowledge. **18.**

secretary (sĕk′rē tĕr′ĭ), 1. a person who writes letters and keeps records, etc. for a person, company, or club. 2. a writing desk. **28.**

security (sē kū′rĭ tĭ), 1. something given as a pledge. 2. safety. **30.**

seems (sēmz), appears; appears to be. **29.**

seize (sēz), 1. to take by force. 2. to take hold of suddenly. **52.**

sense (sĕns), *n.* 1. understanding. 2. judgment; intelligence. 3. a feeling; a sensation.—*v.* to become aware of. **39.**

sensible (sĕn′sĭ bl), 1. wise; having good judgment. 2. that can be perceived by the senses. 3. sensitive. **57.**

sentence (sĕn′tĕns), 1. a group of words that expresses a complete thought. 2. a decision. **45.**

separate (sĕp′ȧ rāt), *adj.* apart from others.—*v.* 1. to divide; to part. 2. to withdraw from. **11.**

series (sēr′ēz), a number of things in order and connected by being alike. **9.**

service (sûr′vĭs), 1. work done for another. 2. a job; a duty; an occupation. 3. a religious ceremony. **13.**

severe (sē vēr′), 1. sharp; violent. 2. very strict; stern. 3. without ornament. **5.**

shepherd (shĕp′ẽrd), *n.* a man who takes care of sheep.—*v.* to guard, as a shepherd guards his sheep. **59.**

sheriff (shĕr′ĭf), an important law-enforcing officer of a county. **25.**

shining (shīn′ĭng), 1. reflecting light steadily. 2. splendid; illustrious. **14.**

shipment (shĭp′mĕnt), 1. the act of shipping goods. 2. the goods shipped. **17.**

shipped (shĭpt), 1. sent by water. 2. transported by any means. **42.**

shoes (sho͞oz), 1. coverings for the feet. 2. something resembling shoes. **42.**

siege (sēj), any long-continued attack. **60.**

sight (sīt), *n.* 1. eyesight; vision. 2. something that is seen.—*v.* to get sight of. **9.**

similar (sĭm'ĭ lẽr), alike; much the same. **41.**

since (sĭns), 1. in time past. 2. because; seeing that. **24.**

sincerely (sĭn sēr'lĭ), honestly; really; genuinely. **58.**

sincerity (sĭn sĕr'ĭ tĭ), honesty; genuineness. **9.**

site (sīt), position or place of anything. **51.**

situation (sĭt'ū ā'shŭn), 1. condition; state; circumstances. 2. location; position. 3. a job. **24.**

society (sō sī'ĕ tĭ), 1. companionship. 2. a group of persons joined together for common purpose. 3. people in general. **28.**

soldier (sōl'jẽr), 1. a man in military service. 2. a person who fights for a cause. **44.**

solemn (sŏl'ĕm), 1. serious; grave. 2. done with form and ceremony. **28.**

sophomore (sŏf'ō mōr), a student in the second year of high school or college. **23.**

soul (sōl), 1. the spiritual part of a person. 2. a human being. **17.**

source (sōrs), beginning; origin. **17.**

special (spĕsh'al), 1. having to do with a single thing or class. 2. unusual. 3. dear; intimate. **9.**

speech (spēch), 1. act of uttering sounds. 2. manner of speaking. 3. a public talk. **20.**

spirits (spĭr'ĭts), 1. state of mind; mood. 2. cheerfulness. **51.**

statement (stāt'mĕnt), 1. the act of stating. 2. a report; an account. **28.**

stating (stāt'ĭng), saying; expressing. **57.**

stationary (stā'shŭn ĕr'ĭ), 1. not changing. 2. fixed in a certain place. **60.**

stationery (stā'shŭn ĕr'ĭ), writing materials. **47.**

steal (stēl), 1. to rob. 2. to move secretly or quietly. **7.**

steel (stēl), 1. iron mixed with carbon. 2. hardness and coldness. **7.**

stomach (stŭm'ăk), the organ in the human body which digests food. **5.**

stopped (stŏpt), 1. halted; blocked. 2. ceased to go on. **25.**

straight (strāt), 1. direct; not curved. 2. honest; upright. 3. correct; in order. **7.**

strength (strĕngth), 1. quality of being strong; power. 2. toughness; firmness. **34.**

stretch (strĕch), *n.* 1. the act of extending. 2. a continuous line or surface.—*v.* to reach out; to extend. **4.**

studying (stŭd'ĭ ĭng), 1. applying the mind to books or learning. 2. thinking seriously. **23.**

style (stīl), 1. manner; method; way. 2. fashion. **4.**

substitute (sŭb'stĭ tūt), *n.* a person or thing put in place of another. —*v.* to put in place of another. **60.**

succeed (sŭk sēd'), 1. to have success; to turn out well. 2. to follow. **43.**

success (sŭk sĕs'), 1. desired result. 2. a person or thing that succeeds. 3. prosperity. **50.**

sufficient (sŭ fĭsh'ĕnt), 1. enough. 2. competent; able. **50.**

sugar (sho͝og'ẽr), *n.* a sweet substance obtained chiefly from sugar cane or beets. — *v.* to sweeten with sugar. **37.**

suggest (sŭg jĕst'), 1. to bring to mind; to mention. 2. to propose. **32.**

superintendent (sū'pẽr ĭn tĕn'dĕnt), a person who oversees or manages anything. **49.**

superstitious (sū'pẽr stĭsh'ŭs), believing in magic, chance, and the like. **59.**

supplies (sŭ plīz'), *n.* provisions; stores.—*v.* 1. to furnish. 2. to fill. **37.**

suppose (sŭ pōz'), 1. to believe; to think. 2. to assume as true. **43.**

sure (sho͝or), 1. certain; free from doubt. 2. safe; secure. **12.**

surprise (sûr prīz'), *n.* 1. an act of taking unawares. 2. something surprising. 3. amazement.—*v.* to come upon suddenly. **41.**

syllable (sĭl'ȧ bl), the part of a word pronounced as a distinct unit. **32.**

sympathy (sĭm'pȧ thĭ), 1. a sharing of another's sorrow or trouble. 2. having the same feeling. 3. favor. **38.**

tariff (tăr'ĭf), 1. system of duties or taxes. 2. a duty or tax. 3. any scale of prices. **37.**

taught (tôt), assisted in learning; instructed. **26.**

temporary (tĕm'pō rĕr'ĭ), not permanent; lasting for a time only. **14.**

terms (tûrmz), 1. conditions; provisions. 2. periods of time. 3. words used in a very limited sense. **30.**

terrible (tĕr'ĭ bl), causing terror; fearful. **38.**

territory (tĕr'ĭ tō'rĭ), 1. land; region. 2. land belonging to a government. **19.**

their (*th*âr), of them; belonging to them. **3.**

theory (thē'ō rĭ), 1. explanation. 2. the principles or methods of a science or art. **7.**

there (*th*âr), 1. into or at that place. 2. in that matter; in that respect. **3.**

therefore (*th*âr'fōr), for that reason; hence. **3.**

thorough (thûr'ō), 1. complete; thoroughgoing. 2. painstaking. **23.**

though (*th*ō), 1. although; despite the fact that. 2. in case that; if. **7.**

thought (thôt), *v.* reasoned; formed the opinion.—*n.* 1. use of the mind. 2. reflection. 3. act of thinking. **25.**

through (thro͞o), *adj.* 1. having both entrance and exit. 2. finished; done.—*prep.* 1. into and beyond. 2. among. **11.**

tired (tīrd), weary. **15.**

to (to͞o), 1. in the direction. 2. as far as; until. 3. for. 4. on; against. **3.**

tobacco (tō băk'ō), prepared leaves used for smoking or chewing. **11.**

together (to͝o gĕ*th*'ẽr), 1. with each other. 2. into one gathering or company. 3. at the same time. **41.**

tomorrow (to͝o mŏr'ō), the day after today. **28.**

too (to͞o), 1. very; exceedingly. 2. also; besides. 3. more than enough. **3.**

tournament (to͝or'nȧ mĕnt), a contest of many persons in some sport. **34.**

toward (tō'ẽrd), 1. in the direction of. 2. about; concerning. **19.**

tragedy (trăj'ĕ dĭ), 1. a sad event. 2. a play or story that arouses pity or terror. **19.**

transferred (trăns fûrd'), 1. conveyed. 2. changed from one car line to another. **44.**

traveler (trăv'ĕl ẽr), a person or thing that travels. **15.**

treasurer (trĕzh'ẽr ẽr), one who has charge of money. **55.**

tries (trīz), endeavors; attempts. **50.**

trouble (trŭb'l), *n.* 1. something or someone that causes distress, annoyance. 2. annoyance; uneasiness.—*v.* to agitate or worry. **21.**

truly (tro͞o'lĭ), in a true manner; honestly. **2.**

Tuesday (tūz'dā), the third day of the week. **14.**

tuition (tū ĭsh'ŭn), 1. money paid for instruction. 2. teaching; instruction. **26.**

twelfth (twĕlfth), 1. next after the eleventh. 2. one of twelve equal parts. **42.**

two (tōō), one more than one. **3.**

unanimous (ū năn'ĭ mŭs), in complete agreement. **37.**

university (ū'nĭ vûr'sĭ tĭ), an institution for teaching and study in higher branches of learning. **23.**

until (ŭn tĭl'), 1. up to the time of (or when). 2. before. **4.**

useful (ūs'fŭl), of use; helpful. **9.**

using (ūs'ĭng), making use of; employing. **11.**

usually (ū'zhōō ăl ĭ), commonly; ordinarily. **6.**

vacation (vā kā'shŭn), 1. time of rest and freedom from work. 2. the act of vacating. **1.**

vacuum (văk'ū ŭm), empty space without even air in it. **59.**

valuable (văl'ū ȧ bl), 1. having money value. 2. full of worth. **47.**

variety (vȧ rī'ĕ tĭ), 1. a varied assortment. 2. a particular kind. **51.**

various (vâr'ĭ ŭs), 1. varied; not all alike. 2. several; many and different. **18.**

very (vĕr'ĭ), 1. much; greatly. 2. exactly. 3. same. **24.**

vicinity (vĭ sĭn'ĭ tĭ), 1. nearness. 2. neighborhood. **57.**

view (vū), 1. a look; a sight. 2. mental picture. 3. opinion. **19.**

village (vĭl'ĭj), a group of houses in the country. **41.**

villain (vĭl'ĭn), a scoundrel; a rascal. **55.**

vinegar (vĭn'ē gẽr), a sour liquid used as a condiment. **33.**

volume (vŏl'ūm), 1. a book, especially one of a series. 2. a space. 3. a quantity; a mass. **18.**

volunteer (vŏl'ŭn tēr'), *v.* to offer one's services.—*n.* a person who offers his services of his own free will. **56.**

waist (wāst), 1. a garment for the upper part of the body. 2. the human body between the bottom of the ribs and the hips. **4.**

wait (wāt), to stay; delay; look for. **6.**

warrant (wŏr'ănt), *n.* 1. a written order giving authority for something. 2. a promise.—*v.* 1. to justify. 2. to guarantee. **25.**

waste (wāst), *n.* 1. the action of wasting. 2. a desert. 3. ruin; destruction.—*v.* 1. to make poor use of. 2. to wear away. **22.**

wear (wâr), *v.* 1. to have on the body. 2. to show. 3. to use up in service.—*n.* the act of wearing. **8.**

weather (wĕ*th*'ẽr), *n.* the state of the air and atmosphere.—*v.* 1. to expose to the air. 2. to come safely through danger. **14.**

Wednesday (wĕnz'dā), the fourth day of the week. **14.**

weigh (wā), 1. to determine the weight of something. 2. to be heavy. 3. to have influence. **6.**

weird (wērd), uncanny; having to do with supernatural things. **24.**

where (hwâr), 1. place in or at which. 2. to what place? 3. from what place or source? **7.**

whether (hwĕ*th*'ẽr), 1. either if. 2. if it be true or possible that. **52.**

which (hwĭch), 1. what one (of two or more)? 2. that; as. 3. any one that; whichever. **4.**

whole (hōl), *adj.* 1. complete. 2. full quantity; entire. 3. in sound condition; not defective. — *n.* something which is whole. **27.**

wholly (hōl'lĭ), entirely; totally; fully. **31.**

whom (hōōm), objective case of *who.* **4.**

whose (hōōz), possessive case of *who.* **4.**

woman (wŏŏm'ăn), a mature female. **8.**

women (wĭm'ĕn), plural of *woman.* 8.

would (wŏŏd), past tense of *will.* 40.

wouldn't (wŏŏd''nt), contraction of *would not.* 12.

write (rīt), 1. to form letters, etc., with pen or pencil. 2. to express on paper. 3. to write a letter to. 3.

writing (rīt'ĭng), *v.* forming letters, etc., with pen or pencil.—*n.* that which is set down. 20.

written (rĭt'n), past participle of *write.* 3.

yield (yēld), *v.* 1. to turn over; to give to. 2. to produce. 3. to give way to.—*n.* that which is yielded. 22.

yours (yŏŏrz), possessive case of *you.* 12.

PROOFREADER'S MARKS*

Mark	Meaning	Mark	Meaning
^,	Insert comma	$\overset{2}{\vee}$	Superscript (number specified)
∨'	Insert apostrophe	$\underset{2}{\wedge}$	Subscript (number specified)
∨''	Insert quotation marks	#	Insert space
⊙	Insert period	hr#	Hair space between letters
⊙:	Insert colon	⊥	Push down space
;/	Insert semicolon	[	Move to left
?/	Insert question mark	]	Move to right
=/	Insert hyphen	⊔	Lower
1/M	One-em dash	⊓	Elevate
2/M	Two-em dash	x	Broken letter
en	En dash	⌒	Ligature (AEsop)
.l.l.l.	Ellipsis (If preceded by a period there will be 4 dots.)	sp	Spell out (U.S.)
ϑ	Delete	stet	Let it stand (some-day)
⊂⊃	Close up	wf	Wrong font
ϑ⌒	Delete and close up	bf	Set in boldface type
9	Reverse; upside-down	rom	Set in roman type
∧	Insert (caret)	ital	Set in italic type
¶	Paragraph	sc	Small capitals
no ¶	No paragraph; run in	caps	Capitals
tr	Transpose (thier, only is)	lc	Set in lower case
=	Align	ld>	Insert lead between lines

*Reproduced (in reduced size) from *The American College Dictionary,* copyright 1959 by Random House, Inc., by permission of the publishers.

PART 2

THE TECHNICAL GATEWAY

PRACTICAL SPELLING AND DICTIONARY HABITS

Complete mastery of the 720 words in Part 1 of this text takes care of most mistakes in spelling. Part 2 is presented for the various students, secretaries, and writers who desire to go beyond the basic list of spelling words. Among the students of this book are those who will write the world's business and social letters, its news, its plays, its poems, and its current books. The lessons ahead are designed to meet the practical needs of all such students.

Part 2 of *Gateways to Correct Spelling* makes three practical contributions to the language needs of its students:

1. It presents an additional set of six hundred words especially useful to general literary and business needs.
2. It shows how to become an expert in the use of the dictionary, thus opening a way to the correct understanding and use of all words.
3. It applies the rules and principles of spelling in an objective manner that contributes to better spelling and improved speech.

The lessons which follow may be studied either individually or in a class group. Students should continue to use the whole-word, hard-spot method of study described in Part 1 of this text. The special Memory Aids no longer appear in the lessons. The Visual Drills appear in abbreviated form. The Basic Dictionary should now be supplanted by some standard larger dictionary which meets the broader language needs of students at this level of study. Indeed, the proper use of a comprehensive dictionary is so important to practical progress in spelling that it becomes a major objective in the lessons to follow.

THE VALUE OF A GOOD DICTIONARY

Nine persons out of ten do not use a dictionary properly. A good dictionary is an essential aid to practical spelling and, in addition, opens the way for general language improvement. The business of buying, selling, advertising, writing letters, using the telephone, preparing reports, and giving orders is dependent upon the correct choice and spelling of words. The lessons which follow in this text show how to use the dictionary as a first aid to correct spelling. Fortunately, the proper use of a dictionary for purposes of correct spelling also contributes to the better use of a dictionary for general language purposes.

The student should, first of all, have a good dictionary close at hand where it can be consulted without moving to another place. A dictionary of average size, published for high school or college students, is likely to prove most satisfactory for general use. A pocket dictionary is frequently helpful for quick reference, and a "big" dictionary should be available somewhere. Sample pages from four helpful dictionaries are shown on pages 88, 90, 94, and 96 of this text.

Once a good dictionary has been selected, it is important to study carefully the Directions in the front part of the dictionary which tell how to use the book. Time thus spent will pay for itself many times over. Dictionaries differ considerably in the information they present and in the exact form and place in which they present it. Most standard dictionaries contain information of the following types:

1. The correct spelling and pronunciation of words.
2. The various meanings of words.
3. The accents and syllables of words.
4. The sources from which words are derived.
5. Prefixes, suffixes, and abbreviations.
6. The use of hyphens and capitals.
7. The different forms of words and parts of speech.
8. Obsolete, informal, and slang words.
9. Synonyms, antonyms, and examples of correct usage.
10. Foreign words and phrases.
11. Names of persons and places.
12. Signs and symbols; weights and measures.
13. Pictures, maps, and charts.

The final value of any dictionary depends upon your ability to locate words quickly and to interpret the accompanying information correctly. The lessons which follow show you how to do this in the most helpful manner. In addition, they correlate closely with the methods and objectives of the secondary school's language arts program and may be used as an effective aid to its successful achievement.

al·pha·bet·ize (ăl/fə bə tīz/), *v.t.*, **-ized, -izing. 1.** to arrange in the order of the alphabet: *to alphabetize a list of names.* **2.** to express by an alphabet. —**al·pha·bet·i·za·tion** (ăl/fə bĕt/ə zā/shən), *n.* —**al/pha·bet·iz/er,** *n.*

alpha particle, *Physics.* a positively charged particle composed of two protons and two neutrons (and therefore equivalent to the nucleus of a helium atom) and spontaneously emitted by some radioactive material such as radium.

alpha ray, *Physics.* a stream of alpha particles.

alpha test, a psychological test measuring learning ability for those able to read and write, used by the U.S. Army in World War I.

Al·phe·us (ăl fē/əs), *n.* *Gk. Myth.* a river god, son of Oceanus and Tethys, who fell in love with the nymph Arethusa and, when she became a fountain to escape him, changed into a river and mingled with her.

alp·horn (ălp/hôrn/), *n.* alpenhorn.

al·pho·sis (ăl fō/sĭs), *n.* *Pathol.* lack of pigment in the skin, as in albinism. [f. s. Gk. *alphós* kind of leprosy + -OSIS]

Al·pine (ăl/pīn, -pĭn), *adj.* **1.** of or pertaining to any lofty mountain. **2.** very high; elevated. **3.** (*cap.*) of or pertaining to the Alps. **4.** *Bot.* growing on mountains, above the limit of tree growth. [t. L: m. s. *Alpīnus*, der. *Alpēs* the Alps]

alpine garden, a rock garden.

Al·pin·ism (ăl/pə nĭz/əm), *n.* mountain climbing, esp. in the Alps. —**Al/pin·ist,** *n.*

Alps (ălps), *n.* a mountain system in S Europe, extending from France through Switzerland and Italy into Austria and Yugoslavia. Highest peak, Mont Blanc, 15,781 ft. [see ALP]

al·read·y (ôl rĕd/ĭ), *adv.* by this (or that) time; previously to or at some specified time. [ME *al redy* all ready. See ALL, READY]

al·right (ôl rīt/), *adv.* all right (not generally regarded as good usage).

Al·sace (ăl sās/, ăl/săs; *Fr.* ȧl zȧs/), *n.* a region in NE France between the Vosges Mountains and the Rhine: a former province.

Al·sace-Lor·raine (ăl/sās lō-rān/, -săs; *Fr.* ȧl zȧs lô rĕn/), *n.* a region in NE France, including the former provinces of Alsace and Lorraine: a part of Germany, 1871–1919 and 1940–44. 1,986,-969 (1954); 5607 sq. mi.

Al·sa·tia (ăl sā/shə), *n.* a district in central London, England, once a sanctuary for debtors and lawbreakers: formerly called Whitefriars. [t. ML, Latinization of G *Elsass*, lit., foreign settlement]

Al·sa·tian (ăl sā/shən), *adj.* **1.** of or pertaining to Alsace. **2.** of or pertaining to Alsatia. —*n.* **3.** a native or inhabitant of Alsace. **4.** an inhabitant of Alsatia (Whitefriars).

Al·sib (ăl/sĭb), *n.* the route for air travel between Montana and Moscow, which lies across Alaska and Siberia.

al·sike (ăl/sīk, -sĭk, ôl/-), *n.* a European clover, *Trifolium hybridum*, with whitish or pink flowers, much grown in the U.S. for forage. Also, **alsike clover.** [named after *Alsike*, in Sweden]

al·si·na·ceous (ăl/sə nā/shəs), *adj.* *Bot.* **1.** caryophyllaceous. **2.** relating to or resembling the chickweed. [f. Gk. *alsín*(ē) + -ACEOUS]

Al Si·rat (ăl sĭ rät/), *Mohammedanism.* **1.** the correct path of religion. **2.** the bridge, fine as a razor's edge, over which all who enter paradise must pass. [t. Ar.: m. *al-ṣirāṭ* the road, from L (*via*) *strata* paved (road). Cf. STREET]

al·so (ôl/sō), *adv.* in addition; too; further. [ME; OE *alswā*, *ealswā* all (wholly or quite) so] —**Syn.** likewise, besides, moreover.

alt (ălt), *Music.* —*adj.* **1.** high. —*n.* **2. in alt,** in the first octave above the treble staff. [t. It.: s. *alto* high]

alt-, var. of **alto-** before vowels, as in *altazimuth.*

alt., 1. alternate. **2.** altitude. **3.** alto.

Alta., Alberta (Canada).

Al·ta·ic (ăl tā/ĭk), *n.* a group of languages made up of the Turkish, Manchurian, and Mongolian families.

Al·tai Mountains (ăl tī/, ăl-), a mountain system in central Asia, mostly in the Mongolian People's Republic and the S Soviet Union in Asia. Highest peak, Belukha, 15,157 ft.

Al·ta·ir (ăl tä/ĭr), *n.* a star of the first magnitude in the constellation Aquila. [t. Ar.: m. *al-ṭā'ir* the bird]

Al·ta·mi·ra (äl/tä mē/rä), *n.* a cave in N Spain, near Santander: Old Stone Age color drawings of animals.

al·tar (ôl/tər), *n.* **1.** an elevated place or structure, on which sacrifices are offered or at which religious rites are performed. **2.** (in most Christian churches) the communion table. **3. lead to the altar,** to marry. [ME *alter*, OE *altar*(*e*), t. LL. Cf. L *altāria*, pl., high altar]

altar boy, acolyte (def. 1).

al·tar·piece (ôl/tər pēs/), *n.* a decorative screenlike piece behind and above an altar; a reredos.

alt·az·i·muth (ăl tăz/ə məth), *n.* a mounting of telescopes or transits which provides two axes, one horizontal and one vertical, so that the instrument may be turned in the plane of the horizon and in any vertical plane. Altazimuths are used to determine altitudes and azimuths of heavenly bodies. [f. ALT- + AZIMUTH]

Alt·dorf (ält/dôrf), *n.* a town in central Switzerland: the legendary home of William Tell. 6576 (1950).

al·ter (ôl/tər), *v.t.* **1.** to make different in some particular; modify. **2.** *Colloq.* to castrate or spay. —*v.i.* **3.** to become different in some respect. [t. F: s. *altérer*, ult. der. L *alter* other] —**Syn. 1.** See **adjust** and **change.**

alter., alteration.

al·ter·a·ble (ôl/tər ə bəl), *adj.* capable of being altered. —**al/ter·a·bil/i·ty, al/ter·a·ble·ness,** *n.* —**al/ter·a·bly,** *adv.*

al·ter·ant (ôl/tər ənt), *adj.* **1.** producing alteration. —*n.* **2.** something that causes alteration.

al·ter·a·tion (ôl/tə rā/shən), *n.* **1.** act of altering. **2.** condition of being altered. **3.** a change; modification.

al·ter·a·tive (ôl/tə rā/tĭv), *adj.* **1.** tending to alter. **2.** *Med.* gradually restoring healthy bodily functions. —*n.* **3.** *Med.* an alterative remedy.

al·ter·cate (ôl/tər kāt/, ăl/-), *v.i.*, **-cated, -cating.** to argue with zeal, heat, or anger; wrangle. [t. L: m. s. *altercātus*, pp., having wrangled]

al·ter·ca·tion (ôl/tər kā/shən, ăl/-), *n.* a heated or angry dispute; a noisy wrangle.

altered chord, *Music.* a chord in which at least one tone has been changed from its normal pitch in the key.

al·ter e·go (ăl/tər ē/gō, ĕg/ō), *Latin.* **1.** a second self. **2.** an inseparable friend. [L: lit., another I]

al·ter i·dem (ăl/tər ī/dĕm), *Latin.* another exactly similar.

al·ter·nant (ôl tûr/nənt, ăl-), *adj.* alternating. [t. L: s. *alternans*, ppr.]

al·ter·nate (*v.* ôl/tər nāt/, ăl/-; *adj.*, *n.* ôl/tər nĭt, ăl/-), *v.*, **-nated, -nating,** *adj.*, *n.* —*v.i.* **1.** to follow one another in time or place reciprocally (usually fol. by *with*): *day and night alternate with each other.* **2.** to change about by turns between points, states, actions, etc.: *he alternates between hope and despair.* **3.** *Elect.* to reverse direction or sign periodically. —*v.t.* **4.** to perform by turns, or one after another. **5.** to interchange successively: *to alternate hot and cold compresses.* —*adj.* **6.** being by turns; following each the other, recurringly, in succession: *alternate winter and summer.* **7.** reciprocal: *alternate acts of kindness.* **8.** every other one of a series: *read only the alternate lines:* **9.** *Bot.* **a.** (of leaves, etc.) placed singly at different heights on the axis, on each side alternately, or at definite angular distances from one another. **b.** opposite to the intervals between other organs: *petals alternate with sepals.* —*n.* **10.** *U.S.* a person authorized to take the place of and act for another in his absence; substitute. [t. L: m.s. *alternātus*] —**al/ter·nate·ness,** *n.* —**Ant. 6.** successive.

Alternate leaves

alternate angles, *Geom.* two nonadjacent angles made by the crossing of two lines by a third line, both angles being either interior or exterior, and being on opposite sides of the third line.

al·ter·nate·ly (ôl/tər nĭt lĭ, ăl/-), *adv.* **1.** in alternate order; by turns. **2.** in alternate position.

alternating current, *Elect.* a current that reverses direction in regular cycles.

al·ter·na·tion (ôl/tər nā/shən, ăl/-), *n.* alternate succession; appearance, occurrence, or change by turns.

alternation of generations, *Biol.* an alternating in a line of reproduction, between generations unlike and generations like a given progenitor, esp. the alternation of asexual with sexual reproduction.

al·ter·na·tive (ôl tûr/nə tĭv, ăl-), *n.* **1.** a possibility of one out of two (or, less strictly, more) things: *the alternative of remaining neutral or attacking.* **2.** one of the things thus possible: *they chose the alternative of attacking.* **3.** a remaining course or choice: *we had no alternative but to move.* —*adj.* **4.** affording a choice between two things, or a possibility of one thing out of two. **5.** (of two things) mutually exclusive, so that if one is chosen the other must be rejected: *alternative results of this or that course.* **6.** *Logic.* (of a proposition) asserting two or more alternatives, at least one of which is true. [t. ML: m. s. *alternātīvus*] —**al·ter/na·tive·ly,** *adv.* —**al·ter/na·tive·ness,** *n.* —**Syn. 1.** option, selection. See **choice.**

al·ter·na·tor (ôl/tər nā/tər, ăl/-), *n.* *Elect.* a generator of alternating current.

Alt·geld (ôlt/gĕld), *n.* **John Peter,** 1847–1902, governor of Illinois, 1892–96.

al·the·a (ăl thē/ə), *n.* **1.** any plant of the genus *Althaea.* **2.** a malvaceous flowering garden shrub, *Hibiscus syriacus;* the rose of Sharon. **3.** (*cap.*) *Gk. Legend.* the mother of Meleager. Also, **al·thae/a.** [t. L, t. Gk.: m. *althaía* wild mallow]

alt·horn (ălt/hôrn/), *n.* a valved, brasswind horn, a fourth or fifth below the ordinary cornet; a tenor saxhorn. Also, **alto horn.**

Althorn

al·though (ôl thō/), *conj.* even though (practically equivalent to *though*, and preferred to it only for euphonic

ăct, āble, dâre, ärt; ĕbb, ēqual; ĭf, īce; hŏt, ōver, ôrder, oil, bŏŏk, ōōze, out; ŭp, ūse, ûrge; ə = a in alone; ch, chief; g, give; ng, ring; sh, shoe; th, thin; th, that; zh, vision. See the full key on inside cover.

Lesson 61 LOCATING WORDS IN THE DICTIONARY

The exercises below are planned to give you practice in finding where different kinds of words are located in *your* dictionary. If you have trouble finding any of the words, consult the Table of Contents or the Directions for Use in the front of your dictionary.

1. Speed in locating a word may be attained by following the two guide words which appear at the top of each page in the dictionary. Note the guide words on the sample dictionary page which faces this one. The first guide word *(alphabetize)* is the first entry on the page; the second guide word *(although)* is the last entry on the page. See how quickly you can find the words which follow in your dictionary.

disagree	**whistle**
accordingly	**luncheon**
leaves	**mechanical**

2. Abbreviations, foreign words, and the names of places and persons are frequently listed separately at the end of a dictionary. Some words, for example, *adios*, may be listed both in the main body and at the end of a dictionary. In *The American College Dictionary* (see the opposite page) all of the words are listed in one vocabulary. Look for the following words in your dictionary. It is quite possible that some of them may not be listed.

Washington	**Moses**
id est	**f.o.b.**
petite	**e pluribus unum**
Charles	**China**
Y. M. C. A.	**Chinaman**

VISUAL DRILLS

As you look at each word below try to see (visualize) the whole word with the missing letters in place. Check your efforts by looking at the word as it appears earlier in the lesson. Finally, test yourself by writing three of the words at a time from memory.

dis - gr - -	w - is - le	- ashin - t - n	Mo - - s
ac - ordin - l -	lun - - e - n	pet - t -	- h - na
le - v - s	me - - anic - -	- harl - -	Ch - n - m - n

tary engine; **2**, a light carriage or vehicle; **3**, an automobile; **4**, one who acts mechanically or at the bidding of another; **5**, a combination of persons acting together for a common purpose; as, the *machine* of government, the social *machine*, etc.; **6**, an unofficial political organization which controls the policies and activities of a party; **7**, in ancient drama, a contrivance for producing certain theatrical effects; hence, in literature, those parts of a plot, etc., introduced as a means of adding dramatic force: **machine tool**, a power-driven tool, as a lathe, for cutting and shaping metals:—*v.t.* [*p.t.* and *p.p.* machined (-shēnd′), *p.pr.* machining], to form or effect by the aid of a machine.

ma-chine gun a small, automatic gun, with a cooling device, capable of firing continuously bullets fed to it by means of a disk or a belt.

ma-chine–made (mȧ-shēn′-mād″), *adj.* fashioned or made by machinery: opposite of *handmade.*

MACHINE GUN

ma-chin-er-y (mȧ-shēn-ẽr-ĭ), *n.* **1**, engines and other appliances collectively, or the parts of them; **2**, any means or combination, not mechanical, by which something is kept in action or the result desired is obtained; as, the *machinery* of church government; **3**, the assemblage of agencies, especially the supernatural, such as demons, ghosts, and gods, employed in the plot of an epic, drama, novel, etc.

ma-chin-ist (mȧ-shēn′ĭst), *n.* **1**, one who makes or repairs machines and other appliances, or is skilled in their design and principles; **2**, one who works about, or attends to, machines or other mechanical appliances; **3**, one skilled in the use of machine tools.

Mach number (mŏk), *Aëro.* [< Ernst *Mach* (1838–1916), Austrian physicist], a number indicating the ratio of speed of a body to the speed of sound at a given altitude. Also **Mach.**

ma-chree (mȧ-khrē′), *n.* [< Ir. *mo*, my + *croidhe*, heart], literally, my heart: an Anglo-Irish term of endearment.

mack-er-el (măk′ẽr-ĕl), *n.* [*pl.* mackerel], [< O.F. *makerel:* source uncertain], an edible, oily fish (*Scomber scombrus*) from twelve to eighteen inches in length, found in schools in the North Atlantic (see *Pisces*, illus.); also, any of various other fishes of the same or a related genus: **mackerel sky**, a sky covered with a mass of small white flecks of cloud of the form called *cirro-cumulus* (see *cloud*, illus.).

Mack-i-naw (măk′ĭ-nô), *adj.* [< Ojibway *Michillimackinac*, turtle: name of island], pertaining to, or derived from, Mackinac, Michigan: **Mackinaw blanket**, a heavy blanket, formerly distributed from Fort Mackinac to local Indians: **Mackinaw boat**, a flat-bottomed, square-sterned, sharp-prowed boat propelled by oars: **Mackinaw coat**, a short, heavy, frequently plaid, coat made of material resembling that of Mackinaw blankets: also called *mackinaw.*

mack-in-tosh (măk′ĭn-tŏsh), *n.* [< Charles *Macintosh* (1766–1843), inventor of cloth], **1**, a kind of waterproof overcoat; **2**, a thin, rubber-coated cloth from which such garments are made.

mac-ra-mé (măk′rȧ-mā; mȧ-krä′mā), *n.* [prob. < Turk. *maqrama*, towel], a kind of trimming made of cord knotted in geometrical designs.

mac-ro-cosm (măk′rō-kŏzm), *n.* [< Gk. *makros*, large + *kosmos*, world], the universe; the world at large, exterior to man: used in contrast to *microcosm*, or man.—*adj.* **mac″ro-cos′mic.**

mac-ro-graph (măk′rō-grăf), *n.* [< Gk. *makros*, large + *graphē*, a writing], a drawing or photograph of an object as seen with but little magnification: opposite of *micrograph.*

ma-crog-ra-phy (mȧ-krŏg′rȧ-fĭ), *n.* **1**, extremely large handwriting, often a symptom of nervous disorder; **2**, examination or study without a microscope: opposite of *micrography.*

ma-cron (mā′krŏn; măk′rŏn), *n.* [< Gk. *makros*, long], a mark [¯] over a vowel, as over the *a* in cāme, to show that it is long in quantity or quality.

mac-ro-scop-ic (măk″rō-skŏp′ĭk), *adj.* [< Gk. *makros*, large + *skopein*, to see], visible to the naked eye: opposite of *microscopic.*

mac-u-la (măk′ū-lȧ), *n.* [*pl.* -læ (-lē)], [Lat. = spot], **1**, a spot, as on the sun; **2**, a stain or blemish, as on the skin: ***macula lutea** (lū′tē-ȧ), [Lat. = yellow spot], *Anat.*, the yellow spot on the retina, the retinal area which is most sensitive (see *eye*, illus.).

mac-u-late (măk′ū-lāt), *v.t.* [*p.t.* and *p.p.* -lated, *p.pr.* -lating], to spot; blot; defile:—*adj.* (-lāt), spotted; hence, impure.—*n.* **mac″u-la′tion.**

mad (măd), *adj.* [*comp.* madder, *superl.* maddest], [< A.S. *gemǣd* < *gemǣdan*, to make mad], **1**, mentally disordered; insane; **2**, blindly excited or infatuated; **3**, furious or frenzied, as with rage or terror; **4**, rabid, as with disease; as, a *mad* dog; **5**, imprudent; foolish; as, a *mad* undertaking; **6**, wild; as, a *mad* scramble: *Colloq.*, angry:—*v.t.* [*p.t.* and *p.p.* madded, *p.pr.* madding], *Rare*, to make furious:—*v.i. Rare*, to act insanely.—*adv.* **mad′ly.**—*n.* **mad′ness.**

Syn., *adj.* crazy, delirious, rabid, violent, frantic, rash, infatuated —*Ant.*, *adj.* sane, rational, reasonable.

mad-am (măd′ăm), *n.* [*pl.* mesdames (mā″dȧm′)], [see **madame**], a complimentary title for a lady, used also as a form of courteous address: *Vulgar*, [*pl.* madams (măd′ămz)], the mistress of a house.

***ma-dame** (mȧ″dȧm′; mȧ-däm′; often, măd′ăm), *n.* [*pl.* mesdames (mā″dȧm′)], [< O.F. *ma dame*, my lady], the French title for a married woman.—*abbr.* **Mme** (without period) [*pl.* Mmes].

mad-cap (măd′kăp″), *n.* [*mad*+*cap*], a wild, thoughtless, rattle-brained person:—*adj.* given to wild follies; recklessly adventurous.

mad-den (măd′n), *v.t.* [see **mad**], to craze or make furious:—*v.i.* to become crazed or furious.

mad-der (măd′ẽr), *n.* [< A.S. *mædere*, madder], **1**, any of a genus (*Rubia*) of herbs allied to the bedstraws; especially, a species (*R. tinctorum*) from the root of which a red dye is extracted; **2**, a pigment originally made from this root: also called *turkey red* and *alizarin*, and now made synthetically from coal tar.

mad-ding (măd′ĭng), *p.adj.* [see **mad**], acting madly; frenzied:—*n. Archaic*, frenzied behavior.

made (mād), past tense and past participle of the verb *make:*—*p.adj.* contrived; artificially produced; as, a *made* dish: *Colloq.*, assured of success.

Ma-dei-ra (mȧ-dē′rȧ; mȧ-dā′rȧ), *n.* [Port. < Lat. *materia*, timber: island so named in allusion to dense woods], wine made in Madeira, an island in the Atlantic Ocean northwest of Morocco.

***ma-de-moi-selle** (măd″mwȧ″zĕl′; măd″ĕ-mō-zĕl′; colloquially, măm″zĕl′), *n.* [*pl.* mesdemoiselles (mād″mwȧ″zĕl′)], [Fr. = my young lady], Miss: a title given in France to an unmarried woman.—*abbr.* **Mlle** (without period) [*pl.* Mlles].

mad-house (măd′hous″), *n.* [*mad*+*house*], an asylum for lunatics.

mad-man (măd′măn), *n.* [*pl.* -men (-mĕn)], [*mad* + *man*], an insane man; a lunatic.

Ma-don-na (mȧ-dŏn′ȧ), *n.* [*pl.* -nas (-ȧz)], [It. *ma donna* < Lat. *mea domina*, my lady, mistress], the Virgin Mary, or a picture or statue of her, usually with the infant Christ: **madonna**, formerly, the Italian equivalent for madam; my lady.

ma-dras (mȧ-drȧs′), *n.* [Fr. < *Madras*, India], **1**, a large, bright-colored kerchief; **2**, a fine, cotton fabric, often of fancy design; also, a curtain material with raised figures, often in color.

***ma-dre** (mä′drā), *n.* [Sp.], in the Philippines and other Spanish-speaking countries, a mother.

mad-re-pore (măd′rē-pōr), *n.* [< It. *madre*, mother + *poro*, pore, coral-like substance], any of a genus (*Madrepora*) of stony, mostly branching, corals that build reefs in tropical seas.

mad-ri-gal (măd′rĭ-găl), *n.* [< It. *madrigale*, short song], a short love poem: *Mus.*, an unaccompanied chorus, in from four to eight parts, based on a theme elaborated with complex counterpoint: very popular in the 15th and 16th centuries.

ma-du-ro (mȧ-dōō′rō), *adj.* [Sp. = mature], of full strength and dark color: said of cigars.

Mæ-ce-nas (mē-sē′năs), *n.* [Lat.: name of the patron (about 68 B.C. – 8 B.C.) of Horace and Vergil], a supporter or patron, especially one who gives largely to the arts.

Mael-strom (māl′strŏm), *n.* [Du. < *malen*, to grind + *stroom*, stream], a whirlpool off the Norwegian coast, described with exaggerated horrors by Edgar Allan Poe: **maelstrom**, any widespread, destructive influence; as, the *maelstrom* of war.

mæ-nad (mē′năd), *n.* [*pl.* -nads (-nădz)], [< Gk. *mainas* (-*ados*), mænad < *mainesthai*, to rave], **1**, *Gk. Myth.*, a nymph or bacchante attendant upon Dionysus, the god of wine; **2**, any frenzied woman.

***ma-es-to-so** (mä″ĕs-tō′sō), *adj.* or *adv.* [It. = with majesty], *Mus.*, majestic or majestically: a direction signifying that a composition is to be performed in a majestic style.

***ma-es-tro** (mä-ĕs′trō; almost mīs′trō), *n.* [*pl.* -tri (-trē)], [It. = master], a master in music: a great composer, conductor, or teacher.

ma-fi-a (mä′fē-ä), *n.* [Sicilian], in Sicily, the popular feeling of hostility to the law; also, a secret but widespread organization, originally political, of persons imbued with this feeling: **Mafia**, a society

Lesson 62 UNDERSTANDING DICTIONARY SPELLING

Each of the words listed in alphabetical order in a dictionary is called an *entry*. Most dictionaries print the entry words with the syllables separated by hyphens or spaces. Look at the entries for *machinery* and *machinist* near the top of *The Winston Senior Dictionary* page which faces this one. The words appear as *ma-chin-er-y* and *ma-chin-ist*. The syllables are separated by short hyphens. These are not real hyphens. A real hyphen is shown by the long hyphen which appears in the second entry, *ma-chine–made*. The correct spelling is *machine-made*.

Note carefully how your own dictionary prints its entries. How does it indicate a real hyphen? Make sure that you understand your dictionary. Consult the Directions for Use.

Each entry in the dictionary is followed by a phonetic spelling in parentheses. Thus on the page opposite you find (mȧ-shēn'ẽr-ĭ) and (mȧ-shēn'ĭst) following *ma-chin-er-y* and *ma-chin-ist*. The phonetic spellings show how the words should be pronounced. Be very careful not to confuse these phonetic spellings with the correct spellings.

Listed below are six words with illustrative sentences to show their meanings. Find each word in turn in your dictionary. Then write the correct spelling, the dictionary entry spelling, and the phonetic spelling of each word on a sheet of paper in a manner similar to the following illustration:

CORRECT SPELLING	DICTIONARY ENTRY	PHONETIC SPELLING
machinery	ma-chin-er-y	mȧ-shēn'ẽr-ĭ
machinist	ma-chin-ist	mȧ-shēn'ĭst

despair	The drowning man gave up in *despair*.
hygiene	The science of *hygiene* deals with health.
luncheon	The *luncheon* was served at noon.
permit	Father would not *permit* me to go.
salmon	The *salmon* is an edible fish.
watch	Be sure to *watch* your pronunciation.

VISUAL DRILLS

d - sp - - r	h - g - - ne	lunc - - - n
p - rm - t	s - - m - n	w - - ch

Lesson 63 HOW TO STUDY WORDS IN THE DICTIONARY

It is very important, both for spelling and speech, that you take the right steps in studying the dictionary. Whenever you look up a word to determine its spelling or how to pronounce it, take the following steps:

1. Make sure that you have the right word.
2. Observe how the word is syllabified.
3. Observe how the word is accented.
4. Observe letters pronounced differently than usual.
5. Observe silent or extra letters.
6. Strengthen your visual image of the word.

The method and importance of these steps will become clearer as you consider them in greater detail in the lessons to follow.

Step 1. Making Sure that You Have the Right Word

Always look at the meanings of a word given in the dictionary to make sure that you are not confusing it with some other word. For example, do not confuse *accept* with *except,* or *essay* with *assay.* Confusion of this sort accounts for a surprisingly large number of spelling errors. (See Lessons 3 and 36.)

Look up the following pairs of words in your dictionary and contrast them as to spelling, pronunciation, and meaning.

biannual A bi an′*nu* al event occurs twice a year.
biennial A bi en′*ni* al event occurs once in two years.

dairy We get our milk at the da*i*′ry farm.
diary I write something in my di′a ry every night.

eligible Morgan was not el′i gi bl*e* for membership.
illegible Mary's handwriting was almost *il* leg′i bl*e*.

eminent The president is an em′i nent man.
imminent Another strike seemed im′*mi* nent.

moral His mor′al acts were right and just.
morale The team's mo ral*e*′ was very low.

receipt The re *ceipt*′ showed that I had paid the bill.
recipe Mother has a good re*c*′i pe for making biscuits.

VISUAL DRILLS

bi - n - - al	di - - y	- min - nt	mor - l -
bi - n - ial	eli - - b - -	- mmin - nt	re - e - p -
d - ir -	ill - - ib - -	mor - -	re - ip -

Lesson 64 MAKING SURE THAT YOU HAVE THE RIGHT WORD

This lesson gives you additional practice in the first step in studying the dictionary. Study the different spellings of the pairs of similar words listed below. Be sure when you look at a word that you have its exact meaning in mind. If you are uncertain about the pronunciation or meaning of any of the words, consult your dictionary.

adapt	You should a dapt′ yourself to new conditions.
adopt	The club refused to a dopt′ the motion.
complement	The office had its com′ple ment of workers.
compliment	A com′pli ment is more sincere than flattery.
continual	The rain kept up a con tin′u al patter.
continuous	There was a con tin′u *o*us stretch of bad roads.
council	The city coun′*c*il has five members.
counsel	A wise man gives good coun′sel.
decease	Finally, de *cease*′ (death) relieved him of pain.
disease	The di*s* *ease*′ was very contagious.
emerge	We saw his head e m*erge*′ from the water.
immerge	We saw the diver i*m* merge′ in the water.
healthy	The laborers were not in a he*a*lth′y condition.
healthful	The climate is he*a*lth′f*u*l in Arizona.
lightening	There was no way of lig*h*t′*e*n ing his load.
lightning	The lig*h*t′ning struck the same tree twice.
practicable	Wooden tires are not pra*c*′ti *c*a bl*e*.
practical	One gains pra*c*′ti *c*al knowledge by experience.
prescribe	We should obey what the laws pre *s*cribe′.
proscribe	Some churches pro *s*cribe′ card playing.
respectfully	I signed the letter, "Yours re spe*c*t′ful ly."
respectively	The stamps cost one, two, and three cents, re spe*c*′tiv*e* ly.
stature	Six feet is more than average stat′ ur*e*.
statute	The legislature passed another stat′ ut*e*.

VISUAL DRILLS

ada - -	coun - il	he - lthf - -	r - spe - - f - - ly
cont - n - a -	d - sea - e	li - - t - ning	r - sp - - t - v - ly
cont - nu - - s	- mmer - e	pra - tic - b - -	st - t - r -

ven′er·y (vĕn′ẽr·ĭ), *n.* [OF. *venerie*, fr. *vener* to hunt, fr. L. *venari.*] Art, act, or practice of hunting; the sports of the chase; hunting.

ven′e·sec′tion (vĕn′ē·sĕk′shŭn; vē′nē-), *n.* [NL. *venaesectio*, fr. L. *vena* vein, gen. *venae* + *sectio* a cutting.] *Med.* Phlebotomy.

Ve·ne′tian (vē·nē′shăn), *adj.* Of or pertaining to Venice in Italy. — *n.* **1.** A native or inhabitant of Venice. **2.** Any of various things suggesting, or named in allusion to, Venice; as: **a** *Colloq.* A Venetian blind. **b** *pl.* A heavy tape or braid used especially on Venetian blinds.

Venetian blind. A blind (capable of being raised or lowered) having numerous thin parallel slats that can be set simultaneously at any desired angle.

Venetian glass. A dainty, delicate, and artistic glassware made at Murano near Venice.

Venetian red. **1.** A red pigment consisting of ferric oxides, artificially prepared. **2.** A brown, reddish red-yellow in hue, of medium saturation and low brilliance. See COLOR.

Venetian school. Painting as practiced in and near Venice in the 15th and 16th centuries, noted for its richness and beauty of color, culminating in the work of Giorgione, Titian, Paul Veronese, and Tintoretto.

venge (vĕnj), *v. t. & i.* [OF. *vengier.*] *Archaic.* = AVENGE.

venge′ance (vĕn′jăns), *n.* [OF., fr. *vengier, venchier*, to avenge, fr. L. *vindicare* to claim, defend, avenge, fr. *vindex* a claimant, avenger.] Punishment inflicted in return for an injury or an offense; retribution; often, passionate or unrestrained revenge.
— ***with a vengeance.*** **a** With great violence, force, or the like. **b** Extremely. **c** In great or excessive amount.

venge′ful (vĕnj′fo͝ol; -f'l), *adj.* Revengeful; as: **a** Vindictive; seeking to avenge. **b** Serving to gain vengeance. — **venge′ful·ly**, *adv.* — **venge′ful·ness**, *n.*

ve′ni·al (vē′nĭ·ăl; 58), *adj.* [OF. *venial*, fr. LL. *venialis*, fr. *venia* forgiveness, grace, favor.] **1.** Capable of being forgiven; excusable; as, a *venial* sin. **2.** *Obs.* Allowed; unobjectionable. — **ve′ni·al′i·ty** (-ăl′ĭ·tĭ), *n.* — **ve′ni·al·ly**, *adv.* — **ve′ni·al·ness**, *n.*

venial sin. *R.C.Ch.* A slight offense against divine law in unimportant matters, or, in grave matters, an offense committed without reflection or full consent.

ven′in (vĕn′ĭn; vē′nĭn), *n.* [L. *venenum* poison.] *Biochem.* Any of a class of toxic substances in snake venom.

ven′i·punc′ture (vĕn′ĭ·pŭngk′tūr; vē′nĭ-), *n.* *Med.* = VENEPUNCTURE.

ve·ni′re fa′ci·as (vē·nī′rē fā′shĭ·ăs), *or* **ve·ni′re**, *n.* [L., make, or cause, to come.] *Law.* A judicial writ or precept used in summoning persons to appear in court to serve as jurors.

ve·ni′re·man (vē·nī′rē·măn; vē·nẽr′ē-), *n.; pl.* -MEN (-mĕn). *Law.* A juror summoned by a venire.

ven′i·son (vĕn′ĭ·z'n; -s'n; *Brit.* vĕn′z'n), *n.* [OF. *veneison*, fr. L. *venatio* hunting, the chase, game, fr. *venari*, past part. *venatus*, to hunt.] The flesh of an animal of the deer kind.

Ve·ni′te (vē·nī′tē), *n.* [L., come, imper. 2d pers. pl.; — so called from its opening word in the Latin version.] The 94th Psalm (Vulgate, in A.V., the 95th), which in the form of a response is said or sung at matins.

‖**ve′ni, vi′di, vi′ci** (vē′nī, vī′dī, vī′sī; wā′nē, wē′dē, wē′kē). I came, I saw, I conquered; — the words with which Julius Caesar announced to the Roman Senate his victory at Zela, 47 B.C.

ven′om (vĕn′ŭm), *n.* [OF. *venim, venin*, fr. L. *venenum* poison.] **1.** *Archaic.* Matter fatal or injurious to life; poison in general. **2.** The poisonous matter which certain animals, such as serpents, scorpions, bees, etc., secrete and communicate by biting or stinging. **3.** That which poisons, embitters, or blights; spite; malice; malignity. — *v. t.* To envenom. — **ven′om·er**, *n.*

ven′om·ous (-ŭs), *adj.* **1.** Full of venom; poisonous; also, virulent; baneful. **2.** Malignant; spiteful; as, a *venomous* writer. **3.** *Zool.* Having a gland or glands for the secretion of venom; able to inflict a poisoned bite, sting, or wound. — **ven′om·ous·ly**, *adv.* — **ven′om·ous·ness**, *n.*

ve′nose (vē′nōs), *adj.* [See VENOUS.] Venous; specif., *Bot.*, having numerous or conspicuous veins.

ve·nos′i·ty (vē·nŏs′ĭ·tĭ), *n.* Quality or state of being venous or venose.

ve′nous (vē′nŭs), *adj.* [L. *venosus*, fr. *vena* a vein.] **1.** Of or pertaining to a vein or veins. **2.** *Physiol.* Designating blood, as that in the veins, which has passed through the capillaries, given up oxygen, and become charged with carbon dioxide. Venous blood in the higher animals is dark red. Cf. ARTERIAL. — **ve′nous·ly**, *adv.*

vent (vĕnt), *n.* [From *fent, fente*, a slit, cleft, fissure, fr. *fendre* to split, fr. L. *findere*; confused with F. *vent* wind, fr. L. *ventus.*] **1.** A small aperture; a hole or opening for passage or escape, as of a fluid. **2.** Opportunity of escape or passage; outlet, as from confinement or privacy; passage; escape; hence, utterance, expression, or publication; as, to give *vent* to one's wrath. **3.** *Ordn.* The opening at the breech of a gun through which fire is communicated to the powder. **4.** *Zool.* **a** The anus. **b** The opening of the cloaca or of the intestine on the surface of the body; esp., that of the lower vertebrates, as fishes.
— *v. t.* **1.** To let out at a vent, or small aperture; give passage or outlet to. **2.** To give vent or expression to; as, to *vent* one's anger; also, to utter; publish; as, to *vent* a grievance. **3.** To furnish with a vent; make a vent in. **4.** To relieve by giving vent; as, to *vent* oneself in grief. — **Syn.** See EXPRESS. — **vent′er**, *n.*

vent′age (vĕn′tĭj), *n.* A small hole; a vent.

ven′tail (vĕn′tāl), *n.* [OF. *ventaille* (F. *ventail*). See VENTILATE.] *Hist.* The lower movable front of a helmet.

ven′ter (vĕn′tẽr), *n.* [L.] **1.** Something suggesting a vent; specif.: *Anat. & Zool.* **a** The belly. **b** A protuberant part, as of a muscle. **c** A broad shallow concavity as in a bone. **2.** *Law.* Womb (of wife or mother).

ven′ti·duct (vĕn′tĭ·dŭkt), *n.* [L. *ventus* wind + *ductus* a leading, conduit, fr. *ducere, ductum*, to lead.] A passage or pipe for wind or air, as for ventilation.

ven′ti·late (vĕn′tĭ·lāt), *v. t.* [L. *ventilatus*, past part. of *ventilare* to toss, fan, winnow, fr. *ventus* wind.] **1.** *Now Rare.* To winnow; fan. **2.** To cause fresh air to circulate through (a room, mine, etc.) so as to replace foul air simultaneously removed; also, of air, to circulate through so as to freshen and replace foul air, gas, etc. **3.** To oxygenate, as blood. **4.** To give vent to; utter; as, to *ventilate* one's grievances; also, to discuss freely and openly; expose by publicity. **5.** To provide with a vent, or escape. — **ven′ti·la′tion** (-lā′shŭn), *n.* — **ven′ti·la′tive** (-lā′tĭv), *adj.*

ven′ti·la′tor (-lā′tẽr), *n.* One who or that which ventilates; esp., a contrivance for drawing off or expelling foul or stagnant air, or for introducing fresh air. — **ven′ti·la·to′ry** (-lȧ·tō′rĭ *or, esp. Brit.*, -tẽr·ĭ), *adj.*

‖**Ven′tôse′** (väN′tōz′), *n.* [F., fr. L. *ventosus* windy.] See REVOLUTIONARY CALENDAR.

ven′tral (vĕn′trăl), *adj.* [F. or L.; F., fr. L. *ventralis*, fr. *venter* the belly.] **1.** Of or pertaining to the belly; abdominal; hence, in *Zool. & Anat.*, designating, pertaining to, or situated on or toward that surface of the body which in man is anterior, but in most other animals is the lower surface; — the opposite of *dorsal*. **2.** *Bot.* **a** Pertaining to or designating that surface of a carpel, petal, etc., which faces toward the center of a flower. **b** Pertaining to the lower side or surface of a dorsiventral organ or thallus; — opposed to *dorsal*. — **ven′tral·ly**, *adv.*

ven′tri·cle (vĕn′trĭ·k'l), *n.* [F. or L.; F. *ventricule*, fr. L. *ventriculus* the stomach, a ventricle, dim. of *venter* the belly.] *Anat. & Zool.* A cavity of an organ; esp.: **a** Either of the chambers of the heart that receive the blood from an auricle (atrium), and deliver it to the arteries. See HEART, *Illust.* **b** In the brain, one of the communicating cavities continuous with the central canal of the spinal cord. See BRAIN, *Illust.*

ven′tri·cose (-kōs), *adj.* Also **ven′tri·cous** (-kŭs). [NL. *ventricosus*, fr. L. *venter* belly.] Having a large belly; *Bot. & Zool.*, swelling out on one side or unequally. — **ven′tri·cos′i·ty** (-kŏs′ĭ·tĭ), *n.*

ven·tric′u·lar (vĕn·trĭk′ū·lẽr), *adj.* **1.** Of or pertaining to a ventricle or ventriculus. **2.** Bellied; bulging out.

ven·tric′u·lus (-lŭs), *n.; pl.* -ULI (-lī). [L. See VENTRICLE.] *Zool.* A ventricle; specif., a division of a compound stomach, as the digestive portion of an insect stomach or the gizzard of a bird.

ven′tri·lo′qui·al (vĕn′trĭ·lō′kwĭ·ăl), *adj.* Also **ven·tril′o·qual** (vĕn·trĭl′ō·kwăl). Of, pertaining to, resembling, or using ventriloquism.

ven·tril′o·quism (vĕn·trĭl′ō·kwĭz'm), *n.* Also **ven·tril′o·quy** (-kwĭ). [From LL. *ventriloquus* a ventriloquist, fr. *venter* the belly + *loqui*, past part. *locutus*, to speak.] Act, art, or practice of speaking in such a manner that the voice appears to come from some source other than the vocal organs of the speaker. — **ven·tril′o·quist** (-kwĭst), *n.* — **ven·tril′o·quis′tic** (-kwĭs′tĭk), *adj.*

ven·tril′o·quize (-kwīz), *v. i. & t.* To utter ventriloquially.

ven′tro- (vĕn′trō-). [L. *venter* belly, paunch.] A combining form denoting: **a** *The abdomen*, as in **ven·trot′o·my** (see -TOMY). **b** *Ventral and*, as in **ven′tro·dor′sal.**

ven′ture (vĕn′tūr; 118), *n.* [Aphetic form of ME. *aventure*. See ADVENTURE.] **1.** An undertaking involving chance or danger; a hazard; risk; specif., a speculative business enterprise. **2.** *Now Rare.* Fortune; chance; contingency. **3.** The thing put to hazard, as in gambling; a stake; a risk; esp., something sent to sea in trade. — ***at a venture*** (orig. *at aventure*). At hazard; at random.
— *v. t.* **1.** To expose to hazard; risk. **2.** To undertake the risk of; to brave; dare, as a voyage. **3.** To put or send on a venture or chance, as a business speculation. **4.** *Rare.* To confide in; rely on. **5.** To dare to advance or put forward, or to expose to criticism or refutation, as an opinion. — *v. i.* **1.** To hazard oneself; dare. **2.** To make a venture; run a risk; as, to *venture* ashore. — **ven′tur·er** (-tūr·ẽr), *n.*

venture capital. Money invested in stocks, esp. new or expanding private enterprises, with the expectation of repayment in profits and dividends but subject to the hazards of ownership, as distinguished from capital loaned by banks; — called also *risk capital* or *equity capital*.

ven′ture·some (-sŭm), *adj.* **1.** Inclined to venture; venturous; daring. **2.** Risky; involving hazard; dangerous. — **Syn.** See ADVENTUROUS. — **ven′ture·some·ly**, *adv.* — **ven′ture·some·ness**, *n.*

Ven·tu′ri (vĕn·to͞o′rē; vän·to͞o′rē). A trade-mark applied to a meter, using a venturi tube, to measure the flow of liquids in pipes.

venturi tube, *or* **venturi**, *n.* [After G. B. *Venturi* (1746–1822), It. physicist, who noted the effect of constriction.] **1.** *Hydraulics.* A short tube, inserted in a pipeline, whose internal surface consists of two truncated cones connected at the small ends by a very short cylinder. As the velocity of flow of the liquid increases in the throat, the pressure decreases. The tube is used to measure the quantity of fluid flowing or, by joining a branch tube at the throat, to produce suction. **2.** *Aeronautics.* A short tube with flaring ends and constricted connecting portion, placed parallel to the air flow, with a branch tube entering at the throat, and used, by virtue of the diminished pressure in the throat, to furnish power, for example, to operate an injector or a gyroscopic instrument.

ven′tur·ous (vĕn′tūr·ŭs), *adj.* **1.** Courting danger; ready to meet risks; daring; bold. **2.** Involving danger or risk; hazardous; dangerous; risky. — **Syn.** See ADVENTUROUS. — **ven′tur·ous·ly**, *adv.* — **ven′tur·ous·ness**, *n.*

ven′ue (vĕn′ū), *n.* [OF., a coming, fr. *venir* to come, fr. L. *venire.*] *Law.* **a** The place or county in which the alleged events from which an action arises took place; also, the place from which the jury is taken, and where the trial is held. **b** The statement in a pleading, laying the place for the trial; also, sometimes, the clause in an affidavit indicating the place where it was sworn to.

ven′ule (-ūl), *n.* [L. *venula*, dim. fr. *vena* vein.] A small vein; a veinlet; specif., *Zool.*, one of the small branches of the veins of the wings in insects. — **ven′u·lar** (-ū·lẽr), *adj.*

ven′u·lose (-ū·lōs), **ven′u·lous** (-lŭs), *adj.* Full of venules.

Ve′nus (vē′nŭs), *n.* [L. *Venus, -eris.*] **1.** *Rom. Relig.* An ancient Italian goddess of bloom and beauty, protectress of gardens, who became identified with the Greek *Aphrodite*; also, a statue or picture of Venus; a very beautiful woman. **2.** A planet moving in an orbit between that of Mercury and that of the earth, at a mean distance from the sun of about 67,000,000 miles. Venus passes through phases similar to those of the moon, and at its brightest is far more brilliant than any fixed star. As morning star, it was called by the ancients *Lucifer*; as evening star, *Hesperus*. Its period of rotation is not exactly known. Symbol, ♀. See PLANET, *Table*. **3.** *Alchem.* The metal copper.

Ve′nus·berg (vē′nŭs·bûrg; *G.* vā′no͝os·bĕrk), *n.* [G., mountain of Venus.] A mountain between Eisenach and Gotha in Germany, in a cave of which, according to medieval legend, Venus held court and kept her victims prisoner by means of sensuous pleasures. The name was also given to various other mountains. See TANNHÄUSER.

Ve′nus of Mi′lo (mē′lō; *It.* -lō) *or* **Me′los** (mē′lŏs). A Hellenistic marble statue representing Venus undraped above the thighs and without arms, found on Melos in 1820, and now in the Louvre.

Ve′nus's–fly′trap′, *n.* An insectivorous plant (*Dionaea muscipula*) of the sundew family, found on the Carolinian coast, having the apex of its leaf modified into an insect trap.

Ve′nus's–hair′, *n.* A maidenhair fern (*Adiantum capillus-veneris*) having a slender black stipe and branches.

ver′a (vĕr′ȧ; văr′ȧ), *adj. & adv.* *Scot.* Very.

Lesson 65 OBSERVING HOW A WORD IS SYLLABIFIED

This is the second step in dictionary study. Always note carefully how the dictionary divides a word into syllables. Careful observation of the different syllables helps both to spell and to pronounce words correctly. Some words are syllabified differently in the phonetic spelling. For example, note the phonetic spelling of the word *vengeance* in the sample page from *Webster's New Collegiate Dictionary* which appears opposite. The syllabified entry *venge'ance* shows the proper place at which the word should be divided when broken at the end of a line. The phonetic syllables shown in *vĕn'jăns* are solely for purposes of pronunciation. Do not confuse the phonetic syllables with the correct syllables.

The words listed below are frequently misspelled or mispronounced because a syllable is overlooked or confused. Note carefully the different syllables; then pronounce each word distinctly. If you are not sure of the pronunciation of a word, look it up in your dictionary.

actually	The dog ac'tu al *l*y walked on two legs.
bachelor	The bach'e l*o*r said that he would never marry.
botany	The subject of bot'a ny is a science.
chocolate	Most persons like choc'o late candy.
diamond	The di'a m*o*nd is a precious stone.
granary	A gran'a ry is a storehouse for grain.
history	The his'to ry traced the rise of civilization.
hungry	The children were hu*n*'gry for dinner.
interrupt	The noise did not in'te*r* rupt' the speaker.
medieval	Me'di e'val history pertains to the Middle Ages.
omelet	The om'e let was made of eggs and milk.
ruffian	The ruf'*fi* an was a lawless fellow.
sentinel	The sen'ti nel kept watch all night.
slippery	The wet pavement was very slip'*p*er y.
temperature	The thermometer showed the exact tem'per a tur*e*.
ticklish	Climbing mountains is a ti*c*k'lish sport.

VISUAL DRILLS

a - t - - l - y	d - - mon -	inte - - up -	sent - n - -
b - ch - l - r	gr - n - ry	med - - v - -	slip - - - y
bot - - y	hist - - -	om - l - t	t - mp - r - t - r -
cho - - lat -	hun - - -	ruf - - - n	ti - k - is -

bab bitt (bab′it), *n.* alloy of tin, antimony, and copper, or a similar alloy, used in bearings to lessen friction. [Am.E; named after Isaac *Babbitt,* 1799-1862, American inventor]

Bab bitt (bab′it), *n.* a self-satisfied businessman who readily conforms to middle-class ideas of respectability and business success. [Am.E; named after the hero of the novel *Babbitt* by Sinclair Lewis]

Babbitt metal, babbitt.

bab bitt ry (bab′it ri), *n.* conformity to middle-class ideas of respectability and business success.

bab ble (bab′əl), *v.,* **-bled, -bling,** *n.* —*v.* **1.** make indistinct sounds like a baby. **2.** talk or speak foolishly. **3.** talk too much; tell secrets. **4.** reveal foolishly: *babble a secret.* **5.** murmur. —*n.* **1.** talk that cannot be understood. **2.** foolish talk. **3.** murmur: *the babble of the brook.* [ME *babel*; imitative] —**bab′bler,** *n.*

babe (bāb), *n.* **1.** baby. **2.** an innocent or inexperienced person; person who is like a child.

Ba bel (bā′bəl or bab′əl), *n.* **1.** Babylon. **2. Tower of Babel,** in the Bible, a high tower built after the Flood to reach heaven. God punished its builders by changing their language into several new and different languages. When they could not understand one another, they had to leave the tower unfinished. Gen. 11:1-9. **3.** Also, **babel. a.** confusion of many different sounds; noise. **b.** place of noise and confusion. [< Hebrew]

Bab el Man deb (bäb′el män′deb or bab′el man′deb), strait that connects the Red Sea and the Indian Ocean. 20 mi. wide.

ba bies'-breath (bā′biz breth′), *n.* a tall plant bearing numerous small, fragrant, white or pink flowers.

bab i ru sa, bab i rous sa, or **bab i rus sa** (bab′ə-rü′sə or bä′bə rü′sə), *n.* a wild hog found in the East Indies. The boar has long, curved tusks. [< Malay *bābi* hog + *rūsa* deer]

ba boo (bä′bü), *n., pl.* **-boos.** in India: **a.** a Hindu title meaning "sir," "Mr.," "gentleman." **b.** native with a smattering of English education. **c.** a native clerk who writes English. [< Hindu. *babu*]

ba boon (ba bün′), *n.* any of various large, fierce monkeys of Arabia and Africa, with a doglike face and a short tail. [< OF *babouin* stupid person]

Baboon (body 2 ft. high, 2 ft. long; tail 18 in.)

ba bu (bä′bü), *n., pl.* **-bus.** baboo.

ba by (bā′bi), *n., pl.* **-bies,** *adj., v.,* **-bied, -by ing.** —*n.* **1.** a very young child. **2.** the youngest of a family or group. **3.** person who acts like a baby; childish person. **4.** *Slang.* term of praise or approval applied to a person or thing. —*adj.* **1.** of or for a baby. **2.** young. **3.** small for its kind; small. **4.** childish. —*v.* treat as a baby; pamper. [ME *babi*] —**ba′by like′,** *adj.*

baby grand, a small grand piano.

ba by hood (bā′bi hu̇d), *n.* **1.** condition or time of being a baby. **2.** babies as a group.

ba by ish (bā′bi ish), *adj.* like a baby; childish; silly. —**ba′by ish ly,** *adv.* —**ba′by ish ness,** *n.*

Bab y lon (bab′ə lən or bab′ə lon), *n.* **1.** capital of ancient Babylonia, on the Euphrates River. Later it was also the capital of the ancient Chaldean empire. Babylon was noted for its wealth, power, magnificence, and wickedness. **2.** any great, rich, or wicked city.

Bab y lo ni a (bab′ə lō′ni ə), *n.* an ancient empire in SW Asia, from 2800 to 1000 B.C.

Bab y lo ni an (bab′ə-lō′ni ən), *adj.* of or having to do with Babylon or Babylonia. —*n.* **1.** inhabitant of Babylonia. **2.** language of Babylonia.

ba by-sit (bā′bi sit′), *v.,* **-sat, -sit ting.** *Informal.* take care of a child during the temporary absence of its parents. —**baby sitter.**

bac ca lau re ate (bak′ə lô′ri it), *n.* **1.** degree of bachelor given by a college or university. **2.** sermon delivered to a graduating class at commencement. [< Med.L *baccalaureatus* < *baccalaureus* bachelor, var. of *baccalarius* because of a supposed derivation from L *bacca* berry + *laurus* laurel]

bac ca rat or **bac ca ra** (bak′ə rä′ or bak′ə rä), *n.* kind of card game played for money. [< F]

Bac chae (bak′ē), *n.pl.* **1.** women companions or worshipers of Bacchus. **2.** priestesses of Bacchus.

bac cha nal (bak′ə nəl or bak′ə nal), *adj.* having to do with Bacchus or his worship. —*n.* **1.** worshiper of Bacchus. **2.** a drunken reveler. **3.** a wild, noisy party; drunken revelry; orgy. **4. Bacchanals,** *pl.,* the Bacchanalia. [< L *bacchanalis* < *Bacchus* god of wine < Gk. *Bakchos*]

Bac cha na li a (bak′ə nā′li ə or bak′ə nāl′yə), *n.pl.* **1.** a wild, noisy Roman festival in honor of Bacchus. **2. bacchanalia,** a wild, noisy party; drunken revelry; orgy.

bac cha na li an (bak′ə nā′li ən or bak′ə nāl′yən), *adj.* **1.** having to do with the Bacchanalia. **2.** drunken and riotous. —*n.* a drunken reveler.

bac chant (bak′ənt), *n., pl.* **bac chants, bac chan tes** (bə kan′tēz). **1.** priest or worshiper of Bacchus. **2.** a drunken reveler. [< L *bacchans, -antis,* ppr. of *bacchari* celebrate the festival of Bacchus]

bac chan te (bə kan′ti, bə kant′, or bak′ənt), *n.* priestess or woman worshiper of Bacchus. [< F]

Bac chic (bak′ik), *adj.* **1.** of Bacchus or his worship. **2.** Also, **bacchic.** drunken; riotous.

Bac chus (bak′əs), *n.* Roman and Greek god of wine. The Greeks also called him Dionysus. [< L < Gk. *Bakchos*]

Bach (bäH), *n.* **Johann Sebastian,** 1685-1750, German composer of music and organist.

bach e lor (bach′ə lər or bach′lər), *n.* **1.** man who has not married. **2.** person who has the first degree of a college or university. Students who complete the regular undergraduate course of four years are usually given the degree of bachelor. **3.** a young knight who served under the banner of another. [< OF *bacheler* < Med.L *baccalarius,* apparently, small landowner]

bach e lor-at-arms (bach′ə lər ət ärmz′ or bach′lər-ət ärmz′), *n., pl.* **bach e lors-at-arms.** bachelor (def. 3).

bach e lor hood (bach′ə lər hu̇d′ or bach′lər hu̇d), *n.* condition of being a bachelor.

bach e lor's-but ton (bach′ə lərz but′ən or bach′lərz-but′ən), *n.* **1.** plant with a flower shaped somewhat like a button; cornflower. **2.** the flower. **3.** any similar flower.

ba cil lar (bə sil′ər or bas′ə lər), *adj.* **1.** of or like a bacillus. **2.** characterized by bacilli. **3.** rod-shaped.

ba cil li (bə sil′ī), *n.* pl. of **bacillus.**

ba cil lus (bə sil′əs), *n., pl.* **-cil li. 1.** any of the rod-shaped bacteria. **2.** any of the bacteria. [< LL *bacillus,* dim. of *baculus* rod]

back[1] (bak), *n.* **1.** part of a person's body opposite to his face or to the front part of his body. **2.** the upper part of an animal's body from the neck to the end of the backbone. **3.** the backbone. **4.** rear, upper, or farther part: *the back of the head, the back of the hand, the back of a hill, the back of the room.* **5.** rear part of an object serving to support or protect: *the back of a chair, the back of a book.* **6.** player whose position is behind the front line in football and certain other games.

behind one's back, without one's knowing it; in one's absence; secretly.

get one's back up, a. make one angry. **b.** become angry. **c.** be stubborn.

on one's back, a. helpless. **b.** sick.

put one's back up, a. make one angry. **b.** be stubborn.

turn one's back on, abandon; forsake.

with one's back to the wall, hard pressed; unable to escape without fighting.

—*v.* **1.** support; help: *Many of his friends backed his plan.* **2.** move backward: *He backed away from the gun.* **3.** cause to move backward: *He backed his car slowly.* **4.** endorse: *back a check.* **5.** bet on: *back a baseball team in the World Series.* **6.** make or be a back for: *Our little farm was backed by woods.*

back and fill, a. trim sails so as to keep a boat in a channel and floating with the current. **b.** *U.S. Informal.* be undecided; keep changing one's mind.

back down, give up an attempt or claim; withdraw.

---

hat, āge, cãre, fär; let, ēqual, tėrm; it, īce; hot, ōpen, ôrder; oil, out; cup, pu̇t, rüle, ūse; ch, child; ng, long; th, thin; TH, then; zh, measure; ə represents *a* in about, *e* in taken, *i* in pencil, *o* in lemon, *u* in circus.

Lesson 66 OBSERVING HOW A WORD IS ACCENTED

This is the third step in dictionary study. When you look at words in the dictionary, be sure to note which syllables are accented. Look for the accent marks in the phonetic spellings. Some words have two syllables accented. See, for example, the word *Babylonia* on the sample page from the *Thorndike-Barnhart High School Dictionary*. The primary (heavy) accent is shown by a heavy mark (ʹ), while the secondary (light) accent is shown by a light mark (ˊ). Some dictionaries use one mark (ʹ) for the primary accent and two marks (ʺ) for the secondary accent.

The accent in certain words changes the pronunciation and meaning. For example, *con duct*ʹ (a verb) means *to guide; con*ʹ*duct* (a noun) means *behavior.* Note the change of meaning in the following words according to the change in accent.

abstract	Abʹstract ideas are difficult to understand. The doctor failed to ab stractʹ the sliver.
accent	The stranger spoke with a foreign acʹ*c*ent. Be sure to ac *c*entʹ the proper syllable.
convict	The conʹvict was imprisoned for life. The jury voted to con victʹ the man.
entrance	There was but one enʹtran*c*e to the room. The music seemed to en tran*c*eʹ the listeners.
essay	James wrote a short but very good esʹ*say*. The boy prepared to e*s* sa*y*ʹ his strength.
increase	Each year brought an inʹcre*ase* in population. The newspaper tried to in cre*ase*ʹ its circulation.
insult	His hard words added inʹsult to injury. The remark seemed to in sultʹ the visitor.
present	John was happy over his birthday pre*s*ʹent. Father will pre *s*entʹ his gift later.
progress	They made slow progʹre*ss* climbing the hill. The truck began to pro gre*ss*ʹ more rapidly.
transfer	Give me a transʹf*e*r to the Chicago bus. Please trans f*e*rʹ my trunk to the depot.

VISUAL DRILLS

ab - tr - c -	conv - - t	e - s - y	in - ul -	pr - gr - s -
a - - ent	- ntr - n - -	- n - re - se	pr - s - nt	tran - f - -

Lesson 67 — OBSERVING LETTERS THAT ARE PRONOUNCED DIFFERENTLY

This is the fourth step in dictionary study. Some letters, particularly in words of foreign derivation, are pronounced differently than they are in most English words. The *Gi* in *Gila monster,* for example, is pronounced *he.* When you discover a word of this type, focus your attention sharply upon the peculiar letters and at the same time pronounce the word distinctly several times.

Practice pronouncing the words listed below while you look at them sharply. If you are uncertain concerning the correct pronunciation of any of the words, consult your dictionary. By mastering this lesson, you can make a big advance in both spelling and speech.

antique	The odd-looking chair was an an *tique*′.
asphalt	The boy skated on the as′*ph*alt pavement.
author	Dickens was the *au*′thor of many books.
beggar	The beg′*ga*r asked everyone for money.
buffet	Mother keeps our best china in a b*uf* fe*t*′.
café	We went to the *ca* fe′ for a cup of coffee.
cello	The *c*el′*lo* looks like a large violin.
collar	Robert's col′*la*r was too large for his neck.
comptroller	The co*mp* trol′*l*er handled all expenditures.
crepe	The coffin was covered with a thin *crepe* cloth.
debris	The storm left piles of de br*is*′ everywhere.
editor	Captain Rogers was also ed i tor′ of a newspaper.
etiquette	A gentleman observes the rules of et′i *quette.*
mirage	The m*i* rage′ of water on the desert seemed real.
reign	Queen Victoria's r*ei*gn lasted sixty-four years.
rumor	There was no truth in the widespread r*u*′ mor.
sphere	A true *sph*ere is perfectly round.
suede	The *sue*de cloth looked like leather.
sword	The s*w*ord had an unusually long blade.
valise	Father packed his va l*ise*′ for a short trip.

VISUAL DRILLS

ant - q - -	caf -	d - br - -	rum - -
as - hal -	c - l - o	ed - t - -	s - - er -
a - th - r	col - - r	et - q - - t - -	s - ord
beg - - r	com - - rol - - r	m - ra - -	su - d -
buf - e -	cr - p -	r - - gn	val - - -

Lesson 68 OBSERVING SILENT LETTERS

This is the fifth step in dictionary study. It would be much easier to spell words correctly if so many of them did not contain silent letters. The phonetic spellings given in the dictionary omit all silent letters, so you must be certain to note any that may be in the original entries. Always look at the true spelling when you practice pronouncing a word. In this way you can avoid associating the wrong image with the correct pronunciation.

Note carefully the silent letters in the words listed below. If you are uncertain of the correct pronunciation of any of the words, consult your dictionary.

achieve	The lawyer failed to a ch*i*ev*e*' his purpose.
commence	Charley should co*m* men*ce*' his work earlier.
coupon	His co*u*'pon entitled him to another ride.
depot	Get your train ticket at the city de'po*t*.
entries	The dictionary contained many new en'tri*es*.
grief	His sudden death caused widespread gr*i*ef.
handkerchief	Mary dropped her silk han*d*'ker ch*i*ef.
indict	There was no evidence to in di*c*t' the suspect.
irrigate	The canal brought water to ir'*r*i gat*e* the farm.
ledger	The clerk posted the charge in the le*d*g'er.
offense	His act was an o*f* fens*e*' against the law.
plague	Many men died as the plag*ue* spread rapidly.
pneumonia	Both lungs were inflamed with *p*n*e*u mo'ni a.
prairie	The grass on the pra*i*'ri*e* caught on fire.
scissors	The new s*c*is'*s*ors have sharp blades.
thief	A th*i*ef stole our garden hose last night.
tongue	The boy stuck his tong*ue* out of his mouth.
vengeance	We swore veng*e*'an*ce* against the cruel Indians.
wrench	The sudden *w*rench broke off the handle.
yacht	They sailed away in the racing ya*ch*t.

VISUAL DRILLS

ach - - v -	gr - - f	of - en - -	th - - f
com - en - -	han - - erch - - -	plag - -	t - ng - -
c - - p - n	ind - - t	- n - umon - a	ven - e - n - e
d - p - t	ir - ig - t -	pr - - r - -	- ren - -
entr - - s	le - - er	s - i - s - rs	ya - - t

Lesson 69 STRENGTHENING THE VISUAL IMAGE

Strengthening the visual image of a word is the final step in studying the dictionary for the purpose of learning to spell and pronounce words correctly. It will be helpful at this point to think of all six steps:

1. Make sure that you have the right word.
2. Observe how the word is syllabified.
3. Observe how the word is accented.
4. Observe letters pronounced differently than usual.
5. Observe letters not pronounced.
6. Strengthen the visual image of the true spelling.

All through this book, emphasis has been placed upon the importance of retaining correct visual images of spelling words. There is a real danger that the syllabified and phonetic spellings in the dictionary may blur rather than strengthen the correct visual image of a word. For this reason, the student should keep the correct image clearly in mind at all times during the six steps of his dictionary study.

Whenever you study a difficult word, give special emphasis to the correct visual image. First, examine the word carefully as directed in the various steps for dictionary study. Then as you look away, strengthen the correct visual image by writing, printing, or typing the word several times.

Find the words in your dictionary which are listed below. Study each word by the six-step method. Keep this practice up whenever you consult your dictionary. Before long, the steps will become automatic. You will have mastered an exceedingly useful method of word study.

boulder	A heavy bo*u*l′der rolled down the mountain.
honorable	The *h*on′*o*r a bl*e* thing to do is to apologize.
dangerous	Automobile racing is a dan′*g*er *o*us occupation.
readily	The singers responded re*a*d′i ly to the request.
drowned	The swimmer dro*w*n*e*d before aid could reach him.
weighed	Frank w*eigh*e*d himself on the new scales.

VISUAL DRILLS

bo - ld - -	dan - er - - s	dr - - n - d
- on - r - ble	r - - d - ly	w - - g - ed

Lesson 70 PRONOUNCING WORDS CORRECTLY

Although the chief emphasis of this book is on correct spelling, students should by no means overlook the contribution that the proper study of spelling makes to correct speech. The first step in clear speech is to utter each word distinctly. Stop running words together. For example, do not say: "Canchew kumere jussa secun?" for "Can't you come here just a second?" In the same manner each syllable of a word should be spoken clearly and distinctly.

Your dictionary is an open road to improved speech. By faithful repetition you can establish the habit of clear and effective speech. Whenever you look up a word, take time to pronounce it slowly, distinctly, and correctly. It is essential that you *know* the sounds indicated by the diacritical marks used in the phonetic spellings in your dictionary.

The Pronunciation Key given below is similar to, although somewhat simpler than, the key found in most dictionaries. It is presented here so that you can use it for quick reference in the next several lessons.

PRONUNCIATION KEY

ā as in āle	(long *a*)	ō as in gō	(long *o*)
ā̇ as in vā̇cation	(modified long *a*)	ō̇ as in prō̇pose	(modified long *o*)
â as in câre	(circumflex *a*)	ŏ as in ŏdd	(short *o*)
ă as in ăt	(short *a*)	ŏ̂ as in clŏ̂th	(medial *o*)
ä as in päl‌m	(Italian *a*)	ô as in ôrb	(circumflex *o*)
ȧ as in ȧsk	(short Italian *a*)	o͞o as in no͞on	(long double *o*)
ē as in ēve	(long *e*)	o͝o as in fo͝ot	(short double *o*)
ē̇ as in dē̇pend	(modified long *e*)	ū as in ūnion	(long *u*)
ĕ as in gĕt	(short *e*)	ū̇ as in ū̇nite	(modified long *u*)
ẽ as in watẽr	(tilde *e*)	ŭ as in ŭnder	(short *u*)
ī as in īce	(long *i*)	û as in bûrn	(circumflex *u*)
ĭ as in hĭt	(short *i*)	th as in thin	(breathed *th*)
		th as in *th*ough	(voiced *th*)

The special symbol ə is used in some dictionaries to indicate obscure vowel sounds, such as the *a* in *alone.* In learning to spell, it is better to give these vowels a short vowel sound, such as the *i* in *easĭly,* the *o* in *gallŏp,* or the *u* in *circŭs.*

(Continued on the next page)

To get the most out of the exercises which follow, first count the syllables and note which ones are accented. Next, check the diacritical marks, referring to the Pronunciation Key on page 101 when uncertain as to the exact sounds. Then read the NOTE which accompanies each drill and speak the word distinctly several times. Finally, read aloud the sentence indicating the correct use of the word.

In the exercises on this page, watch particularly for the pronunciation of the letter *i* and the proper syllable to accent.

allies (ă līz′) The British were our *allies.*
NOTE: Accent the last syllable. Pronounce it *līz,* not *lēz.*

conspiracy (kŏn spĭr′ȧ sĭ) The *conspiracy* was opposed to the Union.
NOTE: Do not say *kŏn spīr′a see.* Both *i*'s are short.

deficit (dĕf′ĭ sĭt) His accounts showed a *deficit.*
NOTE: Accent the first syllable. Do not say *di fĭs′et.*

experiment (ĕks pĕr′ĭ mĕnt) The professor performed the *experiment.*
NOTE: Do not say *ek spear′mint.* Sound all four syllables.

genuine (jĕn′ů ĭn) It was a *genuine* diamond.
NOTE: The last syllable is *in,* not *wine.*

heroine (hĕr′ō ĭn) The *heroine* in the story was pretty.
NOTE: Do not say *heer o een′.* Accent the first syllable.

horizon (hō rī′zn) The sun sank below the *horizon.*
NOTE: Do not say *hor′ĭ zon* or *hor ĭ zon′.* Accent the *ri.*

Italian (ĭ tăl′yȧn) Caruso was an *Italian* singer.
NOTE: Do not say *eyetalian;* say *ĭ tăl′yan.*

italics (ĭ tăl′ĭks) Words may be printed in *italics* for emphasis.
NOTE: The first syllable is *ĭ* in *Italy, Italian, italics,* and *italicize.*

long-lived (lŏng′līvd′) He came from a *long-lived* family.
NOTE: Sound the medial *o* and the long *i.* Observe that both syllables are accented.

pupils (pū′pĭls) Five *pupils* were late to school.
NOTE: Pronounce the last syllable *pills,* not *pulls.*

rinse (rĭns) Be sure to *rinse* the clothes.
NOTE: Do not say *wrench* or *rense,* but *rinse.*

suite (swēt) Father rented a *suite* of four rooms.
NOTE: Pronounce *suit* like *fruit,* but *suite* like *sweet.*

VISUAL DRILLS

al - i - s   - en - in -   - tal - - n   p - p - - s
- onsp - r - - y   her - - n -   - tali - s   r - n - -
e - per - m - nt   hor - z - n   long-l - - - d   s - - t -

Lesson 71 PRONOUNCING THE *O* SOUNDS

If you wish to speak correctly, you must distinguish between the short *o* (ŏ), the circumflex *o* (ô), and the medial *o* (ŏ̂). (See the Pronunciation Key on page 101.) The short *o* is like the *a* sound in *swan, what,* and *squander.* Most people pronounce the *o* correctly in *tŏp, spŏt,* and *rŏt;* but for *fŏg, frŏm, ŏf,* and *ŏrange,* many say *fawg, frum, uv,* and *ōrange.*

The circumflex *o* is like the *o* sound in *lôrd, fôrk,* and *ôrder.* The medial *o* sound, as in *lŏ̂ss, sŏ̂ft,* and *cŏ̂ffee,* is in between the short *o* and the circumflex *o.* Note the three *o* sounds in the following sentence: He was sŏrry fôr the poor dŏ̂g. Some words pronounced correctly with the short *o* change their meaning if given the circumflex *o* sound. For example, *not* becomes *naught* when the ŏ is pronounced with the ô sound. In the same manner *nod* becomes *gnawed, stock* becomes *stalk, pod* becomes *pawed, odd* becomes *awed, clod* becomes *clawed,* and *tot* becomes *taught.*

Watch the *o* sounds in the following exercises:

across (ă krôs′) George swam *across* the river.
NOTE: Sound the circumflex *o.* Do not say *a krôst.*

coyote (kī ōt′ or kī ō′tē) The dogs chased the *coyote.*
NOTE: The first *o* is silent; the second *o* is long.

forehead (fŏr′ĕd) The hair grew down on his *forehead.*
NOTE: Say the *o* as in *hŏt,* not as in *fôr* or *fōre.* Instead of *head,* say *ed.*

Florida (Flŏr′ĭ dȧ) *Florida* is a southern state.
NOTE: Do not say *Flowrida* or *Flawrida.* Sound the *o* as in *blŏck.*

foreign (fŏr′ĭn) The man came from a *foreign* country.
NOTE: Sound the *o* as in *hŏt.* Do not say *fōr′in.*

horrible (hŏr′ĭ bl) The explosion created a *horrible* scene.
NOTE: This is the same short *o* as in *hŏt, fŏrehead,* and *Flŏrida.*

iron (ī′ẽrn) Steel is made from *iron* and carbon.
NOTE: It seems queer, but the *ron* in *iron* is pronounced *ern.*

recognized (rĕk′ŏg nīzd) Mother *recognized* us immediately.
NOTE: Do not say *rĕk′a nīze.* Sound the *og* as in *hog.*

was (wŏz) The hour *was* too late.
NOTE: To say *wŭz* or *wawz* is a speech barbarism.

VISUAL DRILLS

a - ros -	for - - ead	for - - g -	ir - n
co - - te	Fl - r - da	h - r - - ble	re - o - ni - ed

Lesson 72 PRONOUNCING LETTERS AND SYLLABLES

If you study the dictionary as directed, you will be able to avoid speech errors which are frequently made by careless speakers. Sound all of the letters and syllables indicated in the phonetic spelling. Avoid adding letters or syllables which do not appear in the phonetic spelling. The words listed below are frequently mispronounced.

arctic (ärk′tĭc) It is very cold in the *arctic* region.
NOTE: Do not say *artic.* Sound the *k* after the *r.*

attacked (ȧ tăct′) His speech *attacked* the new senator.
NOTE: Two syllables only. Do not say *at tac ted.*

deteriorate (dē tēr′ĭ ō rāt) The perfume seemed to *deteriorate.*
NOTE: Sound all five syllables. Do not say *de ter′i at.*

diphtheria (dĭf thēr′ĭ ȧ) The patient was ill with *diphtheria.*
NOTE: The first syllable is *dif,* not *dip.* Sound the long *e* in *ther.*

evening (ēv′nĭng) The church bells rang Tuesday *evening.*
NOTE: Do not say *ev′en ing.* The syllables are *eve* and *ning.*

library (lī′brĕr ĭ) The *library* loaned many of its books.
NOTE: Do not say *libaree.* Sound the two *r*'s, the short *e,* and the short *i* in *brĕrĭ.*

overalls (ō′vẽr ôlz) The workmen wore heavy *overalls.*
NOTE: Do not say *holls* for *olz.* There is no *h* in *overalls.*

parliament (pär′lĭ mĕnt) A *parliament* deals with legislation.
NOTE: Omit the second *a* sound in *parliament.* Sound the short *i.*

rind (rīnd) The flavor came from lemon *rind.*
NOTE: Say *rind,* not *rine.* Sound the long *i* and the *d.*

secretary (sĕk′rē tĕr′ĭ) His *secretary* answered the letters.
NOTE: The chief accent is on the first syllable. Do not say *sek′re tri* or *sek a tar′ee.*

strictly (strĭkt′ly) The information is *strictly* confidential.
NOTE: Sound the *t* in such words as *strictly, compactly, exactly.*

united (ū nīt′ĕd) *United* we stand; divided we fall.
NOTE: Do not say *yoo ni′ted.* Pronounce the *u* as in *humane.*

VISUAL DRILLS

ar - ti -	di - - th - r - -	over - - ls	se - r - t - ry
at - ac - - -	ev - - in -	par - - - m - nt	stri - - ly
det - r - - r - t -	lib - - r -	rin -	- nit - d

Lesson 73 WATCHING THE ACCENT

Your attention was called in Lesson 66 to the importance of noticing how words are accented. The English language is liberally sprinkled with words which serve as nouns when accented on the first syllable and as verbs when accented on the second syllable. Besides those listed in Lesson 66, such words include:

confine	contrast	imprint	project	refuse
conflict	convert	insert	protest	subject
contest	digest	produce	record	transport

No rules govern the accents given to most words. To avoid embarrassing mistakes, always check the accents given in your dictionary. Many persons give the wrong accent to the words listed in the following exercises.

admirable (ăd′mĭ rȧ bl) His conduct was *admirable.*
NOTE: Accent the first syllable. The *i* in *mi* is short.

applicable (ăp′lĭ kȧ bl) The description is not *applicable.*
NOTE: Do not say *a plĭk′a bŭl.* Sound the *ca* syllable.

bronchial (brŏng′kĭ ăl) The *bronchial* tubes lead to the lungs.
NOTE: Do not say *bronichal.* Be sure to sound the *g.*

contrary (kŏn′trĕr ĭ) They parked *contrary* to the sign.
NOTE: Do not say *kŏn trâr′ē.* Accent the first syllable.

discharge (dĭs chärj′) The soldier received an honorable *discharge.*
NOTE: Both noun and verb accent the last syllable.

exquisite (ĕks′kwĭ zĭt) Your friend has *exquisite* taste.
NOTE: Accent the first syllable. Avoid accenting *skwĭz.*

hospitable (hŏs′pĭ tȧ bl) Southerners are exceptionally *hospitable.*
NOTE: Accent the first syllable. Sound the *o* as in *hŏt.*

interested (ĭn′tẽr ĕs tĕd) Mrs. Jones is *interested* in painting.
NOTE: Accent the first syllable only. Do not say *in tres′ted.*

mischievous (mĭs′chĭ vŭs) Bobby liked *mischievous* pranks.
NOTE: There are only three syllables. Do not say *mĭs chēv′vĭ ŭs.*

museum (mû zē′ŭm) The *museum* was full of curious birds.
NOTE: Do not say *mū′zē ŭm.* Accent the second syllable.

theater (thē′ȧ tẽr) There is a new show at the *theater.*
NOTE: Say *thē′a ter,* not *thē ā′ter.* Sound the *th* as in *thin.*

VISUAL DRILLS

adm - r - b - -	- ont - - - y	h - spit - b - -	mu - e - m
ap - li - ab - -	d - schar - -	int - r - sted	th - - t - -
br - n - - i - l	e - - u - s - t -	mi - ch - - v - - s	

Lesson 74 PRONOUNCING FOREIGN WORDS

Many derived words retain part or all of their foreign pronunciation. The words selected for study on this page are among the foreign words most commonly misspelled, mispronounced, or misused. Remember that in French words the diacritical marks are a regular part of the spelling.

adobe (ȧ dō′bĕ), sun-dried brick; structure made therefrom.
adios (ä′dyōs′), good-by among Spanish-speaking peoples.
ad infinitum (ăd ĭn′fĭn ī′tŭm), to infinity; endlessly.
attaché (ăt′ȧ shā′), member of a staff or an embassy.
au revoir (ō′ rē vwär′), good-by till we meet again.
bona fide (bō′nȧ fī′dē), in good faith; genuine.
chef (shĕf), chief cook; skillful male cook.
clique (klēk), a social set; an exclusive group.
coiffure (kwä fūr′), headdress; the way one's hair is arranged.
connoisseur (kŏn′ĭ sûr′), one who knows a subject thoroughly.
debris (dĕ brē′), fragments; rubbish; remains; ruins.
éclair (ā′klâr′), small, coated cake with a cream filling.
élite (ā′lēt′), people considered socially superior; choice or select part.
ennui (än′wē), extreme boredom; weariness; dissatisfaction.
ensemble (än sŏm′bl), all together; three-piece woman's costume.
entree (än′trā), entrance to society; dish between chief courses.
esprit de corps (ĕs′prē′ dē kôr′), animated group spirit.
faux pas (fō′ pä′), a social blunder; a false step.
hacienda (hä′sĭ ĕn′dä), Spanish American large estate; ranch.
liaison (lē ā zŏn′), a relationship; co-operation; improper intimacy.
lingerie (lăn′zh rē′), linen goods; undergarments worn by women.
menu (mĕn′ū), bill of fare; list of dishes served.
penchant (pän′shän′), strong liking for person or subject.
portiere (pōr tyâr′), a door entrance or drapery.
premiere (prē myâr′), first or chief; first performance.
prima facie (prī′mȧ fā′shĭ ē), at first sight; highly probable.
protégé (prō′tĕ zhā′), one under care of another.
résumé (rā′zū mā′), a summary; condensed outline.
sauté (sō tā′), fried; for example, tomatoes sauté.
sine die (sī′nḗ dī′ē), without appointing a day for reassembling.
table d'hote (tȧ′blē dōt′), complete meal served at a fixed price.
tamale (tȧ mä′lĕ), Mexican dish of chopped meat and corn meal.

Lesson 75 USE OF THE HYPHEN TO SEPARATE SYLLABLES

Many spelling mistakes are made, particularly by typists, in the use of hyphens. The hyphen is used in two distinct ways: (1) to separate syllables and (2) to separate words. This lesson is concerned with the use of the hyphen to separate syllables.

Use of the Hyphen To Separate Syllables in the Dictionary

If your dictionary is the kind that makes use of hyphens to separate the different syllables in the entry words, you must note what substitute symbol is used to indicate a *true* hyphen. Dictionaries of this type usually use a long hyphen (–) or a double hyphen (=). For example, the compound word *go-between* will probably be entered either as *go–be-tween* or as *go=be-tween.*

Look up the following words in your dictionary to see (1) how the syllables are separated and (2) how the hyphen is printed in the compound words.

ammunition	**four-footed**	**quality**
cafeteria	**fresh-water**	**wholesale**
employee	**snowbound**	**muscle**

Use of the Hyphen at the Ends of Lines

A hyphen is always used to separate syllables when a word is broken at the end of a line. Whenever possible, a line should be ended with a complete word. When this is not possible, the last word in the line should be broken at the end of a syllable and a hyphen placed after that syllable. When it is necessary to divide a word, observe the following rules:

1. Never divide a word of one syllable; for example, *rhythm.*
2. Never divide a four-letter word of two syllables; for example, *diet.*
3. Never separate a one-letter syllable at the beginning or end of a word; for example, *a-bout, ever-y.*
4. In a word with three or more syllables, any one-letter syllable should be written on the first line; for example, *privi-lege.*
5. Divide two vowels which are pronounced separately; for example, *situ-ation.*
6. Separate compound words at the hyphen; for example, *blue-eyed.*

VISUAL DRILLS

a - m - n - t - - n	f - - r-f - - ted	- u - l - ty
ca - - ter - -	fr - - h-w - t - -	- hol - sal -
- mpl - y - -	sno - bo - nd	mu - - le

Lesson 76 USE OF THE HYPHEN IN COMPOUND WORDS

Words used together frequently tend in the course of time to become hyphenated and finally to appear as one word; for example, *to day, to-day,* and *today.* Dictionaries vary considerably in the number of compound words included.

1. Consult your dictionary to find out the present practice in spelling the following words:

inasmuch	**in so far**	**to-day**
thereafter	**thereby**	**good-by**
postmark	**post office**	**co-operate**
half-dollar	**one-half per cent**	**percentage**
remark	**re-mark**	**eighty-eight**

2. Study the spelling and composition of the words listed below. Note how each word is built up from two or more words. Consult your dictionary if you are uncertain about the meaning or derivation of any of the words. It is possible that some of the words may not be in your dictionary.

afternoon	**doubtless**	**handkerchief**	**northeast**
aircraft	**dreadful**	**hardware**	**oversight**
bankrupt	**elsewhere**	**hitherto**	**self-control**
battlefield	**everywhere**	**in spite of**	**some one**
chairman	**first-class**	**midnight**	**vice-president**
cheerful	**gentlemen**	**nevertheless**	**wireless**

50-horse power **ten-year-old boy** **pro-British**

There are a number of rules which govern the use of hyphens in connection with compound words, but unless you are very good at remembering rules, it is better in the long run to learn each word by itself. The use of the hyphen, moreover, is to some extent a matter of personal taste. The most helpful rules follow:

1. A hyphen is used in all compound numerals from twenty-one to ninety-nine.
2. When two or more words are used as one adjective *before* a noun, the words are connected with hyphens. For example, a *public-spirited* man.
3. When a verb is made up of two or more words, the words are connected with hyphens. For example, to *blue-pencil* the mistakes.

Lesson 77 THE APOSTROPHE

Frequent mistakes in spelling are caused by the incorrect use of the apostrophe ('). The apostrophe has three chief uses:

1. An apostrophe is inserted in contractions to take the place of one or more omitted letters. For example, John *can't* go; *tomorrow's* too late.
2. An apostrophe is inserted to indicate the plurals of figures, letters, and other symbols. For example, Dot your *i*'s; your 2's look like *Q*'s.
3. An apostrophe is added to indicate possession. (See Lesson 78.)

The materials below are planned to aid you in the correct spelling of contractions and the plurals of symbols.

1. Write the words for which the following contractions stand:

who's	**today's**	**they're**
'twould	**I've**	**we're**
won't	**o'clock**	**don't**
what's	**isn't**	**'twere**

2. Write the contractions of the following words:

I shall	**it is**	**they have**
I have	**we are**	**have not**
she is	**you will**	**did not**
what is	**I would**	**over**

3. Do not use an apostrophe with the following pronouns: *its, hers, his, ours, theirs, yours.* Copy the eight sentences below. Note the difference in the meanings of *their* and *they're; it's* and *its; you're* and *your.*

It's their business, not ours.
They're all here for a vacation.
I can't go because it's raining.
What's its color when it's wet?
You're wrong about it this time.
'Tis hers, not yours or mine.
There are three 5's in 555.
Type a line of x's for practice.

NOTE FOR TYPISTS: The apostrophe ('), the single quotation mark (') and the accent mark (′) are shown by the same symbol (') on the typewriter.

Lesson 78 WORDS THAT SHOW POSSESSION

The apostrophe (') is also used to show possession or ownership. Dictionaries do not usually show the possessive forms of nouns. To spell possessive words correctly, you will have to depend upon general rules and your familiarity with individual words. The following general rules and exercises will be of most help.

1. If a noun, singular or plural, does not end in an *s*, add an apostrophe followed by an *s*. For example, the *girl's* coat, the *world's* champion, the *women's* club. Study the spelling of the following words:

gentlemen's The law was merely a gen'tle men's agreement.
box's The box's top and bottom were broken in.
advertisement's The ad ver'tise ment's language was appealing.
attorney's We paid the at tor'ney's fees at once.

2. If a word ends in a single *s*, add an apostrophe. For example, the *girls'* glee club, *James'* troubles, the *Germans'* prisoners. Study the spelling of the following words:

days' The firm owed the laborer three days' wages.
minutes' The ten min'utes' delay lost the battle.
ladies' Not one lady's complaint, but all la'dies' complaint.

3. Most words ending in *ss* add an apostrophe and an additional *s*. For example, the *princess's* jewels, the *ass's* brays. Exception: for *clearness'* sake. Study the spelling and note the pronunciation of the following words:

witness's The wit'ness's testimony was not trustworthy.
mistress's She always obeyed her mis'tress's command.
boss's It was the boss's duty to keep order.

4. When a phrase is put into the possessive case, the apostrophe or *'s* is added to the last word. For example, his *son-in-law's* manners. Study the spelling of the following words:

half an hour's There was half an hour's delay.
Marshall and Cooper's Mar'shall and Coop'er's store was open.
somebody else's It is usually some'bod y else's fault.

VISUAL DRILLS

Cover the endings of the possessive words. Then write them from memory.

Lesson 79 CAPITAL LETTERS

Many mistakes in spelling are due to lack of knowledge concerning the use of capital letters. Capital letters should be used to begin every sentence, every line of poetry, every important word in the title of a book, every direct quotation, every proper noun or adjective, and all titles attached to the names of individuals. When in doubt consult the dictionary or a good author's or secretary's handbook.

Many spelling errors result from the fact that the same word sometimes begins with a capital and sometimes with a small letter. Study the following examples of correct usage of some of the more troublesome capitals. Note the spelling of all the italicized words.

North	The *North* and the *South* are interdependent.
north	Turn *north,* not *south,* at the crossroads.
Mountains	The Rocky *Mountains* are *west* of the Missouri River.
mountains	Many rivers have their source in the *mountains.*
Tuesday	It happened on *Tuesday,* not *Wednesday.*
February	The month of *February* follows *January.*
winter	The *winter* months were very cold.
University	The *University* of Oregon is in Eugene, Oregon.
university	Every *university* lost a number of students.
Avenue	Dr. Jones lived on *Fourth Avenue.*
avenue	Go to the *third avenue;* then turn *east.*
Capitol	The *Capitol* was the city's highest building.
capital	The *Empire Building* is in the *capital* city.
Venus	The planets include *Venus, Jupiter,* and *Mars.*
earth	We learned about the *earth, moon,* and *stars.*
Superintendent	No one had seen *Superintendent* McClure.
superintendent	A *superintendent* of schools has many duties.
professor	Our most-loved *professor* is *Professor* Jones.
Uncle	All of our family love *Uncle* John.
uncle	He is my only *uncle;* but I have two *aunts.*

VISUAL DRILLS

The - niversity of Chicago is - orth of the Tennessee - ountains. The - inter term included five - uesdays in - ebruary. The - apitol is the largest - uilding in the - apit - l city. It is on the longest - venue in the - apital. The - arth is larger than - enus. Your - ncle William was a - rofessor before he was elected - uperintendent of schools.

Lesson 80 SPELLING BY RULES

Few rules are of permanent help in learning to spell. It is well to know that the letter *q* is always followed by *u* in a word and to realize that proper nouns and adjectives should begin with capital letters. This text, moreover, has listed certain rules which govern the use of periods, hyphens, and apostrophes. Despite the values attached to these and a few other general rules, most students will do better in the long run to learn each word as a distinct word. For this reason the main emphasis of Part 2 will continue to be placed upon words rather than upon rules.

Many spelling rules have to do with the formation of derivatives. A *derivative* is a word formed from another by adding a prefix or a suffix or by internal change. Thus, from the word *use* are formed such derivatives as *misuse, disuse, uses, used, usage, using, user, usable,* and *useless.* Note the following rules which apply to the spelling of certain derivatives:

1. Words ending in silent *e,* drop the final *e* before the addition of suffixes beginning with a vowel.

   Examples: come, coming; use, usable; please, pleasure.

2. Words ending in silent *e,* keep the final *e* before the addition of suffixes beginning with a consonant.

   Examples: care, careful; tire, tireless; like, likeness.

Some important exceptions to the foregoing rules are listed below. Study them carefully. They show how dangerous it is to rely upon spelling rules.

advantage, advantageous	**notice, noticeable**	**judge, judgment**
canoe, canoeing	**outrage, outrageous**	**true, truly**
dye, dyeing	**argue, argument**	**whole, wholly**
mile, mileage	**awe, awful**	**wise, wisdom**

The "*i*-before-e" *Rule*

Another spelling rule frequently quoted is: Put *i* before *e* except after *c,* or where sounded like *a* in *neighbor* and *weigh.*

Since many people apply the above rule, be sure to learn the following exceptions:

ancient	**height**	**leisure**	**seize**	**foreign**
forfeit	**inveigle**	**neither**	**weird**	**counterfeit**

VISUAL DRILLS

mil - - ge	h - - g - t	n - - ther	w - - rd
anc - - nt	inv - - g - -	jud - m - nt	for - - - n
forf - - t	l - - sur -	s - - ze	c - - nterf - - t

Lesson 81 SOME TROUBLESOME *EI* AND *IE* WORDS

Although they conform to the spelling rule quoted in Lesson 80, the words listed below give trouble to many persons who attempt to spell them correctly. Consult your dictionary for the correct pronunciation.

Troublesome *ei* Words

ceiling	The *cei*l'ing of the room was very high.
conceit	Mary's con *ceit*' over her beauty was unfortunate.
conceived	Jane con *ceive*d' many new ideas.
deceit	A liar prefers de *ceit*' to truth.
heir	There is no *hei*r to the estate.
perceive	I did not per *ceive*' his change in attitude.
receipts	The cash re *ceip*ts' exceeded our expectations.
received	The crowd re *ceive*d' him with applause.
rein	His pull on the r*ei*n turned the horse.
veil	Her face was covered by a new v*ei*l.
vein	A v*ei*n carries blood toward the heart.
weighed	The man w*eigh*ed about three hundred pounds.

Troublesome *ie* Words

achieve	Many men do not a ch*ie*ve' their aims.
apiece	They were given three apples a p*iece*'.
diet	The doctor prescribed a limited di'et.
fiend	The lonely woman was murdered by a f*ie*nd.
fierce	The f*ie*r*ce* snarls of the wolves scared him.
grievance	His gr*ie*v'an*ce* was caused by an unjust accusation.
pier	The store p*ie*r jutted out into the lake.
priest	The Catholic pr*ie*st chanted the prayer in Latin.
shriek	The frightened woman uttered a shr*ie*k of terror.
twentieth	We live in the twen'ti eth century.
wield	Some kings w*ie*ld but little power.
fortieth	Tuesday was father's for'ti eth birthday.

VISUAL DRILLS

c - - ling	dec - - t	p - - r	v - - l
ach - - ve	h - - r	rec - - p - s	tw - nt - - th
ap - - ce	f - - nd	rec - - ved	w - - ld
con - - - ved	f - - rce	pr - - st	v - - n
dec - - t	perc - - ve	shr - - k	w - - g - ed
d - - t	gr - - v - nce	r - - n	f - - t - - th

Lesson 82 FORMING PLURALS

Although most plurals are formed according to established rules, there are enough exceptions to make it unsafe to depend entirely on rules. Each plural is a separate problem. The plurals of most English nouns are formed according to three rules:

A. Add *s* to the singular form. Examples:
   1. birth, births 2. burglar, burglars 3. page, pages

B. Add *es* to the singular when it ends with *s* or a similar sound, *ss, ch, x, sh.* Examples:
   1. mass, masses 2. box, boxes 3. dispatch, dispatches

C. Change the *y* to *ies* when the singular ends in *y* preceded by a consonant. Examples:
   1. ally, allies 2. boundary, boundaries 3. baby, babies

Study the spelling of the various plurals given below. They are frequently misspelled because of conflict or confusion with the foregoing rules. The singular form is listed first and is followed by the plural form in an illustrative sentence.

attorney There were more *attorneys* than legal business.
bacterium Soil contains many types of *bacteria.*
basis Religion is founded on many *bases.*
cargo The ships carried *cargoes* of wheat and clothes.
corps Several *corps* of workers sold the new stamps.
datum The writer gathered *data* for his article.
hero Three men that I know were *heroes.*
Kelly Everybody liked the *Kellys.*
loaf Each family was given two *loaves* of bread.
mosquito Some *mosquitoes* carry disease germs.
phenomenon All the *phenomena* of nature were described.
stimulus Our ears are sensitive to sound *stimuli.*
thief The bank was robbed by three *thieves.*
turkey The farmers sold their *turkeys* before Thanksgiving.
valley The river *valleys* were covered with water.
veto The three bills received early *vetoes.*

VISUAL DRILLS

attorn - - -	cor - -	lo - - es	th - - - es
ba - ter - -	dat -	mosq - - t - - -	t - rk - - -
bas - -	her - - -	- henome - -	va - l - - -
cargo - -	Kell - -	stimu - -	vet - - -

Lesson 83 USING ABBREVIATIONS

An abbreviation is the shortened form of a word, such as *Dr.* for *Doctor.* An abbreviation should almost always be followed by a period.* Many abbreviations are the initial letters of foreign words, such as *e.g.* for the Latin *exempli gratia* (for example). Abbreviations should be written with great care for accuracy and legibility as they are easily and frequently misinterpreted. The following list includes fifty-one abbreviations that are used frequently, together with their English meanings.

A.B.	Bachelor of Arts	**Jan.**	January
A.D.	in the year of the Lord	**Jr.**	Junior
		lb.	pound or pounds
a.m.	before noon	**Lieut.** or **Lt.**	Lieutenant
Apr.	April		
Asst.	assistant	**M.A.**	Master of Arts
atty.	attorney	**Mar.**	March
Aug.	August	**M.D.**	Doctor of Medicine
Ave.	Avenue	**memo**	memorandum
B.C.	before Christ	**Mgr.**	manager
B.S.	Bachelor of Science	**Mr.**	Mister
Capt.	Captain	**Mrs.**	Mistress
Co.	Company	**No.**	number
C.O.D.	collect or cash on delivery	**Nov.**	November
		Oct.	October
D.D.	Doctor of Divinity	**oz.**	ounce or ounces
Dec.	December	**Ph.D.**	Doctor of Philosophy
dept.	department	**p.m.**	after noon
doz.	dozen or dozens	**pp.**	pages
Dr.	Doctor	**P.S.**	postscript
e.g.	for example	**Rev.**	Reverend
etc.	and so forth	**Sept.**	September
Feb.	February	**Sr.**	Senior
f.o.b.	free on board	**St.**	Street
ft.	foot or feet	**Supt.**	Superintendent
i.e.	that is	**vs.**	against
in.	inch or inches	**vol.**	volume

*No periods are used after *1st, 2nd, 3rd,* etc.; after *memo, per cent,* or *percent;* or after government agencies commonly known by their abbreviations (TVA, AEC, FDIC, etc.).

Lesson 84 ABBREVIATIONS OF STATES AND TERRITORIES

Abbreviations of states and territories are frequently misspelled with serious results to proper mail delivery. Study carefully the list of abbreviations given below. They are taken from the United States Postal Guide and should be used only in connection with the location of a city. Thus it is generally correct to write, "He went to Sioux Falls, S. Dak.," but it would be incorrect to write, "He went to S. Dak."

Always begin the names of states and their abbreviations with capital letters.

Because of likely confusion with other abbreviations, do not use abbreviations for the following states: Alaska, Idaho, Iowa, Maine, Ohio, and Utah.

Abbre-viation	State or Territory	Abbre-viation	State or Territory
Ala.	Alabama	**Nebr.**	Nebraska
Ariz.	Arizona	**Nev.**	Nevada
Ark.	Arkansas	**N. H.**	New Hampshire
Calif.	California	**N. J.**	New Jersey
Colo.	Colorado	**N. Mex.**	New Mexico
Conn.	Connecticut	**N. Y.**	New York
Del.	Delaware	**N. C.**	North Carolina
D. C.	District of Columbia	**N. Dak.**	North Dakota
		Okla.	Oklahoma
Fla.	Florida	**Oreg.**	Oregon
Ga.	Georgia	**Pa.**	Pennsylvania
H. I.	Hawaiian Islands	**P. R.**	Puerto Rico
Ill.	Illinois	**R. I.**	Rhode Island
Ind.	Indiana	**S. C.**	South Carolina
Kans.	Kansas	**S. Dak.**	South Dakota
Ky.	Kentucky	**Tenn.**	Tennessee
La.	Louisiana	**Tex.**	Texas
Md.	Maryland	**Vt.**	Vermont
Mich.	Michigan	**Va.**	Virginia
Minn.	Minnesota	**Wash.**	Washington
Miss.	Mississippi	**W. Va.**	West Virginia
Mo.	Missouri	**Wis.**	Wisconsin
Mont.	Montana	**Wyo.**	Wyoming

Lesson 85 PREFIXES AND SUFFIXES

A prefix is a word element placed before a word stem to change its meaning, as *un* in *unkind.* A suffix is a word element placed after a word stem to change its meaning, as *ly* in *kindly.* A knowledge of the more common prefixes and suffixes (see lists below) is very helpful in learning word meanings. In many cases—for example, *auto, anti, trans, ful*—such a knowledge is helpful to correct spelling. On the other hand, there are numerous prefixes and suffixes that are spelled differently but have similar meanings (*ible* and *able; ous, ious,* and *tious;* etc.). Words with such beginnings or endings present special spelling problems and need to be studied independently. (See lessons to follow.)

COMMONLY USED PREFIXES

ad, a, ac, af, al, ap, at—to, toward
ante—before
anti—against
con, co, col, com—together, with
de—down, from, away from
dis, di, dif—apart, opposite
ex, e, ec, ef—out of, from, away
in, il, im, ir—in, into, not
inter—between, among
ob, o, oc, of, op—in the way, against
per—through, by means of
post—after, behind
pre—before
pro—before, for, forth, forward
re—back, again
sub, suc, suf, sug, sum, sup—under
trans—across
uni—one

COMMONLY USED SUFFIXES

able, ible, ble—that may or can be
al, ial—relating to, pertaining to
an, ain—pertaining to
ance, ancy, ence, ency—act of, state of being
ant, ent—being
ate, fy, ize, yze—to do or to make
d, ed (past tense, past participle)—did
dom—power, office, state
ee—one to whom
er, or, eer, ier—one who, that which
ful—full of
ing (present participle)—continuing to
ion, sion, tion—act of, state of being
ity, ty, ment—condition, state of being
ness—state of being
ory, ery—place where
ous, ious, tious—full of, having the quality of

Lesson 86 WORDS THAT END IN *ABLE*

As you look at and pronounce the words in this lesson that end in *able,* place special stress on the letter *a.* Try to recall each word as a part of the *able* group of words in contrast to the *ible* group of words which appears in Lesson 87. Refer to your dictionary for the pronunciation or meaning of any words concerning which you are uncertain.

acceptable Mary's poor excuse was not ac cept′a ble.
admirable The conduct of the students was ad′mi ra ble.
applicable The usual rules were not ap′pli ca ble.
breakable The dishes were break′a ble.
capable It will take a ca′pa ble man to fill the position.
chargeable Ellen's purchase was charge′a ble to her account.
charitable Always be char′i ta ble to the poor and needy.
considerable It took con sid′er a ble argument to convince him.
disagreeable His sore throat became more dis′a gree′a ble.
durable This heavy material is very du′ra ble.
enable The money will en a′ble him to travel.
excusable Because of illness, her absence is ex cus′a ble.
favorable The decision was fa′vor a ble to our team.
honorable The officer obtained an hon′or a ble discharge.
peaceable The Indians are not peace′a ble.
miserable The slaves were mis′er a ble.
movable Because of snow the trains were not mov′a ble.
notable The soldiers' return was a no′ta ble event.
probable It is prob′a ble that they will go.
reasonable The price of the lot was rea′son a ble.
reliable The lawyer is a re li′a ble man.
salable The old goods were no longer sal′a ble.
separable Cream and milk are easily sep′a ra ble.
teachable Attentive students are the most teach′a ble.

VISUAL DRILLS

ac - - pt - b - e	char - t - ble	fav - r - - le	prob - - - -
admi - - ble	con - id - r - ble	- on - r - ble	re - s - n - ble
ap - l - c - b - -	dis - gre - - ble	p - - c - able	rel - - b - -
br - - k - ble	dur - - le	mi - er - ble	sal - - - -
cap - b - -	- nab - -	mov - b - -	sep - r - ble
charg - - ble	ex - us - b - -	not - - le	te - ch - ble

Lesson 87 WORDS THAT END IN *IBLE*

As you look at and pronounce the words in this lesson that end in *ible,* place special stress on the letter *i.* Try to recall each word as part of the *ible* group of words in contrast to the *able* group of words which appears in Lesson 86. Refer to your dictionary for the pronunciation and meaning of any words concerning which you are uncertain.

accessible	The mountain stream was not ac *c*es'*s*i bl*e*.
admissible	The judge ruled the evidence ad mis'*s*i ble.
audible	His feeble words were barely *au*'di bl*e*.
collectible	Some of the bills were not col *l*ect'i bl*e*.
contemptible	Striking a woman is a con tempt'i bl*e* act.
convertible	The new car had a con vert'i bl*e* top.
corruptible	His morals were not co*r* rupt'i bl*e*.
defensible	Your theory of the explosion is not de fen'si bl*e*.
destructible	The baby's toy was easily de struct'i bl*e*.
dirigible	The airship was the dir'i gi bl*e* type.
divisible	The number nine is di vi*s*'i bl*e* by three.
eligible	Only girls are el'i *gi* bl*e* for the contest.
feasible	Which plan is the most fe*a*'*s*i ble?
flexible	The flex'i bl*e* tube was bent into a loop.
incredible	Walter's strange story seems in cred'i bl*e*.
indelible	The writing was in in del'i bl*e* ink.
insensible	The blow knocked the boy in sen'si bl*e*.
invisible	The rapid airplane soon became in vi*s*'i bl*e*.
legible	Good handwriting is always leg'i bl*e*.
permissible	Parking at an angle is not per mis'*s*i bl*e* there.
plausible	We believed the boy's pl*au*'*s*i bl*e* story.
responsible	Who was re spon'si bl*e* for the accident?
reversible	Mary purchased a re vers'i bl*e* overcoat.
susceptible	Jane is particularly sus *c*ep'ti bl*e* to colds.

VISUAL DRILLS

a - c - s - - ble	cor - - p - - ble	f - - s - ble	le - - ble
admis - - ble	defen - - ble	fle - ib - -	p - rmis - - ble
a - d - b - -	d - struc - - ble	incr - d - ble	pl - - s - - - -
- olle - - - ble	dir - g - - le	indel - - - -	respon - - ble
con - em - t - - le	div - - i - le	insen - - ble	rever - - ble
conv - rt - b - -	el - g - ble	invi - - ble	su - - ep - - ble

Lesson 88 SOME TROUBLESOME PREFIXES

Prefixes, on the whole, give much less spelling trouble than do the suffixes which have been treated in the preceding lessons. Such prefixes as *bene* (well), *co* (together), *dis* (away), *ex* (out of), *il* (not), *in* (not), *ir* (not), *mis* (amiss), and *un* (not) are used at the beginning of many words but give very little spelling difficulty, particularly when the words are pronounced correctly. Among the words beginning with prefixes which give the most spelling difficulty are the following:

arouse	They could not a rou*s*e′ the sleeper.
beneficial	Charity is ben′e fi′*c*ial.
coincide	The two stories did not co′in *c*id*e*′.
disagree	The speakers dis′a gre*e*′ on the subject.
discovery	The dis *co*v′er *y* of gold was kept secret.
excel	Arthur tried to ex *c*el′ in all sports.
exile	The prisoners were sent into e*x*′il*e*.
exhibit	Three pictures were placed on ex *h*ib′it.
expected	Tom is ex pe*c*t′ed to arrive early.
illiterate	Good schools decrease the *il* lit′er at*e* population.
illustrate	Pictures were used to *il*′lus trat*e* the story.
inability	His in′a bil′ i ty to read is unfortunate.
inauguration	The governor's in *au*′gu ra′*tio*n was delayed.
irrigation	Much water was distributed by ir′*r*i ga′*tio*n.
irreparable	The storm caused *ir* rep′ a ra bl*e* damages.
misfortune	His accident was a great mis for′tun*e*.
misgiving	A sense of mis giv′ing disturbed his hopes.
mishap	The journey ended without mis hap′.
mislay	Where did you mis la*y*′ your glasses?
mispronounce	How many words did you mis′pro noun*c*e′?
mistaken	It was a case of mis tak′*e*n identity.
unnecessary	Let there be no un ne*c*′*e*s sar′y waste.
unusual	Your conduct is quite un u′*s*u al.

VISUAL DRILLS

aro - - -	e - il -	in - - g - ration	m - - la -
ben - fi - - al	e - - ib - t	ir - ep - r - ble	m - - pron - - n - -
co - n - id -	exp - - - ed	i - - - gation	mi - t - ken
dis - gree	il - it - rate	m - sfort - - -	un - e - es - - ry
d - sc - v - ry	il - - strate	m - sg - - - ng	unu - - - l
ex - el	in - bil - ty	mis - ap	

Lesson 89 WORDS ENDING IN *EL, LE,* AND *AL*

There are a number of words ending in *el, le,* and *al* which are pronounced with a similar *l* sound. There are no rules which govern the spelling of these endings. Distinct pronunciation is helpful with words like *mural* with an *al* sound and words like *label* with an *el* sound, but for the most part *l*-sounding endings need to be visualized sharply. Note the endings of the following words carefully:

acquittal The jury voted for the prisoner's ac*q*uit′*t*al.
refusal A quick re fu*s*′al was given to our offer.
angel She was an an′gel from heaven.
barrel The bar′*r*el was full of flour.
bushel We came to buy a b*u*sh′el of oats.
label The la′bel came off the bottle.
novel This is an interesting nov′el.
parcel A par′*c*el came in today's mail.
quarrel Two men engaged in a bitter *qua*r′*r*el.
satchel Doctor Brown left his sa*t*ch′el in his office.
tunnel The train ran through a tun′*n*el.
vessel The ves′*s*el carried cargo to Europe.
angle The an′gl*e* was more than 45 degrees.
axle The rear a*x*′l*e* of the car was broken.
humble The servant's manner was hum′bl*e*.
liable A man is li′a bl*e* for his debts.
meddle Why med′*dle* in other people's affairs?
resemble Twins often re *s*em′bl*e* each other.
struggle The strug′*gle* for existence is unending.
thimble Mary pushed the needle with a thim′bl*e*.
tremble The child began to trem′bl*e* with fear.
trifle The guests were a tri′fl*e* late.
whistle The train's *wh*is′*t*le was long and loud.
wrestle The boys started to *w*res′*t*le each other.

VISUAL DRILLS

ac - - itt - l	n - v - l	angl -	strug - l -
ref - s - l	par - - l	ax - -	th - mbl -
ang - l	qu - - rel	- umble	trem - - e
bar - - l	s - - chel	l - abl -	t - ifl -
b - sh - l	t - nn - l	med - le	w - istl -
lab - l	ves - - l	r - sembl -	wr - stle

Lesson 90 WORDS ENDING IN *AR, ER,* AND *OR*

Many persons confuse the spellings of words which end with an *ẽr* sound. Although the *ẽr* pronunciation is correct for most of these words, it is helpful to give the *ar* endings a slight *a* sound and the *or* endings a slight *or* sound when learning to spell them. Study the following words with special attention upon the final syllable.

beggar	The poor beg′*gar* was wretched.
cedar	They cut down every *ce*′d*ar* tree.
collar	His col′*l*ar was too large for his neck.
polar	The po′l*ar* bear was white as snow.
vinegar	The cider soon turned into vin′e g*ar*.
carrier	Please call the mail car′*ri* er back.
consumer	The sale benefited each con sum′er.
employer	My em pl*oy*′er bought a new typewriter.
jeweler	The j*ew*′el er fixed my watch.
laborer	John is a la′b*or* er at the sawmill.
ledger	The entries were posted in the le*dg*′er.
shoulder	The football player injured his sho*ul*′der.
voucher	A vouch′er indicated the amount of the sale.
ambassador	The foreign am bas′*sa* d*or* was present.
author	The *au*′thor of the book was famous.
aviator	The a′vi a′t*or* owned his airplane.
conductor	The train con du*c*′t*or* collected the tickets.
editor	L. C. Smith is ed′i t*or* of the magazine.
inventor	Edison was a world-famous in ven′t*or*.
investor	The rich man was a heavy in ves′t*or* in bonds.
rumor	The r*u*′m*or* spread throughout the city.
senator	Charley Jones is the new sen′a t*or*.
traitor	The tra*i*′t*or* to his country died in sorrow.
visitor	Our vi*s*′i t*or* stayed only a few days.

VISUAL DRILLS

begg - -	jewel - -	vineg - -	invest - -
carri - -	pol - -	conduct - -	amba - s - d - -
ced - -	aviat - -	edit - -	rum - r
col - - r	con - um - r	sho - ld - -	sen - t - -
auth - -	labor - -	v - - ch - r	tra - t - -
employ - -	le - g - -	invent - -	vis - t - -

Lesson 91 WORDS ENDING IN *ANT* AND *ENT*

The English language contains a considerable number of frequently used words ending in *ant* and *ent*. Many of them are listed in Part 1 of this text. (See, for example, Lessons 39 and 49.) If these two endings are learned and pronounced distinctly as *ănt* and *ĕnt*, most of the spelling difficulties are avoided. Check the list of important words given below to see if you have the endings clearly in mind. Try to combine correct pronunciation with clear visualization.

abundant	There was an a bun′dant supply of food.
applicant	Are you an ap′*pli* *c*ant for the position?
defendant	The de fend′ant was set free.
descendant	Mary is a de *sc*end′ant of Thomas Jefferson.
emigrant	His mother was an em′i grant from Germany.
immigrant	His father was an im′*mi* grant to America.
important	Your health is a very im por′tant matter.
predominant	Industry is the pre dom′i nant activity here.
restaurant	The new res′t*au* rant serves good food.
significant	It is sig nif′i cant that he came early.
tyrant	The mad king became a severe t*y*′rant.
apparent	It is a*p* par′ent that the house needs paint.
current	The June magazine is the cur′*r*ent issue.
deficient	Her daily diet was de fi′*ci*ent in milk.
dependent	Children are de pend′ent upon their parents.
efficient	E*f* fi′*ci*ent work is essential to success.
obedient	Mary was o be′di ent to all rules.
opponent	He finally overcame his strong o*p* po′nent.
ornament	Her picture is an or′na ment to the room.
prevalent	The contagious disease soon became prev′a lent.
resident	The lecturer was not a re*s*′i dent of this city.
violent	The angry man had a vi′o lent temper.

VISUAL DRILLS

abund - - t	t - r - - t	op - on - nt	rest - - r - nt
ap - ar - nt	des - end - - -	import - - -	signif - c - - t
cu - - - nt	im - - gr - - -	prev - l - - t	defi - - - nt
appl - c - - -	ef - ic - - nt	predom - n - - -	d - f - nd - - t
d - pend - - -	obed - - nt	re - id - - t	vi - l - nt
- m - grant		orn - m - nt	

Lesson 92 WORDS ENDING IN *ANCE* AND *ENCE*

What was said in Lesson 91 about words ending in *ant* and *ent* applies equally to words ending in *ance* and *ence*. Careful pronunciation of the *ă* and *ĕ* sounds does much to overcome spelling difficulties with the numerous words of this type.

Review the words listed in Lessons 35 and 45. Then give special study to the words listed below. Mastery of these three sets of words does away with most spelling mistakes due to the confusion of *ance* and *ence*.

abundance	Good weather caused an a bun'dan*ce* of crops.
admittance	Our tickets gave us ad mit'tan*ce* to the first show.
annoyance	The speaker showed an no*y*'an*ce* at the interruption.
attendance	The a*t* tend'an*ce* at the meeting was large.
conveyance	They went in every kind of con v*e*y'an*ce*.
hindrance	Bad roads were a hin'dran*ce* to speed.
ignorance	Lack of study was the cause of his ig'no ran*ce*.
resemblance	The re sem'blan*ce* in looks was remarkable.
resistance	No re *s*ist'an*ce* seemed too great to overcome.
temperance	The preacher advised tem'per an*ce* in all things.
perseverance	Per'se ver'an*ce* will overcome most difficulties.
audience	The *au*'di en*ce* cheered the speaker.
competence	His com'pe ten*ce* for the task was perfect.
excellence	Did you observe the e*x*'ce*l* len*ce* of his manners?
innocence	The accused man claimed complete in'*n*o cen*ce*.
intelligence	High in tel'*l*i gen*ce* leads to correct thinking.
interference	The game ended without further in'ter fer'en*ce*.
negligence	He was discharged for neg'li gen*ce* of duty.
inference	His in'fer en*ce* was based upon facts.
obedience	Strict o be'di en*ce* is demanded in our school.
reverence	The memory of heroes is held in rev'er en*ce*.
violence	The mob continued its acts of vi'o len*ce*.

VISUAL DRILLS

abund - - - -	at - - nd - - - e	interf - - - nce	obed - - nce
admi - t - - ce	conv - - - nce	ign - r - - c -	temp - r - - ce
a - di - - ce	in - o - - nce	negl - g - nce	rever - - - -
an - o - - nce	hindr - - - -	resemb - - - - -	vi - l - nce
comp - t - n - -	intel - - g - nce	res - - t - n - e	per - ev - r - nce
ex - - l - - nce		inf - r - nce	

Lesson 93 WORDS ENDING IN *ISE, IZE,* AND *YZE*

Because of similarity in pronunciation and meaning, frequent mistakes in spelling are made with numerous words ending in *ise, ize,* and *yze.* These words may best be memorized by critical attention to the different endings, accompanied by writing and visual drills. After studying the words listed below, write each one on a separate piece of paper *minus* the ending. Then shuffle the papers and practice completing the words mentally and in writing.

despise Most persons de spi*se*′ lying and cheating.
comprise What items does the outline com pri*se*′?
devise We need to de vi*se*′ a better plan.
disguise His dis *guise*′ entirely changed his appearance.
enterprise They began another business en′ter pri*se*.
franchise The city extended the water fran′chi*se* a year.
revise The writer was asked to re vi*se*′ his story.
supervise Who is to su′per vi*se* our work?
antagonize Let us not an tag′o nize the umpire.
apologize You should a pol′o giz*e* for your unkind remark.
authorize Did the manager *au*′thor iz*e* this change?
baptize The preacher wanted to bap tiz*e*′ the baby at once.
economize Higher costs required us to e con′o miz*e*.
emphasize It is necessary to em′*ph*a size the fact.
equalize The new plan will e′*qu*al iz*e* the tax burden.
organize The boys decided to or′gan iz*e* a club.
standardize Dictionaries help to stand′ard iz*e* pronunciation.
summarize The speaker failed to sum′*m*a rize his points.
sympathize We did not s*y*m′pa thiz*e* with his views.
utilize Many machines u′ti liz*e* electricity for power.
visualize I can vi*s*′u al iz*e* yesterday's storm clearly.
analyze The problem is difficult to an′a l*y*z*e*.
paralyze The blow seemed to par′a l*yze* his arm.

VISUAL DRILLS

antag - ni - e	bapt - - -	eq - al - - -	sup - rv - - -
d - spi - -	enterp - - - -	org - ni - -	ut - li - -
apol - g - - -	e - on - mi - -	revi - -	an - l - - e
dev - - -	em - - asi - e	stand - rd - - -	par - l - - e
d - sg - - se	franc - i - e	sum - ar - - e	compr - - -
a - th - ri - e		s - mp - th - - -	vis - - li - -

Lesson 94 WORDS ENDING IN *ARY, ERY,* AND *ORY*

A confusion which leads to frequent misspellings is due to the similarity of the endings *ary, ery,* and *ory.* In learning these words, special attention should be given to the *a, e,* or *o* sound in the next to the last syllable.

Study the following words in the same manner as directed for the previous lesson. Watch the accents. Pronounce the final syllable *ĭ,* not *ē.*

boundary	The state bound′a ry on the west is a river.
contrary	Your statement is con′tra ry to the facts.
customary	We followed the cus′tom *a*r′y procedure.
elementary	The new el′e men′ta ry school has six grades.
literary	We joined the monthly lit′er *a*r′y society.
ordinary	The trial was just an or′di n*a*r′y affair.
summary	The book sum′*m*a ry reviewed the main points.
voluntary	His contribution was entirely vol′un ta r′y.
artillery	The parade included a piece of ar til′*l*er y.
celery	There was too much *c*el′er y in the salad.
discovery	The dis cov′er y of oil brought prosperity.
recovery	Complete re cov′ er y followed the depression.
millinery	The girls opened a new mil′*li* ner′y store.
misery	The injured man was in great mi*s*′er y.
mystery	The magazine contained two m*y*s′ter y stories.
accessory	He was an a*c* ces′so ry in the crime.
depository	The City National Bank is the chief de po*s*′i to′ry.
directory	His address is in the telephone di rec′to ry.
history	The book contains the his′to ry of slavery.
introductory	Mr. Brown made some in′tro du*c*′to ry remarks.
memory	The old man's mem′o ry for details is remarkable.
preparatory	John went to a college pre par′a to′ry school.
territory	This ter′*r*i to′ry was first settled by the Indians.

VISUAL DRILLS

bo - nd - - y	cust - m - - -	mis - ry	sum - - ry
artil - - ry	disc - v - ry	m - st - - -	hist - - -
cel - - y	mil - - n - - y	ord - n - ry	mem - - -
intr - du - to - y	re - ov - ry	depos - t - - -	prep - r - t - ry
contr - - y	elem - nt - - -	dire - t - - -	vol - nt - ry
ac - es - - - y	lit - r - ry		ter - - t - ry

Lesson 95 WORDS ENDING IN *CIAN, CION, SION,* AND *TION*

As a final illustration of spelling difficulties which arise from similar suffixes, the student's attention is called to certain words ending, respectively, in *cian, cion, sion,* and *tion.* As all of these numerous words end with a *shun,* or similar sound, it is necessary to give each ending intense visual scrutiny and to memorize it as a distinct part of the total word.

The words listed below are among the most frequently used words of the above types. Study them as directed in Lesson 93. Watch the pronunciation of the last two syllables.

magician (jĭsh′ăn) The ma *gi′ci*an used sleight of hand.
musician (zĭsh′ăn) The mu *si′ci*an played skillfully.
physician (zĭsh′ăn) The sick man needed a *phy si′ci*an.
politician (tĭsh′ăn) The pol′i ti′*ci*an asked for votes.
suspicion (pĭsh′ŭn) Our sus pi′*cion* required proof.
admission (mĭsh′ŭn) Ad mis′*sio*n to the game was free.
conclusion (klōō′zhŭn) We came to the same con *clu′sio*n.
confusion (fū′zhŭn) Great con fu′*sio*n followed the wreck.
division (vĭzh′ŭn) There was a di vi′*sio*n of opinion.
expression (prĕsh′ŭn) Accept our ex pres′*sio*n of thanks.
impression (prĕsh′ŭn) Ann made a fine im pres′*sio*n.
permission (mĭsh′ŭn) Norman had per mis′*sio*n to go.
persuasion (swā′zhŭn) He yielded to per *sua′sio*n.
procession (sĕsh′ŭn) We followed the pro *ces′sio*n.
admiration (rā′shŭn) His act deserved ad′m*i* ra′*tio*n.
ammunition (nĭsh′ŭn) The soldiers used much am′*mu* ni′*tio*n.
collection (lĕk′shŭn) John has fine a *col* lec′*tio*n of stamps.
construction (strŭk′shŭn) Con struc′*tio*n of the building stopped.
decoration (rā′shŭn) His dec′o ra′*tio*n was a medal.
fiction (fĭk′shŭn) The story was pure fic′*tio*n.
occupation (pā′shŭn) The store is ready for oc′cu pa′*tio*n.
retention (tĕn′shŭn) Practice improves re ten′*tio*n.

VISUAL DRILLS

suspi - - - n	ph - si - - - n	pol - ti - - - n	confu - - - n
magi - - - n	admis - - - n	con - lus - - n	impre - - - - n
music - - -	o - cupa - - - n	expre - - - - n	adm - ra - - - n
adm - rat - - -	col - ec - - - n	persu - s - - -	dec - ra - - - n
am - unit - - n	construc - - - n	proce - - - - n	fic - - - n

PART 3

THE OPEN GATEWAY

GROWTH IN VOCABULARY

The first gateway in this text opened the way for quick mastery of the 720 most troublesome spelling words in everyday use. The second gateway opened the way to the attainment of the technical spelling and dictionary habits which are most essential to business and literary writing. Students who have mastered these two areas of spelling competence are now ready to build up special spelling vocabularies.

The third gateway into the realm of correct spelling provides a direct approach to the key words which are representative of the leading fields of business and human interest. Part 3 of this book is presented for those special students of spelling who desire to go beyond the conventional standards of good spelling ability. These special students fall chiefly into two groups:

1. Students who wish to learn key words in the leading fields of human interest and business activity.
2. Commercial and secretarial students who desire to extend their spelling vocabulary into new areas of special competence.

For these two groups and all others interested in the study of key words and vocabulary building, Part 3 presents an up-to-date selection of current and vital words taken from the chief work, play, study, and social fields of modern life. The method of selecting these words was based upon a scientific study of word values combined with the judgment of teachers and practical experts.

The mastery of words is the open gateway to the enriched life of mankind. The lessons which follow contain sets of key words which are commonly used and understood by the persons interested in the occupations or human interests selected for study. Mastery of these words will extend your preview of education and business, increase your commercial vocabulary, develop your general language ability, and place you on "speaking" terms with the leading interests of educated men and women.

DIRECTIONS TO STUDENTS

Part 3, "The Open Gateway," includes a lesson of forty key words in each of thirty-eight different fields. A list of the lessons pertaining to these various fields is presented here in order to give you a preview of the different interests covered.

You may not be interested in all of the lessons in Part 3. In general, it will be better for you to select those lessons for study which hold some promise for your future interest as a student or worker. In any event, you may be sure that all of the words are good words to know—words that are commonly used and mean much to large groups of American people and words that are helpful to buyers and consumers everywhere.

You should study these new words by the same *whole-word, hard-spot* method that you used in Parts 1 and 2. By this time, however, you should be able to master a word with fewer direct aids from the textbook. For this reason, the lessons on the new words in Part 3 omit special memory aids and visual drills. Each word is first printed in boldface type. It is then presented in syllabified form showing the primary accent. The silent or unusual letters are indicated in italics. This is followed by a simple definition of the meaning of the word as it is ordinarily used in connection with the topic under consideration.

The meanings given by the text for the words in Part 3 are those selected by experts in each special field. Frequently, these words have other meanings. You should make use of a good dictionary to learn the correct pronunciation and other possible meanings. The words in the text are not the only important words in each business or field of human interest. There are, of course, many other words, some quite technical in character. If especially interested in any of the different fields, you will find it advantageous to consult an encyclopedia concerning the general scope and nature of the field. It is quite probable, too, that your teacher or librarian will be able to locate special pamphlets or books which describe the field of interest in detail.*

---

*Note to Teachers. For helpful references and teaching suggestions, consult Walter J. Greenleaf, *Occupations and Careers,* New York, McGraw-Hill Book Company, 1955, 605 pages.

Lesson 96 ACCOUNTING AND BOOKKEEPING

accountant	a*c* count′ant	Person who examines accounts.
accrual	a*c* cru′al	Process of increasing.
accuracy	ac′*c*u ra cy	Exactness, precision, correctness; freedom from error.
adjust	a*d* just′	Arrange; to make fit.
asset	as′*s*et	Something of value.
auditor	*au*′di tor	One who examines accounts.
budget	bu*d*g′et	Itemized plan for spending.
collection	co*l* lec′*tio*n	Act of collecting money.
columnar	co lum′nar	Written in columns.
contingent	con tin′gent	Possible; liable to occur.
corporation	cor po ra′*tio*n	Group legalized as one person, usually to do business.
credit	cred′it	Enter a favorable payment.
creditor	cred′i tor	One to whom a debt is owed.
debit	deb′it	Charge with debt.
depreciation	de pre *c*i a′*tio*n	Value or price decrease.
discount	dis′count	Deduction for prompt payment.
dividend	div′i dend	Share of business profits.
earnings	*e*arn′ings	Compensation for services.
endorsement	en dors*e*′ment	Approval, as by signature on back of a check.
entry	en′try	Act of recording in a book.
equity	e*q*′*u*i ty	Property value minus claims.
expenditure	ex pend′i tur*e*	Money, time, or energy spent.
income	in′co*me*	Salary; yearly receipts.
installment	in stal*l*′ment	Partial payment.
inventory	in′ven to ry	List of goods in stock.
journalize	jo*u*r′nal iz*e*	Keep a daily record.
ledger	le*d*g′er	Principal account book.
liability	li a bil′i ty	Debt that is owed.
ownership	o*w*n′er ship	Sole right of possession.
payee	pa*y* *ee*′	One to whom money is paid.
posting	post′ing	Transferring journal entries.
profit	prof′it	Amount gained.
proprietorship	pro pri′e tor ship	Legal ownership of something.
receivable	re *cei*v′a bl*e*	Capable of acceptance.
reserve	re *serve*′	Set aside or withhold.
solvent	sol′vent	Able to pay just debts.
stockholder	stock′hold er	Holder of corporation shares.
surplus	sur′plus	Excess of need; not earning.
transaction	trans ac′*tio*n	That which is carried on.
voucher	vouch′er	Form for payment with reason stated.

Lesson 97 ADVERTISING AND PRINTING

alphabet	al'*ph*a bet	Letters used in a language.
brochure	bro *ch*ure'	Any pamphlet or stitched booklet.
bulletin	bul'*l*e tin	Publication appearing regularly.
caption	cap'*tion*	Heading or title.
circular	cir'cu l*a*r	Letter generally distributed.
copyright	cop'y rig*h*t	Exclusive right to publish.
dummy	dum'*m*y	Blank sheets cut and bound like a proposed book.
edition	e di'*tion*	All copies printed at one time.
editorial	ed i to'ri al	Article written by an editor.
electrotype	e lec'tro t*y*p*e*	Plate used in printing.
em	em	Printer's unit of type measure.
emboss	em bos*s*'	Ornament with a raised design.
engraving	en grav'ing	Carved, or cut, in a plate.
etching	e*t*ch'ing	Engraving by means of acid.
folio	fo'li o	Sheet of paper folded once.
font	font	Complete set of printing type.
format	for'ma*t*	General makeup of a book.
galley	gal'*le*y	Narrow tray for holding type.
halftone	ha*l*f'ton*e*	Process to reproduce photographs.
illustrate	il'*l*us trat*e*	Explain with pictures.
imprint	im print'	Mark made by pressure.
indention	in den'*tion*	Space at the beginning of a line.
italics	i tal'ics	Type slanting to the right.
linotype*	lin'o t*y*p*e*	Typesetting machine, casts each line as one piece of metal.
lithograph	lith'o gra*ph*	Print made from an engraved stone.
manuscript	man'u script	Copy submitted for publication.
monograph	mon'o graph	Book written on a single subject.
monotype*	mon'o typ*e*	Typesetting machine, casts letters separately but in lines.
photogravure	*ph*o to gra vur*e*'	Printing from an engraved plate.
pica	pi'ca	Printer's unit of type measure.
placard	plac'ard	Posted notice.
prospectus	pro spec'tus	Printed statement of a plan.
quad	*qu*ad	Square type piece used for spacing.
quire	*quire*	Twenty-four sheets of paper.
ream	re*a*m	Twenty quires of paper.
rotogravure	ro to gra vur*e*'	Printing from a copper cylinder.
royalty	roy'al ty	Payment due or made to an author.
script	script	Type similar to handwriting.
stereotype	ster'e o t*y*p*e*	Plate cast from type or a mold.
typographical	t*y* po gra*ph*'i cal	Relating to printing processes.

*To be capitalized when used as a trade term.

Lesson 98 AGRICULTURE

acre	a′cr*e*	Measure of land.
agriculture	ag′ri cul tur*e*	Art of cultivating the soil.
alfalfa	al fal′fa	Clover-like variety of the pea.
arable	ar′a bl*e*	Fit for tillage.
barren	bar′*r*en	Not producing vegetation.
brooder	brood′er	Heated enclosure for the raising of chicks.
calves	ca*l*ves	Young of the cow family.
cultivate	cul′ti vat*e*	Prepare and use for crops.
dairy	da*i*r′y	Farm producing milk products.
fallow	fal′*low*	Left uncultivated for a year.
fertilizer	fer′ti liz er	Substance put on soil to enrich it.
fodder	fod′*d*er	Coarse food for horses and cattle.
forage	for′*age*	Food for farm livestock.
furrow	fur′*row*	Trench made by a plow.
ginning	gin′*n*ing	Separating cotton from its seeds.
granary	gran′a ry	Storehouse for grain.
grazing	graz′ing	Feeding on growing herbage.
harrow	har′*row*	Implement for smoothing soil.
horticulture	hor′ti cul tur*e*	Art of growing plants.
incubator	in′cu ba tor	Apparatus for hatching eggs.
irrigate	ir′*r*i gat*e*	Supply with water by ditches.
meadow	me*a*d′o*w*	Piece of grassland.
mulch	mulch	Substance used to protect roots.
orchard	or′ch*a*rd	Piece of land growing fruit trees.
pasture	pas′tur*e*	Grassy piece of land.
plantation	plan ta′*tion*	Large farm estate.
potato	po ta′to	Edible underground vegetable.
poultry	po*u*l′try	Domestic fowl—chickens, turkeys, ducks, etc.
prairie	pra*i*r′*ie*	Treeless land covered with grass.
ranch	ranch	Large Western cattle farm.
range	rang*e*	Tract of land for grazing.
reaper	re*a*p′er	Machine that cuts grain.
rural	ru′ral	Pertaining to the country.
shepherd	shep′*h*erd	Man who takes care of sheep.
silage	si′l*age*	Silo-preserved food for farm stock.
stubble	stub′*ble*	Stalks left after grain is cut.
tobacco	to bac′*c*o	Plant bearing leaves which when dried are used for smoking or chewing.
tractor	trac′tor	Engine on wheels used for pulling.
vegetable	veg′*e* ta bl*e*	Plant grown for food.
wheat	*wh*e*a*t	Plant producing cereal grain.

Lesson 99 ARCHITECTURE AND BUILDING

air-condition	air-con di'tion	Furnish with air-cooling system.
aisle	aisle	Passageway.
alcove	al'cove	Recessed portion of a room.
arcade	ar cade'	Series of arches.
architect	ar'chi tect	Expert in the art of planning and designing buildings.
balcony	bal'co ny	High projecting platform.
blueprint	blue'print	Photographic print, white lines on blue.
boudoir	bou'doir	Room to which women may retire.
bungalow	bun'ga low	Low one-storied house.
buttress	but'tress	Projecting support for a wall.
casement	case'ment	Window sash opening on hinges.
ceiling	ceil'ing	Upper surface of a room.
chimney	chim'ney	Structure to carry away smoke.
clapboard	clap'board	Narrow boarding on the outside of a house.
colonnade	col on nade'	Row of columns or pillars.
cornice	cor'nice	Projecting molding near a roof.
facade	fa cade'	Front view of an edifice.
flue	flue	Opening in a chimney for smoke.
gable	ga'ble	Upper end of a building.
jamb	jamb	Side post of doorways or windows.
joists	joists	Timbers supporting a floor or a ceiling.
kitchen	kitch'en	Room for cooking.
lacquer	lac'quer	Artificial varnish, usually colored and sometimes opaque.
mantel	man'tel	Facing about the fireplace.
masonry	ma'son ry	Art of brick or stone construction.
molding	mold'ing	Strip around the upper walls.
mortar	mor'tar	Mixture to bind bricks or stones.
mortise	mor'tise	Hole for tenon in a wood joint.
newel	new'el	Post supporting a stair rail.
panel	pan'el	Rectangular piece set in a frame.
partition	par ti'tion	Interior dividing wall.
patio	pa'ti o	Open inner court.
plaster	plas'ter	Pasty mixture, hardening on drying, used for covering walls.
plumbing	plumb'ing	Pipes and connections for water, etc.
portico	por'ti co	Roof supported by columns.
scantling	scant'ling	Small beam of timber.
stucco	stuc'co	Fine plaster for covering exterior walls.
tenon	ten'on	Projection in a wood joint.
veranda	ve ran'da	Open balcony or porch.
wainscot	wain'scot	Wooden paneling on inner walls.

Lesson 100 ARMY, NAVY, AND AIR FORCE

ambuscade	am bus cade′	Place where troops lie hidden.
armament	ar′ma ment	Body of forces prepared for war.
armistice	ar′mi stice	Brief pause in war by agreement.
arsenal	ar′se nal	Building for the storage of ammunition.
artillery	ar til′ler y	Mounted cannon.
atom bomb	at′om bomb	Extremely powerful explosive bomb.
bayonet	bay′o net	Swordlike instrument at rifle end.
bomber	bomb′er	Airplane used for bombing.
camouflage	cam′ou flage	Disguise on or over a target.
canteen	can teen′	Soldier's store; a Post Exchange.
carrier	car′ri er	Designed to carry; an aircraft carrier.
casualties	cas′u al ties	Losses from death, wounds, etc.
cavalry	cav′al ry	Mounted troops.
chaplain	chap′lain	Clergyman for the armed forces.
citation	ci ta′tion	Honorable mention for bravery.
combatant	com′bat ant	One who fights.
commander	com mand′er	Officer in charge of troops.
commando	com man′do	Special military unit of 584 men.
commissary	com′mis sa ry	Store selling official goods.
convoy	con voy′	Accompany for protection.
corps	corps	Part of an army.
court-martial	court-mar′tial	Military or naval trial.
furlough	fur′lough	Leave of absence from duty.
infantry	in′fan try	Soldiers who fight on foot.
insignia	in sig′ni a	Distinguishing marks.
maneuver	ma neu′ver	Military or naval operation.
military	mil′i ta ry	Pertaining to soldiers or war.
militia	mi li′tia	Reserve of trained citizens.
missile	mis′sile	Object thrown, hurled, or guided.
naval	na′val	Pertaining to warships or navy.
ordnance	ord′nance	Military supplies or stores.
radar	ra′dar	Electronic locating device.
reconnaissance	re con′nais sance	Scouting on land or in the air.
regiment	reg′i ment	Organized body of soldiers.
reveille	re veil le′	Morning bugle call.
sentry	sen′try	Armed guard.
squadron	squad′ron	An air fleet, or an organized group of soldiers in formation.
submarine	sub ma rine′	Vessel operated under water.
tank	tank	Armored caterpillar vehicle.
torpedo	tor pe′do	Elongated explosive projectile.

Lesson 101 ART

batik	ba'ti*k*	Multicolored dyed fabric.
block print	bloc*k*' print	Printed from wood blocks.
brayer	bra*y*'er	Roll used to ink a block print.
canvas	can'vas	Heavy fabric for oil painting.
cartoon	car toon'	Amusing sketch or drawing.
carving	carv'ing	Art of decorating by cutting.
ceramics	*c*e ram'ics	Art of pottery making.
charcoal	char'co*a*l	Draw with a charcoal pencil.
contour	con'to*u*r	Outline; profile.
design	de *s*ign'	Arrangement of form and color; a preliminary sketch.
easel	e*a*'*s*el	Support for an artist's picture.
etching	e*t*ch'ing	Design engraved by acid.
exhibit	ex *h*ib'it	Show of art work.
fresco	fres'co	Painting on fresh plaster.
frieze	fr*i*ez*e*	Ornamental band around a wall.
glaze	glaz*e*	Smooth, glossy surface or coating.
graphic	gra*ph*'ic	Of or pertaining to the arts of drawing and painting.
hue	hu*e*	Variety of any one color.
kiln	kil*n*	Oven for treating pottery.
landscape	land'scap*e*	Scenery picture.
lithograph	lith'o gra*ph*	Print made by use of a prepared stone surface.
media	med'i a	Working materials.
model	mod'el	Form in clay or plastic.
motif	mo t*i*f'	Central or controlling idea.
palette	pal'et*te*	Painter's plate for mixing colors.
pastel	pas tel'	Soft colored chalk.
perspective	per spec'tiv*e*	Drawn so as to show distance.
pigment	pig'ment	Dry coloring matter.
plastic	plas'tic	Moldable substance.
realism	re'al i*s*m	Concerned with actuality.
relief	re l*i*ef'	In sharp outline.
sculptor	sculp't*o*r	One who models or carves.
sculpture	sculp'tur*e*	Art of modeling or carving stone, etc.
sketch	ske*t*ch	Rough outline drawing.
spatterwork	spat'*t*er wo*r*k	Picture or design made by use of coarse paint spraying.
spraying	spra*y*'ing	Scattering a liquid in fine drops.
stencil	sten'*c*il	Mark by use of a perforated pattern.
symmetry	sym'*m*e try	Balance; harmony.
tempera	tem'per a	Opaque paint.
wedging	we*dg*'ing	Working clay to remove bubbles.

Lesson 102 AUTOMOBILES AND BICYCLES

accelerator	ac *c*el'er a t*o*r	Pedal-controlled speed regulator.
axle	ax'l*e*	Shaft connecting opposite wheels.
battery	bat'ter y	Cells producing electric current.
bearing	b*e*ar'ing	Part within which something revolves.
brake	brak*e*	Stopping device.
chassis	*c*has'*sis*	Frame under an automobile.
chauffeur	*c*h*au*f *feu*r'	Paid private car operator.
clutch	clu*t*ch	Device to couple engine with load.
convertible	con ver'ti bl*e*	Car with changeable top.
crankcase	crank'cas*e*	Case inclosing the crankshaft.
crankshaft	crank'shaft	Crank-like shaft turned by the pistons.
cylinder	*c*yl'in der	Piston chamber in an engine; tube.
differential	dif *f*er en'*tia*l	Gears transmitting power to rear axle.
exhaust	ex *hau*st'	Spent gases from an engine.
fender	fen'der	Protective shield over a wheel.
garage	ga rag*e*'	Building for housing cars.
gasket	gas'ket	Thin piece to make joints tight.
generator	gen'er a t*o*r	Machine using electromagnets to produce current for ignition.
hydraulic	h*y* dr*au*'lic	Operated by a fluid under pressure.
ignition	ig ni'*tio*n	System that explodes fuel inside the cylinders of an engine.
limousine	lim o*u* *sine*'	Closed car with driver's seat outside.
lubricate	lu'bri cat*e*	Apply oil or grease.
magneto	mag ne'to	Machine using permanent magnets to produce current for ignition.
manifold	man'i fold	Pipe between cylinders and exhaust.
motor	mo't*o*r	Machine which makes a thing go.
motorcycle	mo't*o*r *cy* cle	Two-wheeled vehicle with a motor.
muffler	muf'*f*ler	Device for deadening exhaust noise.
panoramic	pan *o* ram'ic	Providing unobstructed view.
pedal	ped'al	Lever acted upon by the foot.
piston	pis't*o*n	Cylinder which slides in a tube (called the "cylinder" in a motor).
pneumatic	*p*n*e*u mat'ic	Filled with air; worked by air.
puncture	punc'tur*e*	Hole made by piercing.
radiator	ra'di a t*o*r	Pipes which cool circulating water.
sedan	se dan'	Type of large, closed car.
speedometer	spe*e*d om'e ter	Instrument indicating speed.
synthetic	syn thet'ic	Man-made substance; not natural.
transmission	trans mis'*sio*n	Gears transmitting engine power.
upholstery	up hol'ster y	Covering for seats.
vulcanize	vul'can iz*e*	Weld rubber with heat, using sulphur.
windshield	wind'sh*i*eld	Glass shield for motor vehicles.

Lesson 103 AVIATION

aerial	a er'i al	Pertaining to aircraft.
aeronautics	a er o n*au*'tics	Science of flying.
aileron	a*i*'le ron	Wing-part which balances airplane.
airborne	a*i*r'born*e*	Conveyed by air.
aircraft	a*i*r'craft	Flying machines of all kinds.
airplane	a*i*r'plan*e*	Mechanically flown aircraft.
airport	a*i*r'port	Place for landing aircraft.
altimeter	al tim'e ter	Instrument that measures altitude.
altitude	al'ti tud*e*	Height of aircraft above sea level.
amphibian	am *ph*ib'i an	Airplane, can taxi on land or water.
autogiro	*au* to gi'ro	Airplane with horizontal propellers for providing vertical lift.
aviation	a vi a'*tio*n	Art and science of flying.
aviator	a'vi a t*o*r	One who operates an airplane.
biplane	bi'plan*e*	Airplane with two planes (wings).
blimp	blimp	Non-rigid airship, cabin attached.
ceiling	*cei*l'ing	Top limit of visibility in the air.
cockpit	co*c*k'pit	Compartment for the pilot.
cowling	co*w*l'ing	Metal cover around aircraft engine.
dirigible	dir'i *g*i bl*e*	Gas-filled, cigar-shaped airship with rigid internal frame.
elevator	el'e va t*o*r	Tail-part which controls pitch.
fuselage	fu'se l*age*	Body of an airplane.
helicopter	hel i cop'ter	Aircraft without wings; horizontal propellers cause all its movements.
jet-propelled	jet-pro pel*led*'	Moved by exhaust through rear jet.
monoplane	mon'o plan*e*	Airplane with one plane (wing).
navigation	nav i ga'*tio*n	Science of flying to a destination.
parachute	par'a *ch*ut*e*	Device for slow descent in air.
pilot	pi'l*o*t	Operator of an airplane.
pitch	pi*t*ch	Aircraft's movement up or down.
propeller	pro pel'*l*er	Device for moving an airplane.
retractable	re tract'a bl*e*	Capable of being pulled back.
rudder	rud'*d*er	Hinged device used to turn airplane.
runway	run'wa*y*	Landing strip.
rocket	ro*c*k'et	Tube propelled by escaping gas.
solo	so'lo	Flight made by aviator alone.
stabilizer	sta'bi liz er	Device to keep airplane level.
taxi	ta*x*'i	Drive an airplane on the earth.
torque	tor*que*	Force tending to cause rotation.
turbulence	tur'bu len*ce*	Disturbing, irregular flow of air.
visibility	vi*s* i bil'i ty	Distance of maximum view.
yaw	ya*w*	Sideways shift of flying airplane.

Lesson 104 — BANKING

acceptance	ac *c*ept′an*c*e	Signed draft agreeing to pay.
accrued	a*c* cr*u*e*d*′	Accumulated, but not paid.
bankable	bank′a bl*e*	Receivable at a bank.
bond	bond	Interest-bearing certificate.
broker	bro′ker	Buyer and seller for others.
bullion	bul′*li*on	Uncoined gold or silver.
capitalist	cap′i tal ist	Man with wealth (used in business).
certify	*c*er′ti f*y*	Guarantee by bank authority.
clientele	cli en tel*e*′	Body of patrons.
collateral	co*l* lat′er al	Additional security.
collect	co*l* lect′	Obtain payment.
counterfeit	coun′ter f*e*it	Not genuine.
coupon	co*u*′pon	Interest certificate.
currency	cur′*r*en *c*y	Medium of exchange; money.
defaulter	de f*au*lt′er	Embezzler.
deposit	de po*s*′it	Put into a bank.
discount	dis′count	Deduct for prompt payment; the deduction so made.
dividend	div′i dend	Share of the profits.
dollar	dol′*la*r	One hundred cents.
draft	draft	Written order to pay.
financier	fin an *ci*er′	One skilled in investing money or administering investments.
forgery	for′ger y	False document or signature.
hypothecate	h*y* poth′e cat*e*	Pledge as security.
legal tender	le′gal ten′der	Money legally accepted for debts.
liquidate	li*q*′*ui* date	Settle or pay a debt or claim.
loan	lo*a*n	Money lent at interest.
maturity	ma tu′ri ty	Becoming due, as a note.
negotiable	ne go′*ti* a bl*e*	Transferable.
nickel	ni*c*k′el	Small coin; five cents.
option	op′*tio*n	Choice; alternative.
overdraw	o ver dr*aw*′	Check out more than deposited.
payee	pa*y* ee′	Receiver of payable money.
postdate	post dat*e*′	Date after time of writing.
promissory	prom′i*s* so ry	Containing an agreement, as in a promissory note.
promoter	pro mot′er	Organizer of a company.
specie	spe′*cie*	Coin.
teller	tel*l*′er	Bank employee handling money.
vault	v*au*lt	Safe storage place for valuables.
verify	ver′i f*y*	Confirm.
voucher	vouch′er	One who guarantees as a witness; a receipt; certificate.

Lesson 105 — BIOLOGY

algae	al'gae	Group of the simplest green plants.
alimentary	al i men'ta ry	Pertaining to the organs and functions of digestion.
amphibian	am phib'i an	An animal or plant living both on land and in water.
anatomy	a nat'o my	Study of the structure of organisms.
antenna	an ten'na	Feeler on the head of insects.
anterior	an ter'i or	Toward the head.
biennial	bi en'ni al	Plant which lives for two years.
biology	bi ol'o gy	Study of living organisms.
botany	bot'an y	Science dealing with plants.
carnivorous	car niv'o rous	Flesh-eating.
cell	cell	Unit of living matter.
chlorophyll	chlo'ro phyll	Green coloring substance of plants.
chrysalis	chrys'a lis	Dormant form of some insects.
conifers	co'ni fers	Cone-bearing plants.
embryo	em'bry o	Young of an animal in the earliest stages of development.
evolution	ev o lu'tion	Connected development of all life.
fungus	fun'gus	Non-green plant, as mushroom.
habitat	hab'i tat	Region where plant or animal lives.
heredity	he red'i ty	Transmission of characteristics of parents to their offspring.
instinct	in'stinct	Complex unlearned reaction.
invertebrate	in ver'te brate	Animal without an internal skeleton.
larva	lar'va	Worm-like stage of certain animals.
legume	leg'ume	Pod-bearing plant.
mammal	mam'mal	Animal that gives milk to young.
metabolism	me tab'o lism	Basic processes of living.
microscope	mi'cro scope	Instrument which enlarges object.
neuron	neu'ron	Nerve cell.
nucleus	nu'cle us	Active body of cell protoplasm.
organism	or'gan ism	Individual animal or plant.
parasite	par'a site	Organism which lives on another.
physiology	phys i ol'o gy	Study of the functions of organisms.
pistil	pis'til	Central part of a flower.
pollen	pol'len	Spores on the anthers of flowers.
posterior	pos te'ri or	Toward the rear.
protoplasm	pro'to plasm	Living substance of cells.
psychology	psy chol'o gy	Science of mind and behavior.
species	spe'cies	Special kind of animal or plant.
stamen	sta'men	Pollen-bearing part of a flower.
vertebrate	ver'te brate	Animal which has a backbone.
zoology	zo ol'o gy	Science dealing with animals.

Lesson 106 CLOTHING AND DRY GOODS

apparel	ap par'el	Clothing; dress.
batiste	ba tiste'	Cloth of fine texture.
blouse	blouse	Loose waist.
brassiere	bras siere'	Woman's protecting undergarment.
cashmere	cash'mere	Soft wool of fine grade.
chambray	cham'bray	Gingham woven with linen finish.
chamois	cham'ois	Soft pliable leather.
corduroy	cor'du roy	Cotton fabric with raised cords.
costume	cos'tume	Complete set of outer garments.
cretonne	cre tonne'	Strong cloth of printed cotton.
crinoline	crin'o line	Stiff cloth used for lining, etc.
dacron	da'cron	Strong wool-like synthetic material.
denim	den'im	Coarse cotton fabric.
ensemble	en sem'ble	Several garments worn together, often of different fabrics.
gabardine	gab ar dine'	Fabric resembling serge.
gingham	ging'ham	Cotton cloth of two or more colors.
hosiery	ho'sier y	Stockings and knitted goods.
jersey	jer'sey	Silk, wool, or cotton knitted fabric.
khaki	kha'ki	Light, dull cloth used for uniforms.
linen	lin'en	Fabric made of flax fibers.
lingerie	lin ge rie'	Linen goods collectively; undergarments for women.
mercerize	mer'cer ize	Prepare cotton with a caustic to make it stronger and silky and take dye better.
millinery	mil'li ner y	Women's hats.
necktie	neck'tie	Tie worn under chin.
negligee	neg li gee'	Dressing gown worn by women.
nylon	ny'lon	Strong, smooth synthetic fabric.
organdy	or'gan dy	Kind of thin muslin.
orlon	or'lon	Synthetic fiber used in textiles.
overalls	o'ver alls	Trousers worn by workmen.
percale	per cale'	Closely woven cotton fabric.
pique	pi que'	Ribbed cotton fabric.
rayon	ray'on	Synthetic fiber made chemically from cellulose.
remnant	rem'nant	Small remaining part.
sateen	sa teen'	Cotton fabric with glossy surface.
suspenders	sus pen'ders	Twin straps to hold up trousers.
taffeta	taf'fe ta	Fine smooth silk fabric.
texture	tex'ture	Characteristic structure of fabric.
underwear	un'der wear	Garments worn under outer clothing.
worsted	wor'sted	Yarn spun from long-stapled wool.
zipper	zip'per	Interlocking fastening device.

Lesson 107 — EDUCATION

academic	ac a dem′ic	Pertaining to schools and studies.
accelerated	ac cel′er at ed	Young or rapid for school grade.
accredited	ac cred′i ted	Meets prescribed requirements.
auditorium	au di to′ri um	Room assigned to an audience.
baccalaureate	bac ca lau′re ate	Relating to graduation or degree.
census	cen′sus	House-to-house school canvass.
classics	clas′sics	Literature of the highest class.
compulsory	com pul′so ry	Required; enforced by law.
creative	cre a′tive	Emphasizing originality.
criteria	cri te′ri a	Standards of judging.
curriculum	cur ric′u lum	Total or required school offering.
dean	dean	Directing administrative officer.
department	de part′ment	Any one branch of learning.
evaluation	e val u a′tion	Careful appraisal.
fraternity	fra ter′ni ty	Society of men students.
genius	gen′ius	Person with exceptionally high I. Q.
graduate	grad′u ate	Finish course and receive diploma.
guidance	guid′ance	Special advice to students.
honorary	hon′or a ry	Title held by courtesy.
instill	in still′	Infuse; impart.
instruction	in struc′tion	Teaching; knowledge; education.
I. Q.	I. Q.	*Abbr.* intelligence quotient, measure of children's intelligence.
kindergarten	kin der gar′ten	School just below first grade.
lecture	lec′ture	Instruct by formal talks.
matriculate	ma tric′u late	Enroll as a student.
moron	mo′ron	Person with low mental ability.
normal	nor′mal	Conforming to a standard, or average growth, progress, or mentality.
pedagogy	ped′a go gy	Science of teaching.
philosophy	phi los′o phy	System to guide life or education.
profession	pro fes′sion	Occupation requiring advanced and specialized education.
progressive	pro gres′sive	Emphasizing reform in education.
retarded	re tard′ed	Old or slow for school grade.
rural aid	ru′ral aid	Financial help to country schools.
scholarship	schol′ar ship	Quality of learning.
scientific	sci en tif′ic	Pertaining to science.
sectioning	sec′tion ing	Dividing classes into like groups.
semester	se mes′ter	Half a school year.
sorority	so ror′i ty	Society for women students.
syllabus	syl′la bus	Brief statement of main points.
technical	tech′ni cal	Pertaining to special skills.
traditional	tra di′tion al	Emphasizing past values and methods.

Lesson 108 ELECTRICITY

alternating	*a*l'ter nat ing	Reversing at regular intervals.
ammeter	am'*me* ter	Device for measuring current.
ampere	am'per*e*	Unit of current strength.
amplifier	am'pli fi er	Device to magnify impulses.
amplitude	am'pli tud*e*	Departure from the average.
anode	an'od*e*	Positive electrode.
armature	ar'ma tur*e*	Revolving part of a dynamo.
atom	at'om	Smallest bit of matter retaining properties of a chemical element.
cathode	cath'od*e*	Negative electrode.
circuit	cir'*cu*it	Path of an electric current.
coil	coil	Spiral or ring made by winding.
commutator	com'*m*u ta t*o*r	Device on an armature.
condenser	con dens'er	Instrument for holding a charge.
conductance	con duc'tan*ce*	Ease of flow of a current.
conductor	con duc't*o*r	Good transmitter of current.
conduit	con'd*u*it	Tubing for conductors.
controller	con trol'*l*er	Device controlling current.
converter	con ver'*t*er	Device for changing A.C. to D.C.
coulomb	co*u* lom*b*'	Unit of quantity of current.
current	cur'*r*ent	A flow of electricity.
dynamo	d*y*'na mo	Machine that induces current.
electrification	e lec'tri fi ca *tio*n	Process of supplying current.
electrode	e lec'trod*e*	Terminal of electric source.
electrolysis	e lec trol'y *si*s	Electrical decomposition of matter (the electrolyte).
farad	far'ad	Unit of electric capacity.
frequency	fre'*qu*en *c*y	Number of cycles per second.
fuse	fus*e*	Overcurrent protective device.
incandescence	in can des'*cence*	Condition of glowing with heat.
insulation	in su la'*tio*n	Nonconducting material.
kilowatt	kil'o w*a*tt	One thousand watts.
magneto	mag ne'to	Dynamo with permanent magnets surrounding the armature.
motor	mo't*o*r	Electric engine; self-propelled.
neon	ne on'	Type of tubular electric light.
ohm	o*h*m	Unit of electrical resistance.
rheostat	r*h*e'o stat	Device for varying current.
transmitter	trans mit'*t*er	Device that carries current or sends out electrical energy.
shunt	shunt	Conductor that is a resistor.
transformer	trans for'mer	Device changing current voltage.
volt	volt	Unit of electromotive force.
watt	w*a*tt	Unit of electric power.

Lesson 109 FOODS AND GROCERIES

asparagus	as par′a gus	Tender-stalked plant.
avocado	av o ca′do	Pulpy, pear-shaped fruit.
banana	ba nan′a	Tropical, sweet, pulpy fruit.
biscuit	bis′cuit	Small, dry cake of raised bread.
bologna	bo lo′gna	Large sausage.
broccoli	broc′co li	Variety of cauliflower.
canape	ca na pe′	Piece of bread spread with a relish.
cauliflower	cau′li flow er	Vegetable with solid, white head.
caviar	cav i ar′	Prepared, salted fish eggs (roe).
cayenne	cay enne′	Hot pungent pepper.
cereals	ce′re als	Edible grains.
chile con carne	chi′le con car′ne	Mexican dish of chile, meat, etc.
chop suey	chop su′ey	Chinese dish of meat, vegetables.
cinnamon	cin′na mon	Spicy bark of East Indian tree.
cocoa	co′coa	Powder made from cacao seed.
coconut	co′co nut	Fruit of the coconut palm.
consomme	con som me′	Clear soup made from meat broth.
endive	en′dive	Curled leafed herb used in salads.
fricassee	fric as see′	Dish made of finely cut meat served with gravy.
gelatin	gel′a tin	Animal jelly.
hominy	hom′i ny	Coarsely ground cooked corn.
lentils	len′tils	Seeds of plant of the pea family.
macaroni	mac a ro′ni	Flour paste in form of tubes.
marshmallow	marsh′mal low	Soft, white, spongy candy.
mayonnaise	may on naise′	Thick salad dressing.
nutrition	nu tri′tion	Process of nourishment; food.
oleomargarine	o le o mar′ga rine	Fat butter substitute.
oyster	oys′ter	Mollusk used as food.
raisin	rai′sin	Dried grape.
rhubarb	rhu′barb	Plant with edible stalks.
saccharin	sac′char in	Nonfattening sweetener.
salmon	salm′on	Large soft-finned fish.
sauerkraut	sauer′kraut	Cabbage cut fine and fermented.
sausage	sau′sage	Ground meat with seasoning.
spaghetti	spa ghet′ti	Slender, dried sticks of wheat paste.
sorghum	sor′ghum	Molasses made from sorghum plant.
syrup	syr′up	Concentrated sugar solution.
vermicelli	ver mi cel′li	Wheat paste formed in cords.
vitamin	vi′ta min	Essential constituent in foods.
zwieback	zwie′back	Kind of over-browned toast.

Lesson 110 — FUEL AND OIL

acetone	ac′e tone	Inflammable solvent for fats, resin.
acetylene	a cet′y lene	Explosive gas used in welding.
anthracite	an′thra cite	Hard, lustrous, ashless, smokeless coal.
Bakelite	Ba′ke lite	Compound resembling hard rubber.
benzine	ben′zine	Motor fuel mixture; cleaning solvent.
bituminous	bi tu′mi nous	Soft coal.
butane	bu′tane	Gaseous hydrocarbon fuel.
charcoal	char′coal	Black substance of charred wood.
coke	coke	Distilled coal. It is hard, porous.
colliery	col′lier y	Coal mine.
combustion	com bus′tion	Process of burning.
creosote	cre′o sote	Oily antiseptic fluid.
croppings	crop′pings	Portion of exposed coal vein.
crude	crude	In natural state.
dehydrator	de hy′dra tor	Apparatus for removing water, or moisture, from any material.
derrick	der′rick	Framework over a drill hole.
distil	dis til′	Drive off gas from a liquid or solid.
ethyl	eth′yl	Antiknock fluid in gasoline.
gasoline	gas′o line	Inflammable liquid used as fuel.
graphite	graph′ite	Slippery, greasy, soft form of carbon.
gusher	gush′er	Spouting oil well.
illuminate	il lu′mi nate	Light up.
inflammable	in flam′ma ble	Easily set on fire.
kerosene	ker′o sene	Oil used in lamps, called "coal oil."
lampblack	lamp′black	Fine, black soot.
lignite	lig′nite	Brownish-black coal.
lubricant	lu′bri cant	Substance used to reduce friction.
naphtha	naph′tha	Colorless solvent and fuel.
octane	oc′tane	Evaluative constituent of gasoline.
ozocerite	o zo′ce rite	Waxlike mineral used in candles, etc.
paraffin	par′af fin	Colorless, tasteless wax.
peat	peat	Fuel-forming deposit of plants partly decomposed in water.
petroleum	pe tro′le um	Oily liquid formed in the earth.
pipeline	pipe′line	Line of pipes to carry oil or gas.
pool	pool	Area of rock which yields petroleum.
refinery	re fin′er y	Outfit for separating oil products.
saturation	sat u ra′tion	State of a liquid that has absorbed all that it can of a substance.
screenings	screen′ings	Small particles of sifted material.
seep	seep	Ooze; place where oozing occurs.
thermal	ther′mal	Relating to heat or heating.

Lesson 111 GEOGRAPHY

archipelago	ar *chi* pel'a go	Sea containing many islands.
arctic	arc'tic	Region surrounding the North Pole.
atmosphere	at'mos *phere*	The air that surrounds the earth.
atoll	at'ol*l*	Ring-shaped coral island.
coastal	co*a*st'al	Along a coast or seashore.
continent	con'ti nent	Major body of land; mainland.
doldrums	dol'drums	Region of light winds, near equator.
equator	e *qu*a'tor	East-west circle around the earth and midway between the poles.
equinoctial	e *qu*i noc'*ti*al	When day and night are equally long.
fiord	fiord	Narrow inlet of the sea.
fossil	fos'*s*il	Any trace of ancient life in rock.
geography	ge og'ra *phy*	Study of the earth as man's home.
glacier	gla'*ci*er	Large, natural mass of moving ice.
global	glob'al	Pertaining to the whole world.
harbor	har'bor	Protected body of water for ships.
hemisphere	hem'i *sphere*	Half of the earth.
highlands	hig*h*'lands	Land high above sea level.
inhabitant	in hab'i tant	Person or animal living in a place.
island	i*s*'land	Land surrounded by water.
isthmus	is*th*'mus	Strip joining two bodies of land.
latitude	lat'i tud*e*	Distance from equator in degrees.
longitude	lon'*gi* tud*e*	Distance east or west in degrees.
meridian	me rid'i an	Circle of longitude between poles.
mountainous	moun't*a*in *o*us	Abounding in mountains.
oasis	o a'sis	Fertile green spot in a desert.
ocean	o'*ce*an	Vast body of salt water.
pampas	pam'pas	Grassy plains in Argentina.
peninsula	pen in'su la	Land almost surrounded by water.
physiography	*phys* i og'ra *phy*	Study of physical features of earth.
plateau	pla *teau'*	Tableland, high above the sea.
prairie	pra*i*'ri*e*	Level, grassy land without trees.
stratosphere	stra'to *sphere*	Upper region of the atmosphere.
swamp	sw*a*mp	Wet, soft land; morass.
temperature	tem'per a tur*e*	Measurement of the relative "hotness" or "coldness," in degrees.
terrain	ter ra*i*n'	Land; character of land.
time belts	tim*e* belts	Longitudinal areas with same time.
torrid	tor'*r*id	Equatorial zone; very hot.
tributary	trib'u ta ry	Stream flowing into another.
volcano	vol ca'no	Vent in earth's surface through which steam, lava, etc., issue.
zone	zon*e*	Latitudinal division of the earth.

Lesson 112 GOVERNMENT

alien	al'*i*en	Foreigner.
alliance	a*l* li'an*c*e	Union formed by agreement.
ambassador	am bas'*s*a d*o*r	Official representative of one government to another.
amendment	a mend'ment	Change in the constitution.
assessor	a*s* ses*s*'*o*r	Estimator of value for tax.
autocracy	*au* toc'ra *c*y	Government with absolute rule.
ballot	bal'*l*ot	Method of secret voting.
bureaucracy	bu r*eau*'cra *c*y	Government administered by groups.
cabinet	cab'i net	Chief group of advisory officials.
candidate	can'di dat*e*	One who aspires to an office.
census	*c*en'sus	Numbering of the population.
citizenship	*c*it'i zen ship	Status of being a citizen.
communism	com'*m*u ni*s*m	Governmental ownership of property.
conservation	con *s*e*r* va'*tio*n	Official care of natural resources.
constitution	con sti tu'*tio*n	Basic body of laws and principles.
consul	con'sul	Official foreign representative.
delegate	del'e gat*e*	Person given representative power.
democracy	de moc'ra *c*y	Government run by the people.
department	de part'ment	Special division of government.
disfranchise	dis fran'chi*se*	Deprive of citizenship rights.
domestic	do mes'tic	Pertaining to one's own country.
envoy	en'voy	One dispatched upon a mission.
federal	fed'er al	Pertaining to central government.
foreigner	for'*eig*n er	Person from foreign government.
inauguration	in *au* gu ra'*tio*n	Formal induction into an office.
judicial	j*u* di'*c*ial	Pertaining to justice.
legislation	leg is la'*tio*n	Pertaining to lawmaking.
legislature	leg is la'tur*e*	Lawmaking body.
lobby	lob'*by*	Solicit votes of legislators.
mayor	ma*y*'*o*r	Chief magistrate of a city.
naturalize	nat'u ral ize	Make citizens of aliens.
nominate	nom'i nat*e*	Propose for office.
patriotic	pa tri ot'ic	Tending to love one's country.
protectorate	pro tec't*o*r at*e*	Government or protection of a weak country by a strong one.
reciprocity	re*c* i pro*c*'i ty	Mutually advantageous trade relationship.
reclamation	rec la ma'*tio*n	Restoring wasted resources.
revenue	rev'e nu*e*	General source of state or national income.
socialism	so'*c*ial i*s*m	Production control by government.
suffrage	suf'*frage*	Right to vote.
treasury	tre*a*s'ur y	Place for keeping funds.

Lesson 113 HARDWARE

auger	*au*g′er	Tool for boring holes.
bevel	bev′el	Instrument for marking angles.
cable	ca′bl*e*	Large, strong rope or chain.
calipers	cal′i pers	Measuring compass.
carver	car′ver	Large knife for carving.
chisel	chi*s*′*e*l	Cutting tool with the edge at its end.
cleaver	cle*a*v′er	Small ax for cutting meat.
corrugated	cor′*r*u gat ed	Formed with folds or furrows.
cutlery	cut′ler y	Cutting tools.
emery	em′er y	Dark, hard material, used as powder or in a stone for grinding.
enameled	en am′el*e*d	Covered with hard, glossy paint.
faucet	f*au*′*c*et	Device to control water flow; a tap.
forceps	for′*c*eps	Pincers or tongs for delicate work.
galvanized	gal′va niz*e*d	Iron or steel coated with zinc.
gauge	ga*u*g*e*	Carpenter's tool to mark a line parallel to an edge.
gimlet	gim′let	Small, augerlike tool.
gouge	goug*e*	Chisel with a curved blade.
hammer	ham′*m*er	Tool for driving nails, beating metal.
hatchet	ha*t*ch′et	Small, short-handled ax.
hone	hon*e*	Stone for sharpening tools.
isinglass	i′*s*in glas*s*	Thin, transparent sheets, often mica.
knob	*k*nob	Handle of a door.
level	lev′el	Tool for determining levelness.
mallet	mal′*l*et	Hammer with wooden head.
mattock	mat′*t*o*c*k	Tool used for grubbing.
nozzle	noz′*z*l*e*	Spout or mouthpiece of a hose.
padlock	pad′lo*c*k	Portable lock having a curved bar or bow.
pincers	pin′*c*ers	Long-handled tool for gripping things.
pliers	pli′ers	Pincers with long jaws for bending, cutting, etc.
pumice	pum′*ice*	Abrasive powder used for polishing.
rivet	riv′et	Pin or bolt with head to fasten metal.
screws	screws	Small, threaded bolts.
shovel	sho*v*′*e*l	Long-handled dirt or sand scoop.
sickle	sick′l*e*	Short, curved blade used in cutting.
solder	so*l*′der	Melting metal used to fasten metals.
tongs	tongs	Tool for taking hold of objects.
trowel	tro*w*′el	Tool for shaping a plastic material.
washer	wash′er	Flat ring placed around bolts.
wrench	*w*rench	Tool for turning nuts, bolts, etc.
wringer	*w*ring′er	Machine to press water from clothes.

Lesson 114 HEALTH

abscess	ab'*scess*	Collection of pus in the body.
acidosis	*ac* i do'sis	Excessively acid body condition.
allergic	*al* ler'*gic*	Extra-sensitive to a substance.
anemia	a ne'mi a	Lack of red corpuscles in the blood.
anesthetic	an es thet'ic	Drug causing loss of sensation.
antiseptic	an ti sep'tic	Substance that opposes infection.
antitoxin	an ti to*x*'in	Body substance in blood that combats a specific poison.
appendicitis	a*p* pen di *c*i'tis	Inflammation of the appendix.
artery	ar'ter y	Blood vessel leading from the heart.
asthma	a*sth*'ma	Disease of the bronchial tubes.
bacteria	bac ter'i a	One kind of micro-organisms.
cardiac	car'di ac	Pertaining to the heart.
contagious	con ta'*gio*us	Catching; spread by contact.
corpuscle	cor'pus *cle*	Small mass, such as a blood cell.
diagnosis	di ag no'sis	Recognition of disease by symptoms.
diphtheria	di*ph* the'ri a	Acute infectious throat disease.
disinfectant	dis in fect'ant	Agent that destroys disease germs.
epidemic	ep i dem'ic	Widespread disease, common to many.
hemorrhage	hem'*o*r r*hage*	Discharge of blood from blood vessels.
hygiene	h*y*'*giene*	Science of keeping well.
inflammation	in fla*m* ma'*tion*	Act of being inflamed; redness.
insomnia	in som'ni a	Inability to sleep.
malignant	ma lig'nant	Very infectious; very dangerous.
microbe	mi'crob*e*	Tiny living thing, usually a bacterium.
nausea	n*au*'*s*e a	Sickness of the stomach.
neuralgia	n*e*u ral'*g*i a	Pain along the course of a nerve.
paralysis	pa ral'y sis	Loss of sensation or movement.
penicillin	pen i cil'*l*in	Material made by a mold, kills some kinds of disease bacteria.
pestilence	pes'ti len*ce*	Contagious widespread disease.
plasma	plas'ma	Fluid part of the blood.
pneumonia	*pneu* mo'ni a	Disease involving inflamed lungs.
polio	po'l*i* o	Informal word for poliomyelitis, infantile paralysis.
poultice	poul'ti*ce*	Medical mixture applied to a sore.
sanitarium	san i tar'i um	Institution for sick people.
serum	se'rum	Watery part formed by coagulation.
sulfa drugs	sul'fa drugs	Group of chemicals which inhibit growth of some bacteria.
symptoms	symp'toms	Body changes that indicate disease.
tonsillitis	ton *sil* li'tis	Condition of inflamed tonsils.
tuberculosis	tu b*e*r cu lo'sis	Infectious disease, often in lungs.
typhoid	t*y*'*ph*oid	Abdominal disease with fever, rash.

Lesson 115 HOME ECONOMICS

albumin	al bu'min	Food substance in milk, eggs, etc.
aluminum	a lu'mi num	Light-weight non-corrosive metal used in some cooking utensils.
aniline	an'i lin*e*	Oily liquid used in many dyes.
barbecue	bar'be cu*e*	Animal roasted whole.
baste	bast*e*	Sew with wide stitches.
bobbin	bob'*b*in	Spool for holding thread, yarn, etc.
braise	bra*ise*	To stew in a covered kettle.
casserole	cas'*s*e rol*e*	Covered dish for baking.
cellulose	*c*el'*l*u lose	Solid matter in plants, paper, cotton, etc.
dehydrate	de h*y*'drat*e*	To free from water; to dry.
dextrose	de*x*'tros*e*	Glucose; a sugar present in plants.
diet	di'et	Selected course of food.
dietitian	di e ti'*ti*an	One trained to plan meals.
escalloped	es cal'*loped*	Baked with a cream sauce.
fillet	fil'*let*	Slice of boneless meat or fish.
fluorescent	fl*u* o res'*c*ent	Lamp which glows without heat.
hemstitch	hem'sti*t*ch	Ornamental gathering stitch.
homogeneous	ho mo *ge*'ne *o*us	Composed of similar parts.
homogenize	ho mog'en iz*e*	Break up fat globules in milk and cream to increase digestibility.
lactic	lac'tic	Pertaining to milk.
lactose	lac'tos*e*	Type of sugar present in milk.
legume	leg'um*e*	Podlike fruit such as peas.
overcast	o ver cast'	Sew over raw edges of a seam.
pepsin	pep'sin	Substance that helps digestion.
pinking	pink'ing	Edge cut in a zigzag manner.
puree	pu r*ee*'	Thick soup.
Pyrex	P*y*'rex	Heat-resistant glass.
ramekin	r*a*m'e kin	Deep dish for serving food.
refectory	re fec'to ry	Table with two drop-leaves.
riboflavin	ri bo'flav in	Vitamin B_2.
Sanforize	San'for iz*e*	Treatment to prevent shrinkage.
sanitary	san'i tar y	Free from filth and infection.
sear	se*a*r	Expose meat to intense heat.
shuttle	shut'*tle*	Part which carries bobbin.
souffle	sou*f* *fle*'	Dish made with beaten egg whites.
spatula	spat'u la	Implement with broad, flat blade.
thermostat	ther'mo stat	Device for regulating temperature.
utensil	u ten'sil	Useful tool or equipment.
vitamin	vi'ta min	Substance needed in small amounts for proper growth and health.
warp	warp	Vertical thread in weaving.

Lesson 116 HOME FURNITURE

antique	an tique'	Relic; something old.
buffet	buf fet'	Cabinet for china, etc.
burnish	bur'nish	Cause to shine.
cabinet	cab'i net	Case for holding or displaying valuables, radio, television, etc.
chaise longue	chaise longue	Chair with a long seat.
chintz	chintz	Printed cotton cloth, often glazed.
Chippendale	Chip'pen dale	Furniture designed by Chippendale, English cabinetmaker.
colonial	co lo'ni al	Pertaining to the Colonial period.
cupboard	cup'board	Closet for dishes.
curtain	cur'tain	Material hung at a window.
Deepfreeze	Deep'freeze'	Freezer for quick-freezing and storage of food.
divan	di'van	Large, low couch.
drapery	dra'per y	Fabric used for decoration.
Empire	Em'pire	Heavy, ornate style of furniture.
hassock	has'sock	Footstool.
Hepplewhite	Hep'ple white	Furniture designed by Hepplewhite, English cabinetmaker.
highboy	high'boy	Tall chest of drawers on legs.
Jacobean	Jac o be'an	Seventeenth century design.
jardiniere	jar di niere'	Ornamental jar for flowers.
laminated	lam'i nat ed	Thin layers of wood glued together with matching grains.
linoleum	li no'le um	Type of floor covering.
mahogany	ma hog'a ny	Reddish-colored hardwood.
maple	ma'ple	Hard, light-colored wood.
mattress	mat'tress	Stuffed, tufted pad for a bed.
mirror	mir'ror	Reflector; a looking glass.
modern	mod'ern	Functional, undecorated furniture.
mohair	mo'hair	Fabric woven from Angora goat hair.
ottoman	ot'to man	Stuffed seat without a back.
porcelain	por'ce lain	Translucent china or earthenware.
radiator	ra'di a tor	Device for diffusing heat.
refrigerator	re frig'er a tor	Cabinet for keeping food cool.
Sheraton	Sher'a ton	Furniture designed by Sheraton.
traditional	tra di'tion al	Furniture following period styles.
upholstery	up hol'ster y	Textile fittings for furniture.
veneer	ve neer'	Thin layer of wood.
Venetian blind	Ve ne'tian blind	Inside shutter.
wainscot	wain'scot	Wooden paneling on inner walls.
walnut	wal'nut	Dark, hard wood.

Lesson 117 INSURANCE AND REAL ESTATE

abstract	ab′stract	Summary of title to land.
actuary	ac′tu a ry	Expert computer of insurance risks and premiums.
adjuster	ad just′er	One who adjusts claims.
annuity	an nu′i ty	Sum of money payable per year.
arson	ar′son	Purposely setting fire to property.
assessment	as sess′ment	Amount to be paid.
beneficiary	ben e fi′ci a ry	Person receiving insurance benefit.
casualty	cas′u al ty	Unforeseen event; type of insurance against loss from accident.
compensate	com′pen sate	Make amends for; to pay.
convertible	con vert′i ble	Capable of being exchanged, as one security for another.
conveyance	con vey′ance	Deed transferring title.
disability	dis a bil′i ty	State of being disabled.
emblements	em′ble ments	Annual growing crops.
encumbrance	en cum′brance	Charge or lien upon land.
endowment	en dow′ment	Money or property settlement.
estate	es tate′	Person's property.
expectation	ex pec ta′tion	Prospect of the future.
forfeiture	for′fei ture	Act of losing possession.
indemnity	in dem′ni ty	Security against loss.
insure	in sure′	Make safe from financial loss.
landlord	land′lord	One who rents to another.
lapse	lapse	Ending of neglected right.
lessee	les see′	Person to whom a lease is granted.
mortality	mor tal′i ty	Death percentage or rate.
occupancy	oc′cu pan cy	Act of dwelling in a place.
perpetuity	per pe tu′i ty	Existence forever.
policy	pol′i cy	Insurance contract.
premises	prem′is es	House or building and its grounds.
premium	pre′mi um	Money paid for insurance; a sum above face value.
protection	pro tec′tion	Preservation against loss.
quitclaim	quit′claim	Relinquishment of claim.
realty	re′al ty	Real estate property.
recipient	re cip′i ent	One who receives against loss.
section	sec′tion	640 acres of land.
solicit	so lic′it	Ask for business or trade.
survivor	sur vi′vor	One who remains alive.
tenant	ten′ant	One who rents property.
title	ti′tle	Legal right to property.
underwriter	un der writ′er	Person in insurance business.
warranty	war′ran ty	Guarantee of title or contract.

Lesson 118 JEWELRY

alloy	*al* loy′	Two or more metals mixed and fused.
amethyst	am′e thyst	Purple quartz.
baguette	ba g*u*et*te*′	Stone cut in an oblong, narrow form.
bracelet	bra*ce*′let	Ornament worn around the wrist.
brooch	br*o*och	Large ornamental pin.
cameo	cam′e o	Gem carved in relief, often onyx or shell.
carat	car′at	Unit of weight for precious stones; a twenty-fourth part in an alloy.
carnelian	car nel′*i*an	Bright, red stone, hard and tough.
crystal	crys′tal	Colorless, transparent quartz or diamond.
diamond	di′a mond	Precious stone that is crystalized carbon.
earring	e*a*r′ring	Ornament worn on the ear lobe.
electrum	e lec′trum	Alloy of gold and silver, pale yellow.
embossed	em bos*sed*′	Ornamented with raised work.
emerald	em′er ald	Brilliant-green precious stone.
engraved	en grav*e*d′	Cut or carved in sunken patterns.
facet	fa*c*′et	One of the sides of a cut gem.
filigree	fil′i gre*e*	Ornamental work of fine wire.
garnet	gar′net	Brittle mineral of deep-red color.
hallmark	hal*l*′mark	Official mark of purity on gold and silver articles.
inlay	in′la*y*	Decoration or design set in a surface.
jade	jad*e*	Tough, green or whitish stone.
loupe	lo*upe*	Magnifying glass used by jewelers.
marquise	mar *quise*′	Gem cut as an oval with pointed ends.
niello	ni el′*l*o	Black, metallic alloy of silver, copper, lead, containing sulphur.
onyx	on′*y*x	Quartz in layers of various colors.
pearl	pe*a*rl	Round, lustrous gem formed by oysters. Is blue, black, gray, pink, or white.
pendant	pen′dant	Any hanging ornamentation.
pewter	pe*w*′ter	Alloy that includes tin.
platinum	plat′i num	Heavy, precious, silver-white metal.
relief	re l*i*ef′	Carving projecting from a background.
rhinestone	r*h*in*e*′ston*e*	Colorless imitation stone, high luster.
rosette	ro *s*et*te*′	Design shaped like a rose, circular.
ruby	ru′by	Highly valued red stone.
sapphire	sa*p*′*ph*ir*e*	Transparent, rich-blue precious stone.
solitaire	sol i ta*i*r*e*′	Single gem set alone.
tiara	ti a′ra	Decorative band for the head.
topaz	to′paz	Yellow mineral used as a gem.
tourmaline	t*o*ur′ma lin*e*	Semiprecious stone, usually black.
turquoise	tur′*quoise*	Opaque green to blue stone.
vanity	van′i ty	Cosmetic bag or box.

Lesson 119 — LAW

adjudicate	ad ju'di cate	Settle judicially.
affidavit	af fi da'vit	Sworn declaration in writing.
allegation	al le ga'tion	Statement of what one undertakes to prove.
appeal	ap peal'	Refer one's cause to a higher court.
apprehend	ap pre hend'	Arrest; understand; fear.
arraign	ar raign'	Call before court for trial.
chattel	chat'tel	Movable personal property.
clemency	clem'en cy	Mercy; leniency; mild treatment.
client	cli'ent	Patron of a lawyer.
decree	de cree'	Edict; law; command.
defendant	de fend'ant	One who is sued in a court.
docket	dock'et	List of impending lawsuits.
domicile	dom'i cile	Place of residence.
duress	du'ress	Imprisonment; restraint by force.
evidence	ev'i dence	Material to determine truth.
executor	ex ec'u tor	One appointed to carry out a will.
felony	fel'o ny	Crime involving penalty more severe than a misdemeanor.
garnish	gar'nish	Warn, or bring into court.
homicide	hom'i cide	Person who kills another; a killing.
incriminate	in crim'i nate	Charge with a crime or a fault.
indictment	in dict'ment	Formal criminal accusation.
injunction	in junc'tion	Court order controlling action.
jurisdiction	ju ris dic'tion	Right to give out justice; territorial or other limits of such right.
larceny	lar'ce ny	Act of stealing.
legacy	leg'a cy	Bequest by will.
libel	li'bel	Written defamation or slander.
lien	li'en	Legal claim on property.
litigation	lit i ga'tion	Act of carrying on a lawsuit.
misdemeanor	mis de mean'or	Petty crime involving a penalty less than that for a felony.
plaintiff	plain'tiff	One who begins a lawsuit.
probate	pro'bate	Official proving of a will.
prosecute	pros'e cute	Bring legal suit against.
quash	quash	Abate; annul; overthrow.
subpoena	sub poe'na	Writ summoning a witness.
testator	tes ta'tor	Man who leaves a will.
testimony	tes'ti mo ny	Words of a witness in a court.
tort	tort	Civil wrong involving damages.
trespass	tres'pass	Intrude, as on property.
verdict	ver'dict	Decision of a jury.
versus	ver'sus	Against.

Lesson 120 LITERATURE AND JOURNALISM

appendix	a*p* pen'di*x*	Matter added at the end of a book.
autobiography	au to bi og'ra *ph*y	One's life story written by himself.
ballad	bal'*l*ad	Romantic story, often sung.
bibliography	bib li og'ra *ph*y	List of related literature.
biography	bi og'ra *ph*y	Study of one person's life.
chronicle	c*h*ron'i cl*e*	Historical story or account of events in order of time.
classic	clas'*s*ic	Literature of the highest quality.
columnist	col'um nist	Writer of a special newspaper department, using his own opinions.
comedy	com'e dy	Amusing, light drama.
copy	cop'y	Manuscript to be set in type.
drama	dra'ma	Play.
editor	ed'i tor	Arranger of copy for publication.
elegy	el'*e* gy	Mournful poem; funeral song.
essay	es'*say*	Literary composition on one subject.
fable	fa'bl*e*	Fictitious story with a moral.
fiction	fic'*tio*n	Imagined story.
frontispiece	fron'tis p*iece*	Illustration facing a title page.
idyll	i'dyl*l*	Description in verse.
illustrated	il'*l*us trat ed	Text accompanied by pictures.
index	in'de*x*	Alphabetical list of contents.
introduction	in tro duc'*tio*n	Preliminary part of a publication.
issue	is'*sue*	Copies sent forth at one time.
journal	j*o*ur'nal	Newspaper or magazine.
literature	lit'er a tur*e*	Field of writing, printed matter.
lyric	lyr'ic	Emotional poem, often sung.
manuscript	man'u script	Author's copy submitted to editor.
narrative	nar'*r*a tiv*e*	That which is told; a story.
novel	nov'el	Fictitious tale of book length.
paragrapher	par'a gra*ph* er	Person who writes short unit thoughts, often humorous.
preface	pref'a*ce*	Explanatory chapter or section.
prologue	pro'log*ue*	Introduction to a literary work.
proof	proof	Trial printing for correction.
review	re v*iew*'	Critical account of a publication.
royalty	roy'al ty	Percentage paid to an author.
satire	sat'ir*e*	Literature used to ridicule.
sequel	se'*qu*el	Continuation of previous article.
serial	se'ri al	Story published in parts.
soliloquy	so lil'o *quy*	Act of talking to one's self.
sonnet	son'*n*et	Lyric poem of fourteen lines.
tragedy	trag'e dy	Serious drama.

Lesson 121 MATHEMATICS

angle	an'gle	Figure made by intersecting lines.
area	a're a	The contents of a figure's surface.
bisector	bi sec'tor	Straight line bisecting a segment.
circumference	cir cum'fer ence	Line bounding a circular area.
coefficient	co ef fi'cient	Number or symbol that multiplies another.
coordinates	co or'di nates	Quantities specifying positions.
correlation	cor re la'tion	Relation between series of data.
data	da'ta	Collected facts or statistics.
decimal	dec'i mal	Numbered or proceeding by tens.
denominator	de nom'i na tor	Lower part of a fraction.
diameter	di am'e ter	Straight line across through the center of a circle.
equation	e qua'tion	Expression of two equal quantities.
exponent	ex po'nent	Figure denoting use of quantity.
formula	for'mu la	Equation expressed by symbols.
fraction	frac'tion	Part of an integer.
graph	graph	Diagram of mathematical relations.
hypotenuse	hy pot'e nuse	Long side of a right triangle.
infinity	in fin'i ty	Quality of being without extent.
integer	in'te ger	Whole number.
linear	lin'e ar	Having length only.
median	me'di an	Middle number of a series.
multiple	mul'ti ple	Number exactly divisible.
negative	neg'a tive	Quantity less than zero; minus.
numerator	nu'mer a tor	Upper part of a fraction.
perimeter	per im'e ter	Outside boundary of a figure.
perpendicular	per pen dic'u lar	Forming a right angle.
positive	pos'i tive	Quantity more than zero; plus.
proportion	pro por'tion	The equality of ratios.
quotient	quo'tient	Result obtained by division.
radius	ra'di us	Line from the center of a circle to the circumference.
ratio	ra'ti o	Relative magnitude.
segment	seg'ment	Part cut off.
semicircle	sem'i cir cle	Half of a circle.
solution	so lu'tion	Act of solving a problem.
statistics	sta tis'tics	Classified numerical facts.
symmetrical	sym met'ri cal	Figure having corresponding parts.
tangent	tan'gent	Touching lines, not intersecting.
unit	u'nit	Least whole number; one.
variation	va ri a'tion	Deviation from average or type.
vertical	ver'ti cal	Perpendicular to the horizon plane; upright.

Lesson 122 MINING ENGINEERING

alignment	a lign′ment	Horizontal plan, not the profile.
alloy	al loy′	Two or more metals mixed and fused.
altitude	al′ti tude	Vertical elevation; height.
amalgam	a mal′gam	Alloy of mercury and another metal.
antimony	an′ti mo ny	Brittle, silver-white metal.
aqueduct	aq′ue duct	Channel made to carry water.
bonanza	bo nan′za	Rich mine vein.
bullion	bul′lion	Gold or silver in the mass.
centrifugal	cen trif′u gal	Flying away from the center.
concrete	con′crete	Artificial stone made of cement, sand, and gravel or crushed rock.
corrosion	cor ro′sion	Eating away due to chemical action.
derrick	der′rick	Machine for lifting heavy objects.
dredge	dredge	Machine to dig up sand from water.
dynamite	dy′na mite	Blasting explosive containing TNT.
fissure	fis′sure	Narrow opening, crack, cleft, or split in rock.
flux	flux	Substance that helps to fuse metals and minerals, such as silica, lime.
hydrometer	hy drom′e ter	Device to find specific gravity.
infiltration	in fil tra′tion	Process of slow penetration.
ingot	in′got	Mass of cast metal.
limestone	lime′stone	Rock composed of calcium carbonate.
lode	lode	Rock fissure containing mineral; vein of ore in rocks.
metallurgy	met′al lur gy	Art of separating metals from ores.
millimeter	mil′li me ter	One-thousandth part of a meter.
mineralogy	min er al′o gy	Science which treats of minerals.
nugget	nug′get	Lump or mass of precious metal.
placer	plac′er	Place where gold is washed out.
pneumatic	pneu mat′ic	Operates by compressed air or gas.
reservoir	res′er voir	Place where water is stored.
resilience	re sil′i ence	Power of rebounding or recovering.
siphon	si′phon	Bent tube for withdrawing liquids.
slag	slag	Refuse from the smelting of ore.
sluice	sluice	Trough to separate gold from dirt.
stratum	stra′tum	Layer of sedimentary rock or soil.
surveyor	sur vey′or	One who measures land.
tensile	ten′sile	Capable of tension; ductile.
topographical	top o graph′i cal	Related to detailed mapping.
turbine	tur′bine	Rotary engine spun by fluid force.
uranium	u ra′ni um	Radioactive metallic element used in atom bombs.
vertex	ver′tex	Summit, top, or crown.
viaduct	vi′a duct	Bridge-like road or railway.

Lesson 123 MOTION PICTURES AND PHOTOGRAPHY

achromatic	ach ro mat′ic	No color; no distortion of color.
aperture	ap′er ture	Picture-taking opening in camera.
binocular	bin oc′u lar	Adapted to use of both eyes.
camera	cam′er a	Instrument used to take pictures.
censor	cen′sor	Person to affirm motion picture.
chromo	chro′mo	Picture printed in all colors.
Cinemascope	Cin′e ma scope	Wide-angle screen projection.
contrasty	con′tras ty	Having contrast of dark and light.
director	di rec′tor	One in charge of filming picture.
emulsion	e mul′sion	Coating on photographic film.
exposure	ex po′sure	Subjecting of film to light.
film	film	Thin, coated strip of acetate.
filming	film′ing	Photographing a motion picture.
focus	fo′cus	Point at which image is formed.
Klieg light	Klieg light	Arc light used on sets; bright.
kodak*	ko′dak	Popular name for hand cameras.
lens	lens	Glass in camera to form image.
microphone	mi′cro phone	Device used to "pick up" sound.
miniature	min′i a ture	Set built on a reduced scale.
movie	mov′ie	Motion picture; a theatre.
negative	neg′a tive	Reversed image on film; used for printing of positives.
newsreel	news′reel	Short film portraying the news.
orthochromatic	or tho chro mat′ic	Producing correct color values.
photograph	pho′to graph	Picture made with a camera.
playwright	play′wright	Writer of plays or scripts.
portraiture	por′trai ture	The making of portraits.
positive	pos′i tive	Photograph showing natural image.
producer	pro duc′er	One in general charge of the making of a motion picture.
projection	pro jec′tion	Throwing pictures on a screen.
reel	reel	Spool for film; spool of film.
reflector	re flec′tor	Surface for reflecting light.
scenario	sce na′ri o	Outline of a play or book.
screen	screen	Smooth surface upon which pictures are projected.
script	script	Dialogue with filming directions.
shorts	shorts	Short films to fill up a program.
silhouette	sil hou ette′	Profile portrait in black.
stereophonic	ster e o phon′ic	Three-dimensional sound.
studio	stu′di o	Place where pictures are made.
take	take	Filming of a picture scene.
Technicolor	Tech′ni col or	Trade name of colored movies.

*To be capitalized when used as a trade term.

Lesson 124 MUSIC

accompany	ac com'pa ny	Play a musical background for a soloist.
accordion	ac cor'di on	Keyed wind instrument with reeds and bellows.
adagio	a da'gio	Slowly; slow part in music.
allegro	al le'gro	Brisk and lively.
alto	al'to	Low female or high male voice.
anthem	an'them	Song of praise and gladness.
baritone	bar'i tone	Male voice between tenor and bass.
bass	bass	Lowest male voice.
carol	car'ol	Song of joy.
cello	cel'lo	Baritone of the violin family.
choir	choir	Organized group of singers.
chord	chord	Three or more tones played at once which blend harmoniously.
chorus	cho'rus	Group of singers.
concerto	con cer'to	Composition for an instrument with an orchestral accompaniment.
contralto	con tral'to	Lowest female voice.
crescendo	cre scen'do	Gradually increasing in loudness.
encore	en'core	Number performed because of applause.
forte	for'te	Loud.
fortissimo	for tis'si mo	Very loud.
fugue	fugue	Musical composition in which two or more parts announce the theme.
guitar	gui tar'	Musical instrument with six strings.
harmony	har'mo ny	Pleasing, tuneful blend.
hymn	hymn	Song of praise.
legato	le ga'to	Sustained; smooth and connected.
melody	mel'o dy	Agreeable succession of sounds.
obbligato	ob bli ga'to	Accompanying part.
opera	op'er a	Drama wholly or mostly sung.
operetta	op er et'ta	Light musical opera.
oratorio	or a to'ri o	Musical Biblical drama.
rhythm	rhythm	Regular recurrence of accent.
saxophone	sax'o phone	Wind instrument with finger keys, brass.
serenade	ser'e nade	Music performed outdoors.
sonata	so na'ta	Composition with four movements.
soprano	so pra'no	Highest singing human voice.
scherzo	scher'zo	Sprightly composition.
staccato	stac ca'to	Short and crisp; detached.
symphony	sym'pho ny	Composition for a full orchestra.
tenor	ten'or	Highest male voice.
tune	tune	Musical tones making a complete theme.
violin	vi o lin'	Stringed instrument played with bow.

Lesson 125 OFFICE SUPPLIES

addressograph*	ad dres'so graph	Machine for addressing letters, etc.
adhesive	ad he'sive	Sticky; a sticky material.
almanac	al'man ac	Book of current useful information.
atlas	at'las	Books of large charts or maps.
bristol* board	bris'tol board	Cardboard with smooth surface.
cabinet	cab'i net	Case or set of drawers.
calculator	cal'cu la tor	Machine for calculation.
comptometer*	comp tom'e ter	Type of calculating machine.
copyholder	cop'y hold er	Device holding matter to be copied.
crayon	cray'on	Wax or chalk stick for drawing.
dictaphone*	dic'ta phone	Device for recording dictation.
directory	di rec'to ry	Book of names and addresses.
duplicator	du'pli ca tor	Machine for making copies.
eradicator	e rad'i ca tor	Solution to remove ink chemically.
eyelet	eye'let	Small metal ring.
fastener	fas'ten er	Device for fastening papers.
file	file	Orderly storage space for papers.
glue	glue	Brownish adhesive material.
hectograph	hec'to graph	Duplicator using a layer of gelatin.
indelible	in del'i ble	Incapable of being erased.
index	in'dex	Alphabetical list.
itinerary	i tin'er a ry	Route or plan of travel.
label	la'bel	Attached descriptive slip.
looseleaf	loose'leaf	Having detachable leaves.
memorandum	mem o ran'dum	Informal record.
mimeograph*	mim'e o graph	Duplicator that uses a stencil.
multigraph*	mul'ti graph	Printing machine using movable type in grooves on a cylinder.
parchment	parch'ment	Vellum; superior type of paper.
perforated	per'fo rat ed	Pierced.
photostat*	pho'to stat	Machine for photographing on paper without using film.
portfolio	port fo'li o	Portable case for papers.
recorder	re cord'er	Device for making records.
ruler	rul'er	Strip used to measure or draw lines.
sharpener	sharp'en er	Device for sharpening pencils.
stapler	sta'pler	Device to fasten papers with wire.
stencil	sten'cil	Kind of paper typed or drawn on for use in one kind of duplicator.
stylus	sty'lus	Sharp tool for marking on stencils.
switchboard	switch'board	Device to connect telephones.
tissue	tis'sue	Thin, translucent paper.
typewriter	type'writ er	Machine for writing in print.

*To be capitalized when used as a trade term.

Lesson 126 PHYSICS AND CHEMISTRY

acid	ac'id	Class of substances that are sour.
alkali	al'ka li	Substance with marked basic properties.
analyze	an'a lyze	Separate the parts of a compound.
atom	at'om	Smallest bit of matter retaining properties of a chemical element.
barometer	ba rom'e ter	Instrument measuring air pressure.
cellophane	cel'lo phane	Transparent material of cellulose.
celluloid	cel'lu loid	Inflammable plastic made from camphor.
centigrade	cen'ti grade	Temperature scale, 100 degrees from freezing to boiling points of water.
chemistry	chem'is try	Study of the composition of matter.
cohesion	co he'sion	Act of sticking together.
compound	com'pound	Chemical combination of several things.
crucible	cru'ci ble	Vessel for melting minerals, etc.
crystallize	crys'tal lize	Form crystals; to deposit crystals.
density	den'si ty	Ratio of mass to volume.
distillation	dis til la'tion	Separation by evaporating a portion.
effervesce	ef fer vesce'	Give off bubbles of gas.
electron	e lec'tron	Electrified particle that is negative.
element	el'e ment	Distinct, fundamental variety of matter.
experiment	ex per'i ment	Find out by trial.
Fahrenheit	Fahr'en heit	Temperature scale, 180 degrees from freezing to boiling points of water.
filtrate	fil'trate	Liquid that has passed through a filter.
friction	fric'tion	Resistance to rubbing.
fulcrum	ful'crum	Point of support.
gaseous	gas'e ous	Having the nature of a gas.
gravitation	grav i ta'tion	Force of attraction between all bodies.
inertia	in er'tia	Tendency not to move or stop moving.
magnetism	mag'net ism	The power to attract, as a magnet.
matter	mat'ter	That which occupies space.
mechanics	me chan'ics	Study of action of forces on bodies.
molecule	mol'e cule	Smallest unit of element or compound.
oxidation	ox i da'tion	Act of combining with or adding oxygen.
physics	phys'ics	Study of heat, sound, light, etc.
plastic	plas'tic	Moldable synthetic substance.
radiation	ra di a'tion	Diffusion of rays.
reaction	re ac'tion	Chemical or physical responses.
refract	re fract'	Change direction of rays, mainly light.
substance	sub'stance	Material; stuff; matter.
synthetic	syn thet'ic	Man-made substance, not natural.
vapor	va'por	Gaseous form of a substance.
velocity	ve loc'i ty	Rate of motion in given direction.
volatile	vol'a tile	Evaporates very quickly.

Lesson 127 PSYCHOLOGY

after-image	af'ter-im'age	Continuance of sensory impression after removal of stimulus.
abnormal	ab nor'mal	Wide deviation from average.
achievement	a chieve'ment	Status in skill or knowledge.
amnesia	am ne'sia	Loss of memory.
aptitude	ap'ti tude	Capacity in skill or knowledge.
attention	at ten'tion	Act of heeding anything.
attitude	at'ti tude	Mental set in kind of response.
auditory	au'di to ry	Pertaining to sense of hearing.
capacity	ca pac'i ty	Potentiality for improvement.
complacency	com pla'cen cy	Contentment; complete satisfaction.
concept	con'cept	General notion of related objects.
ego	e'go	The "I" or self of any person.
emotion	e mo'tion	Stirred-up state of mind as in joy, sorrow, or the like.
faculty	fac'ul ty	Mental function such as memory.
frustration	frus tra'tion	Condition of being thwarted.
habit	hab'it	Fixed learned response.
impulse	im'pulse	Sudden drive to action.
inhibition	in hi bi'tion	Restraint of response.
instinct	in'stinct	Inborn pattern of activity.
intelligence	in tel'li gence	Mental capacity or efficiency.
interest	in'ter est	Feeling of preference or concern.
involuntary	in vol'un tar y	Performed without intent.
maladjustment	mal ad just'ment	Disturbance of personality.
mental age	men'tal age	Average intelligence of persons at a given age.
morale	mo rale'	Enthusiasm for group endeavor.
nostalgia	nos tal'gia	Homesickness.
olfactory	ol fac'to ry	Pertaining to sense of smell.
perception	per cep'tion	Awareness of sensory stimulus.
personality	per son al'i ty	One's total social-stimulus value or pattern of behavior.
phobia	pho'bi a	Abnormal or morbid fear.
psychiatry	psy chi'a try	Treatment of mental disorders.
psychology	psy chol'o gy	Science of mental life.
psychometrics	psy cho met'rics	Mental testing.
psychosis	psy cho'sis	Grave mental disorder.
reasoning	rea'son ing	Act of logical thinking.
self-conscious	self-con'scious	Aware of one's own identity.
sensitivity	sen si tiv'i ty	Responsiveness to stimulation.
somatic	so mat'ic	Pertaining to the body.
tactile	tac'tile	Pertaining to sense of touch.
therapy	ther'a py	Remedial treatment of disease.

Lesson 128 RADIO AND TELEVISION

announcer	an nounc′er	Person who introduces a program.
antenna	an ten′na	Sending or receiving conductor.
audibility	au di bil′i ty	Intensity of a received signal.
audio	au′di o	Pertaining to sound broadcasting.
audition	au di′tion	Trial record or hearing.
broadcast	broad′cast	Send out by radio.
channel	chan′nel	Narrow band of frequencies.
commentator	com′men ta tor	One who interprets news events.
decibel	dec′i bel	Unit for measuring loudness.
detector	de tec′tor	Device that rectifies radio waves.
distortion	dis tor′tion	Undesired changes in wave form.
electronic	e lec tron′ic	Pertaining to behavior of electrons.
frequency	fre′quen cy	Number of waves per second.
interference	in ter fer′ence	Confusion of received signals.
kilocycle	kil′o cy cle	Unit for measuring frequency.
loud-speaker	loud-speak′er	Receiver to produce loud sounds.
microphone	mi′cro phone	Device to convert sound waves into varying electrical impulses.
modulation	mod u la′tion	Alteration of amplitude or frequency.
network	net′work	Chain of broadcasting stations.
newscaster	news′cast er	One who broadcasts news.
oscillator	os′cil la tor	Device to generate radio signals.
radiogram	ra′di o gram	Message transmitted by radio-telegraphy.
reception	re cep′tion	Process of receiving radio signals.
recording	re cord′ing	Phonograph record.
resonance	res′o nance	Increased amplitude because the circuit has the same frequency.
screen	screen	Surface for receiving pictures.
script	script	Manuscript used for a broadcast.
selectivity	se lec tiv′i ty	Ability to "tune in" frequencies.
socket	sock′et	Support for holding tube or lamp.
sponsor	spon′sor	One who pays for a program.
static	stat′ic	Interfering electrical discharges.
studio	stu′di o	Room used for broadcasting.
telecast	tel′e cast	Broadcast by television.
television	tel′e vi sion	Transmission of pictures by radio.
transcription	tran scrip′tion	Recording made for broadcasting.
transmitter	trans mit′ter	Equipment to produce radio signals.
tube	tube	Evacuated container in which electricity passes between electrodes.
tuning	tun′ing	Selecting radio signal by dialing.
video	vid′e o	Pertaining to TV broadcasting.
wave length	wave length	Space between two successive waves.

Lesson 129 RECREATION AND ATHLETICS

amateur	am a teur'	Athlete who plays for pleasure.
amusement	a muse'ment	Diversion; entertainment.
arena	a re'na	Place for shows or combats.
athletic	ath let'ic	Pertaining to games and sports.
bleachers	bleach'ers	Seats for spectators.
caddie	cad'die	One who carries golf clubs.
challenge	chal'lenge	Invitation to contest.
coach	coach	Athletic instructor, trainer.
competitive	com pet'i tive	Pertaining to rivalry in contest.
contest	con'test	Trial to see which can win.
court	court	Place marked off for a game.
diamond	di'a mond	Area inside the base lines in baseball.
entertainment	en ter tain'ment	Giving or receiving hospitality or amusement.
fatigue	fa tigue'	Weariness.
gridiron	grid'i ron	Football field.
hurdle	hur'dle	Barrier to be leaped over.
intercollegiate	in ter col le'gi ate	Between colleges.
intramural	in tra mu'ral	Within a college or a school.
league	league	Association of teams.
linesman	lines'man	One who marks distances.
medalist	med'al ist	Golfer with lowest score.
megaphone	meg'a phone	Trumpet used for speaking.
Nimrod	Nim'rod	Great hunter.
novice	nov'ice	Inexpert beginner.
pastime	pas'time	Diversion for passing time.
pennant	pen'nant	Flag symbolizing victory.
piscatorial	pis ca to'ri al	Pertaining to fishing.
pool	pool	Tank of water for swimming.
prize	prize	Award for winning or for competing.
recreation	rec re a'tion	Play or pastime, in contrast to work.
referee	ref er ee'	Judge of play in games.
scrimmage	scrim'mage	Lined-up play in football.
spectacular	spec tac'u lar	Unusual display.
sportsman	sports'man	One engaged in sports.
stadium	sta'di um	Structure used for sports.
target	tar'get	Mark set up which is to be hit.
tournament	tour'na ment	Sport contest with many players.
trophy	tro'phy	Prize for victory.
turf	turf	Race track for horses.
umpire	um'pire	Official who rules on plays.

Lesson 130 RELIGION

atheist	a'the ist	One who denies existence of a god.
baptism	bap'tis*m*	Ceremony of proclaiming one a Christian by the application of water.
benediction	ben e dic'*tio*n	Asking of God's blessing.
Bible	Bi'bl*e*	Book of sacred Christian writings.
bigot	big'*o*t	Intolerant, prejudiced person.
bishop	bish'*o*p	Clergyman of high rank.
blessing	bles*s*'ing	Giving of God's favor.
brethren	breth'ren	Fellow members of a church.
cardinal	car'di nal	High Catholic official.
ceremony	*c*er'e mon y	Rite; special set of formal acts.
chapel	chap'el	Place of worship.
Christianity	C*h*ris'ti an i ty	Religion of Christians.
commandment	co*m* mand'ment	One of the ten in the Decalogue.
confess	con fes*s*'	Tell one's sins to be forgiven.
confirmation	con fir ma'*tio*n	Ceremony of admission.
congregation	con gre ga'*tio*n	Assembly to worship.
deacon	de*a*'con	Church official.
deity	de'i ty	Divine nature; a god or goddess.
disciple	dis *c*i'pl*e*	Follower; a follower of Jesus.
divine	di vin*e*'	Pertaining to God.
dogma	dog'ma	Doctrine; belief held by a church.
evangelist	e van'ge list	Traveling preacher of the gospel.
heathen	hea'then	Pagan; one who does not believe in the God of the Bible.
heresy	her'e sy	Belief opposed to church doctrine.
idolatry	i dol'a try	Worship of idols or images.
invocation	in vo ca'*tio*n	Prayer opening a church service.
Judaism	Ju'da is*m*	Religion of the Jews.
missionary	mis*'sio*n ar y	One sent to spread religion.
pagan	pa'gan	Heathen.
paradise	par'a dis*e*	Heaven; the garden of Eden.
parochial	pa ro'*ch*i al	Pertaining to a parish.
parsonage	par'son age	Home of a minister.
Reverend	Rev'er end	Title for a clergyman.
Scripture	Scrip'tur*e*	The Bible; any sacred writing.
sermon	ser'm*o*n	Religious address, usually grounded on some passage of Scripture.
spiritual	spir'i tu al	Sacred; religious.
superstition	su per sti'*tio*n	Fear of the mysterious.
synagogue	syn'a gog*ue*	Place of Jewish worship.
theology	the ol'o gy	Science of religion.
worship	wor'ship	Religious honor and reverence.

Lesson 131 SOCIAL STUDIES

Word	Pronunciation	Meaning
allegiance	a*l* le'*gi*ance	Duty of loyalty.
Americanization	A mer i can i za'*tion*	Process of making immigrants into typical Americans.
assimilation	a*s* sim i la'*tion*	Absorption of other cultures.
barter	bar'ter	Trade by exchange of goods.
bolter	bolt'er	Person who deserts his party.
boycott	boy'cot*t*	Refusal to buy from someone.
charter	char'ter	Document granting rights.
civics	*c*iv'ics	Study of community life.
competition	com pe ti'*tion*	Rivalry of two or more groups.
confederacy	con fed'er a *cy*	Union of countries or states.
conservation	con ser va'*tion*	Wise use of natural resources.
economy	e con'o my	Practicing habit of thrift.
emancipate	e man'*ci* pat*e*	Set free from bondage.
epoch	ep'oc*h*	Time of distinctive events.
exploration	e*x* plo ra'*tion*	Discovery in unknown areas.
housing	hou*s*'ing	Provision of houses as homes.
illiteracy	*il* lit'er a *cy*	Being unable to read or write.
interdependence	in ter de pend'en*ce*	Relying on each other.
isolation	i so la'*tion*	Remaining alone; separate.
juvenile	ju've nil*e*	Pertaining to youth, children.
leisure	le*i*'*s*ur*e*	Spare time; freedom from work.
migration	mi gra'*tion*	Moving from one place to another periodically or for residence.
naturalization	nat u ral i za'*tion*	Becoming a citizen through law.
patriot	pa'tri ot	One devoted to his country.
pioneer	pi o n*e*er'	Person who goes first.
politics	pol'i tics	Science and art of government.
proclamation	proc la ma'*tion*	Public, official announcement.
production	pro duc'*tion*	The making of goods for man.
propaganda	prop a gan'da	Systematic efforts to mould opinion or an attitude.
ratify	rat'i f*y*	Confirm; approve.
reclamation	rec la ma'*tion*	Making waste land usable.
revolution	rev o lu'*tion*	Complete change in government.
safety	saf*e*'ty	Keeping one's self and others safe from accidents.
settlement	set'*tle* ment	Colonization of new territory.
tenancy	ten'an *cy*	Practice of renting property.
territory	ter'*r*i to ry	Large tract of land.
transportation	trans por ta'*tion*	Movement of people and goods.
treason	tre*a*'*s*on	Betrayal of one's country.
vandalism	van'dal i*s*m	Willful destruction of property.
zoning	zon'ing	Sectioning a city by law.

Lesson 132 — TRANSPORTATION

airway	air'way	Fully equipped air route.
baggage	bag'gage	Valises, bags, trunks, etc.
berth	berth	Sleeping place on a train or a ship.
bus	bus	Motor vehicle for passengers.
caboose	ca boose'	Railroad car for the train crew.
cargo	car'go	Merchandise shipped by vessel.
coastwise	coast'wise	Along the coast.
consignee	con sign ee'	One to whom something is shipped.
depot	de'pot	Railway station.
destination	des ti na'tion	Place where one is going.
dirigible	dir'i gi ble	Gas-filled, cigar-shaped airship with a rigid internal frame; directable.
drawback	draw'back	Rebate from regular charges.
embargo	em bar'go	Law or order restricting ship movements.
en route	en route'	On the way.
excursion	ex cur'sion	Short pleasure trip.
express	ex press'	Rapid method of conveyance.
interurban	in ter ur'ban	Between cities or towns.
junction	junc'tion	Meeting or crossing of railroads.
lading	lad'ing	Act of loading; freight.
locomotive	lo co mo'tive	Engine for pulling railroad cars.
navigator	nav'i ga tor	One trained to guide a ship or aircraft from one point to another.
pilot	pi'lot	One who steers a vessel or operates and guides an airplane.
prepaid	pre paid'	Charges paid in advance.
Pullman	Pull'man	Trade name for certain sleeping cars.
radiophone	ra'di o phone	Radio that operates like a telephone.
railroad	rail'road	Railway transportation system.
reckoning	reck'on ing	Calculation of a ship's position.
semaphore	sem'a phore	Apparatus for signaling.
streamliner	stream'lin er	Transport shaped for less air resistance.
terminal	ter'mi nal	End of a railroad line.
tonnage	ton'nage	Freight-carrying capacity.
tourist	tour'ist	One who travels for pleasure.
trackage	track'age	Lines of track, collectively.
traffic	traf'fic	Business done by a carrier line.
transport	trans port'	Act of conveying.
tunnel	tun'nel	Underground passage.
vehicle	ve'hi cle	Any land conveyance.
vessel	ves'sel	Ship; large boat; airship.
voyage	voy'age	Journey by air or water.
waterway	wa'ter way	Water that ships travel on.

Lesson 133 VOCATIONS AND INDUSTRIES

applicant	ap'*p*li cant	A candidate for a position.
apprenticeship	a*p* pren'ti*ce* ship	Time during which one is learning an art or trade.
bankruptcy	bank'rupt *c*y	Failure in business.
budgeting	bu*dg*'et ing	Making a plan for spending.
capitalist	cap'i tal ist	Person whose money or property enables a business to operate.
career	ca re*er*'	The general course of a life.
code	cod*e*	A system of business conduct.
compensation	com pen sa'*tion*	Pay; remuneration.
contractor	con trac't*o*r	A large-scale constructor.
counselor	coun'sel *o*r	A person who gives advice.
craftsman	crafts'man	Skilled workman; an artist.
dealer	de*a*l'er	One who buys and sells.
employee	em ploy *ee*'	One who is given work and pay.
employer	em ploy'er	A person who employs others.
enterprise	en'ter pri*se*	An important undertaking.
ethics	eth'ics	Rules of right and wrong.
income	in'*come*	Receipts of a business or person.
industry	in'dus try	The productive occupations.
installment	in st*all*'ment	A part payment.
integrity	in teg'ri ty	Honesty; stability.
inventory	in'ven to ry	Detailed list of stock or items.
laborer	la'b*o*r er	Worker with little skill.
occupation	oc *c*u pa'*tion*	Business; employment; trade.
overtime	o'ver tim*e*	Work beyond regular hours.
personality	per s*o*n al'i ty	The sum of one's characteristics.
personnel	per s*o*n nel'	Persons employed in a business.
profession	pro fes'*sio*n	Vocation requiring education.
profitable	prof'it a bl*e*	Paying; yielding gain.
promotion	pro mo'*tio*n	Advance in rank or position.
proprietor	pro pri'e t*o*r	Owner.
qualification	*qua*l i fi ca'*tion*	That which fits one for a job.
schedule	s*ch*ed'ule	A timetable.
security	se cu'ri ty	Condition of being safe.
specifications	spe *c*i fi ca'*tio*ns	Detailed statement of particulars.
strike	strik*e*	Cease work to get higher wages.
syndicate	syn'di cat*e*	Association to promote an enterprise, usually financial or industrial.
transaction	trans ac'*tion*	Business deal.
union	un'*io*n	An organized group of workmen.
vocation	vo ca'*tio*n	An occupation, business, or trade.
workmanship	work'man ship	Quality or manner of work.